AF856134

MERGERS, MARKETS AND PUBLIC POLICY

Studies in Industrial Organization

Volume 21

Series Editors:
H. W. de Jong, *University of Amsterdam, Amsterdam, The Netherlands*
W. G. Shepherd, *University of Massachusetts, Amherst, U.S.A.*

Advisory Board:
W. Adams, *Michigan State University, East Lansing (Mich.), U.S.A.*
R. E. Caves, *Harvard University, Cambridge (Mass.), U.S.A.*
K. D. George, *University College of Swansea, Singleton Park, U.K.*
E. Heusz, *Friedrich Alexander University, Erlangen-Nürnberg, Germany*
A. P. Jacquemin, *University of Louvain, Louvain, Belgium*, and
Commission of the European Communities, Brussels, Belgium
E. Kantzenbach, *University of Hamburg, Hamburg, Germany*
H. W. Lambers, *Erasmus University, Rotterdam, The Netherlands*
R. Prodi, *University of Bologna, Bologna, Italy*, and
Istituto per la Ricostruzione Industriale, Bologna, Italy
F. M. Scherer, *Harvard University, Cambridge (Mass.), U.S.A.*

Mergers, Markets and Public Policy

edited by

Giuliano Mussati
Bocconi University, Milan, Italy

SPRINGER-SCIENCE+BUSINESS MEDIA, B.V.

Library of Congress Cataloging-in-Publication Data

Mergers, markets, and public policy / edited by Giuliano Mussati.
p. cm. -- (Studies in industrial organisation ; v. 21)
Papers originally presented at a seminar held at Bocconi University's Furio Cicogna Centre for Entrepreneurial Studies, Milan, May 10, 1991.
ISBN 978-94-010-4173-7 : alk. paper)
1. Consolidation and merger of corporations--Congresses.
2. Competition--Congresses. 3. Antitrust law--Congresses.
I. Mussati, Giuliano, 1945- . II. Series: Studies in industrial organization ; v. 21.
HD2746.5.M437 1995
338.8'3--dc20 95-31703

ISBN 978-94-010-4173-7 ISBN 978-94-011-0387-9 (eBook)
DOI 10.1007/978-94-011-0387-9

Printed on acid-free paper

All Rights Reserved
© 1995 Springer Science+Business Media Dordrecht
Originally published by Kluwer Academic Publishers in 1995
Softcover reprint of the hardcover 1st edition 1995
No part of the material protected by this copyright notice may be reproduced or utilized in any form or by any means, electronic or mechanical, including photocopying, recording or by any information storage and retrieval system, without written permission from the copyright owner.

Table of contents

List of Tables

List of Figures

Contributing Authors

Fabio Gobbo
Member of the Commission
Autorità Garante della Concorrenza e del Mercato
Via Calabria 48
00187 Rome
Italy

Alexis Jacquemin
Professor of Economics
Departement of Economics
Université Catholique de Louvain
Place Montesquieu 3
B-1348 Louvain-la -Neuve
Belgium

Frédéric Jenny
Professor of Economics
E.S.S.E.C.
Département d'Economie
Boîte Postale 105
95201 Cergy Pontoise
France

Dennis C. Mueller
Professor of Economics
Department of Economics
University of Wien
BWZ - Brünner Straße 72
A-1210 Wien
Austerreich

Giuliano Mussati
Direttore
"Furio Cicogna" Center for Entrepreneurial Studies
Bocconi University
Via Sarfatti 25
20136 Milan
Italy

Manfred Neumann
Professor of Economics
Volkswirtschaftliches Institüt
Universität Erlagen - Nürnberg
P.O. Box 3931
D-8500 Nürnberg 1
Germany

Robert H. Smiley
Ph.D. Dean and Professor of Management
Graduate School of Management
University of California
95616 Davis - California
United States

Tommaso Salonico
Researcher
Autorità Garante della Concorrenza e del Mercato
Via Calabria 48
00187 Rome
Italy

Cento Veljanovski
Professor of Economics
Waverley International Limited
3207 Peregrine Tower
Lippo Centre
89 Qeensway Central
Hong Kong

Introduction

GIULIANO MUSSATI

Why do mergers occur, which are their effects on social welfare and which is the best economic policy toward them? These three questions have been puzzling industrial economists since the end of the last century when the first great merger wave has come about in the US. They have returned at the centre of the stage of the theoretical and empirical economic research during the last decade when merger and acquisition activity became one of the most evident firms' activities in all industrialised countries, being fostered by some general and country specific facts. These facts have been identified in the appearance of new financial instruments facilitating fund raising by firms, in the benevolent behaviour of the authorities in charge of competition policy during the Reagan administration in the US, while internal market completion has become a strong incentive for European firms to reach a true continental dimension in the UE through external growth.

However a robust and univocal answer to these questions has not yet been found in spite of its importance not only from the theoretical point of view, but also from the normative one. In fact the correct identification of firms' motivations in pursuing merger and acquisition operations and of their consequences on social welfare would help the choice by administrative authorities of different possible options in competition and industrial policies. The lack of this unique answer might be one of the reasons why we observe differences in the antitrust legislation and regulations adopted in various countries, together with discrepancies in administrative and industrial traditions and in general policy objectives.

As it is well known, the principal classical controversy is whether merger operations result in an efficiency increase, or in a market power increase, or in both. In very simple terms, from the social point of view, if the efficiency increase prevails, they are good, if the market power one they are bad. If both, the net welfare gain must be carefully assessed. Thus the argument is between those who consider mergers and take-overs as a necessary and vital part of the competitive process and those who consider these operations only as means to reach dominant positions in the economic system. The former group suggests a sort of a "laissez-faire" competition policy, while the latter a strict administrative control of those operations.

The recent merger and hostile take-over boom, whose social consequences have been demonstrated to be totally negative, has changed a little the

G. Mussati (ed.), Mergers, Markets and Public Policy, 1–8.
© 1995 *Kluwer Academic Publishers.*

focus of the debate. In fact this boom has been seen as largely driven not by real industrial programs, but by financial and strategic concerns. In this new contest the key policy issue remains how to preserve the socially beneficial mergers operations and to prevent the rest. Neither a total ban on all mergers and take-overs, nor a totally liberal policy is likely to be the first best. The existence of both an efficient capital market and the opportunity to exchange shares helps creating a competitive market in ownership which makes it possible to put pressure on ill managed companies to act efficiently thus avoiding any hostile take-over. Relative to this possibility the American choice has been to prevent all those actions that can curb managerial discretion, while allowing the friendly mergers, which often are its most egregious manifestation through a set of measures.

Moreover the debate about mergers possesses a peculiar European dimension, which is relevant to industrial policy also. European firms have always suffered from a smaller dimension with respect to their international competitors. At each country level and at the UE level, the trade-off between an industrial policy goal to create firms big enough to stand international competition and a competition policy one to preserve the market competition has always been present and still waits for a clear solution.

Mergers control is not the only one field of application of competiton policy. Others concern the control of horizontal agreements, vertical restraints and abuses of dominant positions, which stimulated also a debate around their capability to hamper competition. As it results from the papers, in the UE and in some of its adhering countries these topics have been deeply debated and have become the subject of some administrative actions.

The seven papers collected in this volume extensively cover the different subjects related to competition policy by presenting a critical and updated overview of the different economic theories of mergers and of their consequences formulated and tested in the literature, by analysing not only the hypotheses on which antitrust legislation is based in different countries, but also its time evolution in connection with that of its objectives and the empirical experience of the antitrust authorities in its enforcement. This permits an exhaustive comparative analysis of mergers theories and policies in the western hemisphere, which represents this book's main objective.

The papers were originally presented at a Seminar on "Mergers, Markets and Public Policy", promoted by Bocconi University's Furio Cicogna Centre for Entrepreneurial Studies held in Milan, 10th May, 1991. During the time span between their presentation and the conclusion of the lengthy publishing procedure one has been updated by his author due to the appearance of a new set of rules governing horizontal mergers.

As pointed out in the first and second Chapters by Mueller and by Smiley, three basic theoretical hypotheses about mergers motives have been suggested and empirically tested in the literature. The first, the market power hypothesis, asserts that every kind of merger (horizontal, vertical or conglomerate) leads to market power increase and thus to higher prices (and profits) as in the Cournot's classic oligopoly model in which prices vary inversely with the number of sellers in a market. In the second, the efficiency motive hypothesis, mergers are identified as the easiest way to reduce production and transaction costs, thus increasing efficiency in an industry with significant scale economies, where at least one of the merging firms is of less than minimum efficient size, or as a mean to rationalise production. The last hypothesis, the managerial hypothesis, considers the possibility of mergers conducted not in the interest of the company shareholders, but in those of the management whose objective is not profit maximisation but firm's growth, because of the linkage between this objective and their private rewards. The experience teaches us that these operations not only do not create real wealth, but leave the shareholders of the acquiring firm always worse off.

All these three mergers explaining motives have proved not to be very robust when tested because empirical findings have not confirmed their hypotheses. The market power motive for instance seems to be lacking because mergers' timing does not correspond to the one suggested by the motivation to eliminate competiton. Most mergers occur during stock market upswing and crests, when the economy is improving and is expected to become even stronger, while the incentives to merge to suppress competition or to cheat an agreement to price uncompetitively are strongest in a recession. This finding confirms also that horizontal mergers do not have an important impact on industry concentration, because they occur in times of prosperity, when the net entry of firms is positive. Regarding the efficiency motive, the most cited, but also the least effective, the pitfalls awaiting the large merged organisation are legendary, confirming specially large firms' inability to exploit a common organisation. The only advantage of the last hypothesis is that it is broadly consistent with the positive correlation between stock price movements and merger activity, while it does not explain why managers, who are expected to behave in such a way as to maximise the wealth of their shareholders, would choose to participate in an operation where the winners always lose, as broadly demonstrated.

In his paper Smiley starts by examining the nature of the merger activity in the US during the last decade, or what has been called "The Market for Corporate Control" by the American academic community, which affected a surprising large number of firms. A peculiarity of these operations was the quite large premiums paid by the managers of the acquiring firm to the shareholders of the acquired firm in order to convince them to tender.

The author observes that unprecedentedly the Reagan administration's relaxed attitude toward merger operations based on the rethinking of the basic paradigm of industrial economics, i.e. the structure conduct performance one, may have favoured the intensive activity of this period. In fact the possibility of a tightening of antitrust policy under a new president that could challenge mergers which would have passed unchallenged under the Reagan administration, probably has convinced many managers to complete mergers before the January 20, 1989 change in administration.

The key element of this new relaxed attitude was the issue of an entirely new set of merger guidelines, first released in 1982, and then revised in 1984, whose approach to the decision of which merger to challenge and which not was innovative since for the first time rigorous economic analysis was used in decision supporting. The 1984 guidelines were very careful in their description of how product and geographic markets were to be defined. Then they specified the mergers to be challenged or not on the terms of the Hirschman-Herfindal Indices (HHI) rather then on concentration ratio. Contestability theory came into action because it was recognised that if the market was contestable, i.e. entry was free, a merger which might otherwise not be allowed to become effective was instead allowed. Finally a merger bringing substantial efficiency gains was allowed even though it would have created or enhanced the market power of the surviving firm. Market power was defined as the ability of a single firm or group of firms to raise price above the competitive level (5%) for an extended period of time (one year) without experiencing entry. In its assessment for the first time a full weight also was given to foreign competition.

The positive consideration of efficiency gains represents one of the differences between the American and the European antitrust legislation. As pointed out by Jacquemin in his paper, until the beginning of this decade the European antitrust administrative action was based on the interpretation of Articles 85 and 86 of the Treaty of Rome, the two pillars of UE-competition policy, by the Commission and the European Court of Justice in such a way as to make them partly applicable to mergers. A specific Regulation on merger control has been adopted in 1990 and implemented since 1991. It is founded upon two main points. The first states that its aim is to prevent both the creation and the enlargement of dominant market positions and the second that it does not provide for authorisation in derogation from the prohibition on the basis of efficiency effect of merger, but that efficiency becomes one element in the overall appraisal. Another difference between the two legislations concerns the fact that in the European one there is no explicit use of numerical guidelines as a mean of judgement such as a certain change in the Herfindal Index. This deficiency might favour the rise of surreptitious compromises within the Commission.

However,in Jacquemin's opinion, it is hard to believe that in practice such a strict policy will be fully implemented ignoring the role of potential dynamic efficiency gains. In fact three aspects relative to horizontal mergers are relevant in the European context and must be taken into account: first consideration of the new industry structure following mergers; second the international trade dimension within the Common Market and with the rest of the world; third the role of mergers in high technology activities. Concerning the first aspect, the key element is the evaluation of the adjustments of prices and quantities in response to a merger. These depend from the response of non-participant firms to any output reduction by the merging parties. The actual European context seems to favour output expansions by non-participating firms, thus providing significant welfare gain in response to a merger operation. It has also been proved that imports, mainly extra UE, exert a significant disciplinary effect on price-cost margins. The third aspect considered is particularly relevant in Europe. Over the recent past, the Union has lost world market shares in high-tech sectors, where the intensity of R&D and the short-lived nature of the product require the achievement of a sufficient scale of operation in order to exploit scale and scope economies. It has been proved that mergers in these industries should raise fewer concerns than similar mergers in industries which have entered their stable phase.

The following four papers collected in the book, deal with antitrust legislation and policy in the four European major countries, Germany, United Kingdom, France and Italy. Differences arise both because of different political goals assigned to competition policy and administrative experiences depending on the length of the period the antitrust legislation has been into force in each country.

As emerges from Neumann's paper, among the antitrust legislation considered the German one possesses the oldest origin. In fact, upon an accelerated increase in the number of cartels during the later decades of the 19th century in this country, the Court of Justice of the German Empire ruled in 1897 that cartels were principally legal since freedom of business activity was deemed to encompass freedom to enter contracts which regulate prices in a particular industry. This decision made in a short span of time Germany the country of cartels. In 1923 only a law against the abuse of cartels was enacted, while the present legislation dates back to 1957 and has demonstrated to be a good instrument to realise the so called Social Market Economy, which is the main policy goal of Germany. Its guiding principle is twofold: competition maintenance is considered to be the only way to safeguard individual freedom of economic activity and to harness self-interest for serving the public interest. It is presumed to do so, first, by enhancing efficiency in production and distribution of commodities and services, and, second, by being an extremely powerful method to discover new ways and means of economic activity. Thus it is clear that the kind of competition which really counts in this context is the one which introduces new products and processes, not price competition.

This author's opinion is that German competition policy, although not always immune from temptations of ill-advised industrial policy, has on the whole been fairly successful in maintaining a competitive order which has been working for the benefit of consumers and significantly contributed to enhance the efficiency of German economy. This policy can be criticised only for the fact that small and medium sized firms have been compensated for the few favours granted to large firms in very special situations which give them comparative advantages vis-à-vis smaller firms which have the privileges to set up cartels which would be prohibited for large firms. This seems a bad policy because tends to lessen competiton and provokes rent seeking behaviours.

Concerning the control of mergers, its practice by the Federal Cartel Office of Germany suggests that it has been cautiously exercised. In fact although a large number of mergers has been notified only a rather small number of them has been disallowed: from a total of 14403 notified mergers only 98, less than one per cent, have been prohibited, and of those only 40 interdictions became valid in law upon litigation.

Veljanovski's paper describes a quite different situation for the UK. This country entered the 1980s as a corporatist state and left the decade through its privatisation programme a more open and competitive economy. This programme has been used to introduce a proper competitive environment in this economic system, becoming the cornerstone of competition policy. It brought with it both the prospect of greater competition and a new approach to the control of monopoly abuse-regulation. It has been so widespread to interest important sectors of the economy such as telecommunications, gas, electricity, airport and water industries. The introduction of competitive forces has been fostered through a combination of re-structuring the previously nationalised industry into a number of separate companies, fostering of service competition through interconnection agreements using the transmission network of the privatised companies, and supporting new entries in order to provide direct competition to the privatised entity.

In spite of this liberalisation process, the acceptance of the fact that the privatised utilities were still able to wield significant market power has given rise to a new body of regulatory law designed to reach a number of objectives ranging from universal service and consumer protection to enhancing competition. As an example price regulation in each utility entails that retail prices pay the rate of inflation minus X percentage points to reflect the ability of the utility to improve efficiency. This combination of competition law and regulatory approaches has created a complex administrative and legal structure consisting of competition agencies with general responsibility and industry regulators charged with economic regulation, consumer protections and competiton promotion in the privatised utilities.

This author notices that also in the UK merger policy has been quite permissive in the past. During the 1980s the UK experienced its third merger boom and it stood out in Western Europe as having the most permissive and conducive environment for merger and acquisition activity. 85% of take-overs in the UE has occurred in the UK, while this country also had the larger number of successfully contested or hostile mergers and the largest capitalised stock market in Europe.

The French experience is described in Jenny's paper. The enactment of the first French competition antitrust statutes dates back to 1953. Following this country centralising administrative tradition, its principal objective was price control. At that time it was believed that anti competitive behaviour should be opposed because it led to higher price levels and therefore contributed to inflation, rather than because competition would lead to a more efficient allocation of resources. A significant change took place in the 1977 and 1986 reforms. The shift was toward the promotion of competition through the establishment of different practices such as merger control, the prohibition of anti competitive cartel agreements and of abuse of market power by dominant firms and of other business practices restraining competition.

Different factors contributed to the enactment of these reforms. One of which was the willingness of French bureaucracy in charge of industrial policy still busily involved in promoting mergers among French firms to subtract the control of these practices to the European colleagues.

In addition to mergers control this country's experience in promoting competition has dealt with the prohibition of other business practices such as resale price maintenance, refusal to deal, price discrimination and reselling at a loss. Especially the problems related to the relationships between industry and large scale retailers on one side and industry and small scale distributors on the other have received much attention, because of their capability to distort competition. More recently the control of horizontal agreements has become very specialised so to treat also the case of establishment and publication of recommended or suggested tariffs by trade professional organisations. The prohibition of this practice and its motivations may serve as an example for other European administrative bodies.

The last paper concerns the Italian recent experience and was presented by Gobbo, who actually is one of the five members of the Italian antitrust authority. Italy was the last European country to adopt the antitrust legislation in 1990, after a period of gestation lasted twenty years. The main characteristic of the Italian administrative authority in charge of competition policy is its independence on the government. The two main activities carried out by the authority are competition protection and competition promotion. As concerns the former, controlling of concentrations has been the authority's main activity in terms of numbers during the three years of its operation: 1014 concentrations have been examined, but only two prohibited; 42 agreements and few cases of abuses of dominant position have been taken into account also. As concerns the latter, the authority has carried out some sectors' investigations and submitted to the government some reports indicating the uncompetitive situations to be corrected and the remedies proposed. This activity is another peculiarity of the Italian legislation. Turnover values fix the boundaries between European and domestic merger operations. The only criticism that can be advanced to the activity of the Italian authority is that it has dealt almost entirely with horizontal mergers, while living small room to other matters related to competiton policy. But this might be explained by its short period of activity.

This volume's attempt has been to present an exhaustive and, hopefully, fresh look at the current situation concerning competition policy both from the points of view of its basic hypotheses and its different applications in the industrialised countries. The hope is that it could be useful not only to correctly understand each country's situation, but to be the point of departure for a thorough comparative research. In the globalisation era, the objective of this research might be an exchange of experience so to reach uniform positions on the most important subjects at an European and possibly at an industrialised countries level. A second hope is that it becomes the point of reference for all those countries, i.e. Eastern Europe countries, that are actively seeking advice about how to establish a competitive market system, how to develop appropriate antitrust laws and how to set up an efficient regulation system.

1. Mergers: Theory and Evidence

DENNIS C. MUELLER

I. Introduction

The merger of two large corporations or a hostile take-overs of one by another are without question the most dramatic events to transpire on the industrial landscape, and have been so for a century. When the leading cigarette manufacturer, Philip Morris, acquires giants from the food industry like Kraft and General Foods it is front page news, just as the assemblage of cigarette companies by James B. Duke was a century ago. Although the introduction of innovations like the transistor, xerography, and the disposable diaper have arguably had a much greater impact on social welfare than any three mergers or take-overs, the latter grab the headlines and it would seem an increasing fraction of the time and energy of those attracted into business.

Figure 1.1 depicts the volume of mergers and take-overs[1] in the United States over the last century. In the most recent years the aggregate amounts of assets acquired via mergers have averaged $234 billion. This figure might be compared with the $500 billion a year spent on new plant and equipment purchases over the same period, and the $130 billion on R and D. Beyond the sheer magnitude of aggregate merger activity, two facts stand out: mergers have come in great waves around, at least since World War II, a secular upward trend.[2] The wave-like pattern of merger activity has also been observed in other countries.[3] Those whose recollection of economic history spans 100 years will recognize that merger waves tend to correspond to waves in stock market prices (Nelson 1959, 1966; Melicher Ledolter and D'Antonio 1983, pp. 423-30; Geroski 1984, pp. 223-33). Any *general* theory of mergers will have to account, or at least be consistent with, both the wave pattern of merger activity and its association with stock price movements.

In the following section the leading hypotheses as to why mergers occur are reviewed. In Sections III through VI the various micro and macro effects of mergers are discussed. The final section draws some policy implications.

II. Hypotheses about why Mergers Occur

The most appealing and influential description of the competitive process is

G. Mussati (ed.), Mergers, Markets and Public Policy, 9–43.
© 1995 *Kluwer Academic Publishers.*

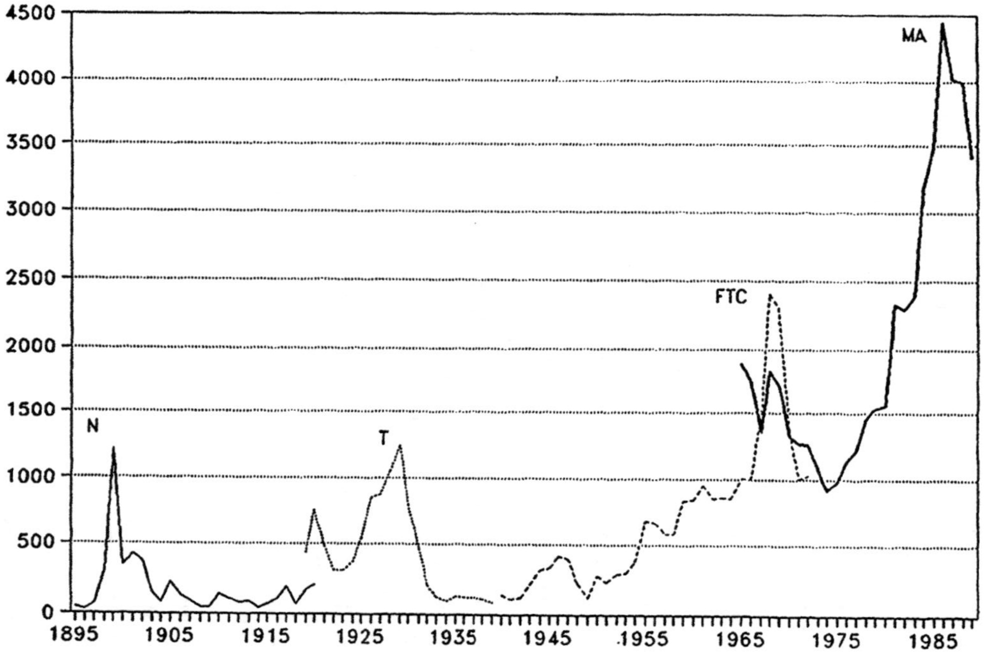

N-NELSON'S SERIES - T-THORP'S SERIES - FTC-FEDERAL TRADE COMISSION SERIES - MA-MERGERS AND ACQUISITION DATA BASE

Fig. 1.1. Numbers of mergers

Sources: Nelson (1959); Thorp, Willard and Crowdler. The structure of industry. Monograph 27, Washington D.C., 1941, pp. 231-4; *Federal Trade Commission*, Current Trends in Merger Activity, 1970, 1971; *Mergers and Acquisitions*, Sep/Oct. 1990, vol. 25.

probably that of Joseph Schumpeter (1934) in which firms come into existence by introducing new products and other innovations, and disappear under the relentless pressure of the competitive process. Mergers fit rather awkwardly into this picture of an economy, since no assets are created or destroyed when two firms combine. Only the names and legal identities of the merging firms are altered. Any *real* consequences of a merger must come about through changes in the development of one or both joining units that can be attributed to the merger in the following years. If the market values of the two merging firms correctly reflect the present discounted values of their respective profit streams, and the managers of the acquiring (surviving) firm maximize profits, then a merger occurs only if it is expected to lead either to an increase in price for one or more of the firm's products, or a reduction in its costs. Numerous hypotheses have been put forward as to why each might occur.

II.1. Mergers that Increase Market Power

Horizontal mergers

The first great merger wave at the end of the 19th century witnessed the creation through merger of such near-monopolies as American Tobacco, Standard Oil of New Jersey, and American Sugar. The increases in market power that these mergers generated were sufficiently transparent to result in their subsequent undoing through the enforcement of the newly passed Sherman Antitrust Act. That some mergers have occurred for the purpose of raising price is unquestionable.

The prediction that price rises following a horizontal merger follows directly from Cournot's classic oligopoly model in which price varies inversely with the number of sellers in a market. Therefore, the demonstration by Salant, Switzer, and Reynolds (1983, pp. 185-99) that, short of a merger between two duopolists, horizontal mergers in a homogeneous product industry characterized by Cournot equilibria are *unprofitable* for the merging firms caught the profession by surprise. Not surprisingly, it generated a medium sized literature of its own.[4]

The counter-intuitive result of Salant, et al., comes about because of the twin assumptions that the reactions of firms are Cournot and the equilibrium is symmetric. Thus, the reduction in industry output that comes about because of the reduction in the number of firms caused by the merger leads the nonmerging firms to *expand* their outputs. The acquiring firm benefits from the merger, but its benefit is no greater than that of the other firms in the industry. Moreover, the profits of the acquired firm are lost entirely in the movement from one symmetric equilibrium to the other. If either of the two assumptions are relaxed, the possibility of horizontal mergers that profit the merging firms begins to appear. For example, if fixed capital results in the merged firm being larger than the others the merger may profit it (Perry and Porter 1985, pp. 219-27). If the firms are price setters rather than quantity setters, the reaction functions are positively sloped, and the rise in optimal price for the merging firms will induce a rise in rival firms' prices and the merger will profit the merging companies (Deneckere and Davidson 1985, pp. 473-86). Perhaps the most important reason for suspecting that horizontal mergers will lead to higher prices is the likelihood that the reduction in the number of firms will facilitate greater cooperation among those remaining. Most of the recent theoretical literature on horizontal mergers assumes either Cournot or Bertrand interactions. More cooperative modes of behavior can be envisaged.

Vertical mergers

The only anticompetitive effects of vertical mergers that have not by now been totally discredited are that they can raise entry barriers by requiring that an entrant at one stage in the production chain enter at all others, or that they can facilitate predatory actions (Comanor 1967, pp. 254-65).

Conglomerate mergers

Conglomerate mergers form the residual category mergers between firms that are not in the same industry, and are not in industries that are vertically linked. The term came into vogue in the late '60s, when mergers between firms in unrelated industries occurred in great numbers. Although mergers of this type would seem to be the least likely to produce market power increases, they can under certain circumstances. John Scott (1982, pp. 368-75) has found that firms that compete against one another in several markets earn higher profits than otherwise predicted, and has hypothesized that this form of "multimarket contact" leads to greater cooperation among firms and may explain some conglomerate merger activity (1989, pp. 35-47). Evans and Kessides (forthcoming) find that multimarket contact among airlines leads to higher air fares. Other hypotheses concerning the anticompetitive effects of mergers are more speculative, although examples of anticompetitive behavior through reciprocal price relationships, or from the elimination of a potential entrant do exist.[5]

Commentary

That some horizontal, vertical and conglomerate mergers can and have led to market power increases and higher prices cannot be questioned. But as a general theory of mergers the market power motive seems to be lacking.

The pressure to cheat on an overt or tacit agreement to price uncompetitively is strongest in a recession, so too, therefore, should be the incentive to merge to suppress competition.[6] But most mergers occur during stock market upswings and crests, when the economy is improving and is expected to become even stronger. The timing of mergers is not what one expects, if their primary motivation is to eliminate competition.

II.2. Mergers that Increase Efficiency

Horizontal mergers

The easiest efficiency gain to envisage is between two firms in an industry with significant scale economies, where at least one of the merging firms is of less than minimum efficient size. Technological changes that greatly expand the minimum efficient size of a firm have led to merger waves within industries. The gains from horizontal merger in the presence of scale economies are greatest for the smallest companies. This explanation of mergers leads one to expect the smaller firms in an industry to be most active in combining. But merging firms tend to be if anything bigger than the average company, and this fact casts a shadow on the general nature of scale economies as an explanation for horizontal mergers (Mueller 1980a and 1980b, pp. 299-314; Huges 1989, pp. 30-98).

Merger waves can also occur in declining industries to rationalize production by assuring that the least efficient production capacity is retired first (Dutz 1989, pp. 11-33).

Vertical mergers

Vertical integration through merger can increase efficiency by (1) eliminating price distortions in factor inputs, when upstream producers have market power, (2) reducing the transactions costs of contracting between vertically linked firms, when asset specificity is present, and (3) reducing bargaining costs between vertically linked firms in the presence of asymmetric information (Williamson 1989, pp. 135-82; Perry 1989, pp. 415-73).

Conglomerate mergers

A variety of hypotheses concerning efficiency gains from diversification mergers were advanced at the time of the first conglomerate merger wave, although not all of these necessarily require that the merger be conglomerate.[7] Most of these have been discredited either theoretically or empirically.

Consider, for example, the finance-related hypotheses advanced by John

Lintner in 1971. He claimed that diversification through merger improved the welfare of acquiring firm shareholders by (1) giving the smaller acquired firm the lower borrowing costs of the acquiring firm, (2) reducing the variance of the acquiring firm's earnings by pooling them with those of the acquired unit, and (3) eliminating the costs of bankruptcy should that befall the smaller company. But surely the larger firm should *lend* to the smaller one, if it believes that the latter has investment projects on the margin with expected returns greater than the larger's cost of capital, rather than acquire the entire company at a premium in 1971 of between 15 and 25 percent, and in the late '80s of 50-100 percent (Mueller 1969, pp. 643-59). Similarly, it is cheaper for shareholders to create their own portfolios to pool risks, especially with the availability of mutual funds, than to have their company pay the premia required to accomplish this end through merger (Levy and Sarnat 1970, pp. 795-802; Smith 1970, pp. 451-71; Azzi 1978, pp. 161-72) although conglomerate mergers can be an attractive way for the managers of the acquiring company to reduce their risks (Amihud and Baruch 1981, pp. 605-17). That the desire to avoid bankruptcy costs would reach feverish heights as the stock market peaks, and then decline precipitously as the economy goes into recession as it did in the '70s, or depression as in the '30s seems implausible. If one assumes that the market value of the acquired firm prior to merger is an upper bound for the transaction costs of bankruptcy, then the probability of its going bankrupt would have to equal the percentage premium paid 50-100 percent in the late '80s. This prediction does not square with the overwhelming evidence that acquired firms in the United States are performing about the same as other firms of similar size in their same industry.[8]

Lintner (1971, pp. 101-11) also listed tax savings, accounting gimmicks to deceive shareholders, and "P/E magic" (the reevaluation of an acquired company's earnings at the higher price/earnings ratio of the buyer) as possible explanations for diversification mergers. Tax considerations appear to be *a* factor in less than 10 percent of mergers, and *the decisive* factor in a much smaller number of cases (Auerbach and Reishuis 1987, pp. 300-13; Gilson, Scholes and Wolfson 1987, pp. 271-99) although they may figure more predominantly in management buyouts (Kaplan 1989e, pp. 611-32). The latter two explanations presume capital market inefficiency, or at least limits on the market's capacity to process accounting information, a presumption most finance people would question. Thus, from Lintner's original list the only viable contender as a general hypothesis as to why diversification mergers occur is the risk-spreading hypothesis as amended by Amihud and Lev (1981, pp. 605-17) to make it refer to the risks faced by the managers of the acquiring firm and not its shareholders.

By far the most widely held view regarding the efficiency gains from mergers and take-overs is the hypothesis that they are motivated to replace managements that fail to maximize shareholder wealth by those that will. As first put forward by Robin Marris (1963, pp. 185-209 and 1964) it was intended to explain hostile take-overs, not mergers in general, but most observers holding this hypothesis apply it to evidence on both mergers and take-overs (Jensen and Ruback 1983, pp. 5-50). Following Henry Manne's (1965, pp. 110-20) appellation, it has come to be called the "market for corporate control" hypothesis. Those who espouse this hypothesis presume this market to be efficient, and thus the premia paid reflect the expected gains from replacing the acquired firm's management with that of the buyer. Although it is the most popular and viable of the efficiency-related hypotheses as to why conglomerate mergers occur, it need not be restricted to mergers of this form, obviously.

II.3. Merger Hypotheses that do not Presume Profit Increases

The managerial hypothesis

Schumpeter (1934, p. 93) placed "the dream ... to found a private kingdom" at the head of his list of entrepreneurial goals. Robin Marris (1964, ch. 2) reviewed considerable evidence linking both the pecuniary and nonpecuniary rewards of managers to the growth in size of their firm. Mergers are the quickest and surest way to grow, and thus may be undertaken by managers even if they do not promise profit and shareholder wealth increases. Young firms or those in rapidly growing industries may have sufficient opportunities to grow internally so that they need never resort to mergers to achieve this managerial goal. Mergers to increase a company's size or to avoid an eventual decline in size are most likely to be undertaken by mature firms and those in slow-growing or declining industries with sufficient cash to finance this type of expansion (Mueller 1969, pp. 643-59 and 1972, pp. 199-219; Jensen 1986, pp. 323-29).[9] Although this managerial hypothesis about mergers is usually associated with the "managerial corporation" in which ownership and control are separated, as first described by Berle and Means in 1932, it should be noted that Schumpeter's description of entrepreneurs as empire builders was based on his observations of owner-entrepreneurs at the beginning of the century. For those seeking to govern a "private kingdom" a sacrifice of profits for size may be made, even when it is one's own profits that are being given up.

The economic disturbance hypothesis

A merger occurs quite simply because the buying company is willing to pay more for another firm than its owners think it is worth. Michael Gort (1969, pp. 624-42) hypothesized that this transaction in turn reflected a difference in expectations between the two parties regarding the future profit stream of the acquired unit: no new profits were expected to be created for any of the reasons given above. Such divergences in expectations are most likely to occur when stock prices are changing rapidly, or in industries in which future profits are difficult to predict (e.g., R and D intensive or fast growing industries).

The "hubris" hypothesis

As we shall see in Section V, acquiring firm shareholders are not better off as a result of a merger at the time it is announced, and generally become worse off with the passage of time. The premia paid to acquire other companies totally exhaust or over-exhaust any gains the mergers might generate. Richard Roll (1986, pp. 197-216 and 1988, pp. 241-52) has hypothesized that the market for corporate control is characterized by the "winner's curse". The company, whose management has the highest expectations of the profit potential of the target, wins the bidding, but pays on average more than the true profit potential of the company justifies. Although the winner's curse hypothesis explains why acquiring firm shareholders lose from mergers, it does not explain why managers, who would seek to maximize the wealth of their shareholders, would choose to participate in a bidding game when the "winner" always loses. Here is where hubris enters. Acquiring firm managers believe that the odds do not apply to them: they can beat the curse.

Commentary

An advantage of all three of the hypotheses that assume that mergers do not create wealth is that they are broadly consistent with the positive correlation between stock price movements and merger activity. The constraint on managerial pursuit of unprofitable growth by mergers is the possibility that their firm will in turn be taken over and they will be replaced. Stockholders are least likely to want to displace a management in a time of prosperity, when things are going well. This observation is consistent with the fact that acquiring firms tend to be out performing the market by a substantial amount over a sustained period *prior* to undertaking an acquisition (Mueller 1977, pp. 315-47; Magenheim 1987, pp. 171-93). What better time could there be to announce an acquisition that will lower your shareholders wealth than at a time when the market is doing well, and your firm has been outperforming the market? Moreover, if company's shares have been outperforming a bull market, internal cash flows are likely to be high, and the cost of raising external capital will appear low.

The economic disturbance hypothesis predicts high merger activity when stock prices are changing rapidly. Since stock prices tend to fall more rapidly after a market breaks, than during the climb to the peak, one might expect this hypothesis to imply merger peaks during market collapses. Gort (1969, p. 628) rationalizes the procyclical pattern of merger activity with the argument that shareholders suffer from the sunk cost fallacy. In a falling market the price bid for a company's shares, although substantially above their current market price, may be lower than the price paid for them. Recalling the price paid for them, their owners pass up the chance to earn a premium today, and refuse to sell.

In a bull market all players may suffer from hubris. Recent price increases confirm the wisdom of one's past investment decisions and lead to overconfidence and overoptimism (Shiller 1981, pp. 421-36 and 1984, pp. 457-98). The behavior Roll posits for acquiring firm managers is quite common during a stock market upswing.[10]

III. The Effects of Mergers on Profitability

A surprising finding about mergers is that they do not *generally* result in increases in the profits of the merging firms. What is most surprising for the United States is that this finding is true even for the first two great merger waves, which were dominated by horizontal and vertical acquisitions, events that Stigler (1950, pp. 23-34) once dubbed waves to create monopolies in the first instance, oligopolies in the second.[11]

One of the first investigations of the effects of mergers, following the tightening of the Cellar-Kefauver Act that closed off horizontal and vertical acquisitions for many firms, concluded that they resulted in substantial *increases* in profitability. Weston and Mansinghka (1970, pp. 919-36) examined a sample of 63 manufacturing firms, which between 1958 and 1968 undertook a substantial number of diversification mergers. They found that these "conglomerates" went from having significantly lower profit rates than other industrial firms to having about the same profit levels at the end of the decade. They concluded that the mergers represented a successful "defensive diversification" strategy by a group of large mature companies that transformed them into the "conglomerates", the hallmark of the merger wave of the late '60s.

Although conglomerate mergers did raise the profit rates of the acquiring firms, one cannot conclude from that alone that the mergers succeeded in creating additional profits for the merging firms, or that they benefited the acquiring company's shareholders. Mergers have an inevitable averaging ef-

Table 1.1 The effects of mergers on profitability

Country	Authors	Time Period	Merger Sample	Control Group	Profitability Measure	Profit Change Relative to Control Group
United States	Piper & Weiss, 1974	1947-67	102 acquisitions by 30 bank holding companies	None	After-tax eamings per share	≈ 0
	Conn, 1976	1964-70	28 firms acquired by 4 conglomerates	Base industry acquired firm	After-tax profit/total assets	≤ 0
	Mueller, 1980	1962-72	247 manufacturing mergers	Base industry;	Before-tax profit/assets	≤ 0
			280 manufacturing mergers	merging firms, size and industry matched tirms	After-tax profit/assets	≥ 0
	Mueller, 1986	1950-72	Merger activity in 551 manufacturing firms	Companies making no acquisitions	After-tax profit/total assets	≤ 0
	Rhoades, 1987	1968-78	413 acquired banks	3600 non-acquired banks	After-tax profit/assets	≈ 0
	Ravenscraft and Scherer, 1987	1950-77	5966 acquired manufacturing companies	Base industry (line of business)	Before-tax profit/total assets	< 0
United Kingdom	Singh, 1971	1955-60	77 horizontal mergers	None	Before-tax profit/assets	≈ 0
					After-tax profit/assets	≈ 0
	Meeks, 1977	1950-71	1000 + mergers	Base industries	After-tax profit/assets	< 0
	Cosh, Hughes, Singh, 1980	1967-70	225 manufacturing mergers	Size and industry matched firms	After-tax profit/assets	≥ 0
					Before-tax profit/assets	
	Kumar, 1985	1967-74	241 mergers	Base industries	After-tax profit/assets	≤ 0

Table 1.1. cont.

Country	Authors	Time Period	Merger Sample	Control Group	Profitability Measure	Profit Change Relative to Control Group
	Cosh, Hughes, Kumar Singh, 1985	1972-6	66 mergers	Base industries	After-tax profit/assets	≈ 0
Australia	Mc Dugall and Round 1986	1970-81	88 takeovers	Size and industry matched firms	Before-tax profit/assets	≈ 0
Belgium	Kumps and Witterwulghe, 1980	1962-74	21 mergers	Size and industry matched non-merging firms	After-tax profit/assets	≈ 0
Canada	Baldwin, 1991	1970-79	1,575 acquired plants	Non acquired plants in same industry	Value-added per worker/shipments	≥ 0
France	Jenny and Weber, 1980	1962-72	40 mergers	Size and industry matched non-merging firms	After-tax profit/assets	≈ 0
Germany	Cable, Palfrey, and Runge, 1980	1964-74	50 mergers	Size and industry matched non-merging firms	After-tax profit/assets	≈ 0
Japan	Ikeda and Doi, 1983	1964-75	49 mergers	None	Before-tax profit/assets	> 0
The Netherlands	Peer, 1980	1962-73	31 mergers	Size and industry matched non-merging firms	After-tax profit/assets	< 0
Sweden	Ryden and Edberg, 1980	1962-76	26 mergers	Size and industry matched non-merging firms	After-tax profit/assets	≈ 0
				Base industry		≤ 0

fect on accounting profit measures. Firms with above (below) average profits typically acquire companies with profit rates below (above) their own. Given enough acquisitions a company's profit rate would approach the average, even if there was no change in the profitability of the merging units as a result of the mergers. I have estimated that the differences in profit rates across firms that would persist indefinitely are reduced on average by 25 percent because of the averaging effect of mergers (Mueller 1986, ch. 8, and 1990).[12] Given that the conglomerates started their large acquisition programs with below average profits, the mergers would almost certainly have had to raise their profit rates.

The proper way to measure the effects of mergers on profitability is to compute the weighted average profit rate of the merging firms *before* the merger and compare it to the profit rate of the merged company *after* the merger. Since economic conditions may differ after the merger from those that held before in a way that effects the profitability of the merged units, one should also control for this factor by comparing the change in profits of the merged firms with a control group of otherwise similar nonmerging firms, or the industry averages of the merging firms (Hughes and Singh 1980, pp. 1-26). Table 1.1 summarizes the results from 19 studies drawn from 10 countries over the post-World War II period that generally follow this methodology (a few omit the control groups, or focus on the profitability of only one part of the merging pair).

The most reliable conclusions can be drawn for the United States and the United Kingdom, since there are more studies for these countries and larger sample sizes. The only study for the United States that found an increase in profits was my study of mergers between 1962 and 1972 using after-tax profits (Mueller 1980, pp. 271-98). But for essentially the same sample of companies, *before*-tax profits fell following the mergers relative to changes in the merging firms' home industries. Since both market power and efficiency changes should effect before-tax profitability, one concludes that these did not increase and at least one probably fell. The improvement in after-tax profitability would appear to indicate that the mergers did result in tax savings in some instances. The most ambitious of all of the studies in terms of sample size, time span, and care in handling the data was that of Ravenscraft and Scherer (1987). They concluded unequivocally that the profitability of acquired firms declined after they were acquired.

The largest study of mergers in the UK reached the same conclusion (Meeks 1977). Once again one study observed profit increases following mergers (Cosh, Hughes and Singh 1980 pp. 227-70), but the preponderance of evidence for the UK as for the US points toward no increase and probably some decline in the profitability of merging firms after they merge.

No distinct pattern emerges in the studies from other countries. Profit increases were observed in Canada (Baldwin 1991) and Japan (Ikeda and Dari 1983, pp. 257-66), profit decreases in Holland (Peer 1980, pp. 163-91) and Sweden (Ryden and Edberg 1980, pp. 193-226). In all other countries the differences were statistically insignificant. The latter is perhaps not too surprising given the small sample sizes in most cases. But even if one ignores formal statistical tests and looks just at the pattern of changes, it is difficult to draw a firm conclusion that mergers have *increased* profitability. Where mergers seem to result in increases in one country (e.g., Germany), they result in declines in another (e.g., France). This lack of systematic evidence of profit increases following mergers in countries other than the US is, as with the similar finding for the first two merger waves in the US, particularly noteworthy, since in all other countries the mergers were predominately horizontal in nature.

IV. Effects of Mergers on Market Share, Growth, and Productivity

A merger that increases one or both joining companies' efficiency should lower the price of their products and lead to an expansion in their output over what would otherwise be expected. Market power increases, in turn, should result in higher prices and reduced outputs. Thus, one can test whether a merger has increased efficiency or market power by testing whether output expands by more or less than one would expect from the joining of the two firms (Hughes and Singh 1980, pp. 1-26; Mueller 1986).

A comparison of market shares before and after a merger controls for changes in economic conditions by using all other firms in the industry as a control group. Three studies of the effects of mergers on market shares exist. Goldberg (1973, pp. 137-58) observed insignificant changes in market shares for a sample of 44 advertising intensive firms over an average of 3 1/2 years following the merger. I (Mueller 1985, pp. 259-67 and 1986, ch. 9) observed significant declines in market shares for a sample of 209 manufacturing companies over an average of 11 years following the mergers. Baldwin and Gorecki (1990, pp. 53-73) find significant declines in market shares for plants acquired in horizontal mergers, but no significant changes for plants acquired in other sorts of mergers, and conclude that the results are consistent with the mergers having increased market power. The declines in market share I observed were for both horizontal and non-horizontal mergers, however, and were too large even for the former to be attributable to the rational exercise of market power. Thus, none of the studies presents evidence that mergers increased efficiency, one implied a significant reduction in efficiency perhaps coupled with an increase in market power, and the third suggested a possible increase in market power.[13]

The same conclusion is reached if one examines changes in the growth rates of merging firms following the mergers using either their industries or matched nonmerging firms as control groups. No significant change in growth rates was observed in studies of Australia (Mc Dougall and Round 1986, pp. 157-9), Belgium (Kumps and Witterwulghe 1980, pp. 67-97), France (Jenny and Weber 1980, pp. 133-62), Germany (Cable, Palfrey and Runge 1980, pp. 99-132), Sweden (Ryden and Edberg 1980, pp. 193-226), the United Kingdom (Cosh, Hughes and Singh 1980, pp. 227-70), and acquired banks in the United States (Rhoades 1983). Mergers in Holland (Peer 1980, pp. 163-91) and the United States (Mueller 1980) were followed by significant declines in the growth rates of merging companies.

Both Caves and Barton (1990) and Lichtenberg (1992) have estimated plant productivity to be significantly lower for more diversified firms. This finding is consistent with the results summarized so far suggesting that diversification mergers in the United States have lowered the efficiency of the acquired companies. Lichtenberg and Siegel (1987, pp. 643-73) challenge the latter conclusion, however, with evidence that changes in plant ownership between 1972 and 1981 were preceded by declines in productivity and followed by increases in productivity. They claim that their evidence indicates that mergers in the '70s were fundamentally different from those in the '60s.

They do not distinguish, however, between changes in ownership resulting from a spinoff of part of a continuing firm, and those resulting from the acquisition of an entire firm. The findings of negative effects on efficiency from mergers are based largely on analyses of mergers in the '50s, '60s, and early '70s. Consistent with this view, a large "wave" of spinoffs was observed in the '70s. Ravenscraft and Scherer (1987, chs. 5, 6) document that spun off units were performing badly at the time of their sale, and had declining performance leading up to it, the same pattern reported by Lichtenberg and Siegel. What is not apparent is whether the improvements in productivity Lichtenberg and Siegel observed occurred for plants involved in complete mergers and in spinoffs, or just for the latter. If they did apply to full mergers, one would expect the acquired firms to be performing badly, but this generally has not been the case (see n. 7).

Baldwin (1991) also estimates productivity changes for plants in Canada that experienced an ownership change between 1970 and 1979. He finds that plants undergoing ownership changes of all types had higher than average productivity than other plants in 1970. However, only plants spun off from a continuing company, or acquired by a firm in the same industry experienced a significant increase in productivity. Plants acquired from an exiting firm by an entering firm, i.e., those involved in a diversification merger, experienced no significant change in productivity.

In a second study Lichtenberg and Siegel (1990b, pp. 383-408) report the effects of changes in the ownership of "auxiliary establishments". These establishments house managerial personnel, as well as those doing R and D, warehousing, data processing, etc. (p. 390). They find significant reductions in both employment and wages for these establishments, and interpret these results as strengthening their earlier conclusions about the positive effects of mergers on productivity. Since some of these establishments may be parts of divisional spinoffs (e.g., R and D laboratories, warehouses), one again has the possibility that these changes may be correcting inefficiencies resulting from earlier mergers. Moreover, even when the establishments house the central management team of a completely acquired firm, the efficiency effects of the changes in employment and wages cannot be judged without knowing what happened to the other parts of the company. If some production plants were closed or quickly spun off following a company's acquisition, as often occurs, a downsizing of the managerial and administrative staff could occur without an increase in output per administrative input.

In a third paper Lichtenberg and Siegel (1990a, pp. 165-94) show that plants that change ownership as a result of a leveraged buyout also experience significant productivity increases. This finding has the unambiguous implication that this form of ownership change improves the efficiency of the company in question. Since leveraged buyouts are often of companies that have previously been engaged in extensive merger activity, and the efficiency gains they produce would appear to be from undoing the effects of these past mergers, one again has the difficulty of judging whether this positive result should be interpreted as evidence in favor or against the general proposition that mergers enhance efficiency.

V. The Effects of Mergers on Share Prices

The desire to report results on the most recent mergers occurring forces studies that compare before and after operating performance to limit their comparisons to but a few years after the mergers. The price of a company's common stock should reflect the market's expectations of the future dividend payments of the firm and, if dividends are linked to profits, its future profits. Thus, changes in share prices resulting from merger announcements should indicate the market's expectation of the effect of the merger on future profits. A large literature estimates these anticipated effects of mergers by examining the changes in stock prices occurring on and around their announcement. Various control groups have been used to control for contemporaneous events that might be affecting share prices during the interval being examined to ascertain the impact of the merger. Table 1.2 (Salinger 1992, pp. 39-53) summarizes the main findings of 28 studies from different countries and time periods listing their control groups in each case. The returns reported are always presented relative to that of the control group.

The easiest results to summarize and interpret are for the acquired firms. Even in a merger there is almost always one company that is being bought, and another doing the buying. The buyer offers a premium for the acquired company's shares to induce its owners to sell. In the late '60s these were running at between 15 and 25 percent of the premerger market value of the acquired firm, in the '80s these rose to between 50 and 100 percent. The acquired firm's share prices rise to reflect these premia. This rise often begins a month or two before the public announcement of the merger suggesting the existence of insider knowledge and trading. On average mergers are consummated six months after announced. Thus, in the matter of a few months, shareholders of acquired firms earn returns substantially *above* what otherwise would be expected. The median gain to acquired firm shareholders in the studies of Table 1.2, a group heavily weighted toward the mergers in the '60s, was 19.6 percent.

The dramatic rise in acquired firm share prices occurring at or a month or two before their announcement allows us to identify that short interval as the time when the "market" learns of the mergers. The impact this information has on acquiring company share prices should be observed over this same interval. This impact is of conflicting signs, and often statistically insignificant. The median gain to acquiring firm shareholders is .002.

This lack of positive response by the market to the announcement that a firm plans to acquire another stands in stark contrast to the performance of the acquiring firms shares *prior* to the announcement. In 14 of the 15 studies that examined acquiring firm share performance for at least 12 months before the merger announcement, positive cumulative returns were recorded. These run-ups begin as far as 5 or 6 years before the mergers occur, and cumulate to as much as 57 percent more than that of the control group. The median cumulative abnormal gain is +13.2 percent. Moreover, several studies (Dodd and Ruback 1977, pp. 351-74; Malatesta 1983, pp. 155-81; Firth 1980, pp. 315-47; Franks, Broyles and Hecht 1977, pp. 1513-25; Eckbo 1986, pp. 236-60) calculate residuals prior to the merger announcements not relative to the market portfolio over this period, *but relative to the performance of the acquiring firm as predicted by the CAPM* estimated over a different time period. Dodd and Ruback's (1977) study is typical of this approach. The CAPM is estimated over a period before the merger announcement, months -72 to -13 where the announcement is month

Table 1.2. Returns to acquiring and acquired firm's shareholders

Study	Time Period (country)	Returns Prior to Merger Announcement, Acquiring Firms	Returns in Announcement Day (*d*) Month (*m*) Year (*y*) Acquiring Firms	Post-Merger Returns in Days (*d*), Month (*m*) Years (*y*) After Merger Acquiring Firms	Acquired Firms' Returns	Sample	Control Group
Hogarty (1970b)	1953 -64 (USA)			-0.05 (*y* varies from + 1 to +11)		43 nonconglom-erates engaged in heavy merger activity	Firm in acqui-ring company's base industry
Lev and Mandelker (1972)	1952-63 (USA)	0.135[b] (*y* = -5, -1)	0.083 (*y* = 0)	0.056 (*y* = +1 to + 5)		69 firms making large acquisition	Nonmerging firms matched by industry and size
Halperne (1973)	1950- 65 (USA)		0.063 (*m* = -7.0)[c]		0.304 (*m* = -7 to 0)[c]	78 mergers by nonconglomerates	Market portfolio
Mandelker (1974)	1941-63 (USA)	0.048[b] (*m* = -34, -1)	0.003[b] (*m* = 0,6)	-0.015[b] (*m* = 7,46)	0.120*	241 large mergers	Market portfolio
Ellert (1976)	1950-72 (USA)	0.233* (*m*=-100 to -1)[c]	0.018*[d]	-0.016 (*m* = +1,48)		205 mergers chal-lenged by Justi-ce Dept.or FTC between 1950 and 1972	Market portfolio
Franks, Broyles, Hecht (1977)	1955-72 (UK)	-0.048 (*m* = -40, -1)	0.001 (*m* = 0)	-0.014 (*m* = 1,2)	0.179	70 mergers by brewers and dis-tilleries	CAPM (*m* = -29,+8)
Dodd & Rubak (1977)	1958-78 (USA)	0.117* (*m* = -60, -1)	0.028 (*m* = 0)	-0.059[b] (*m* = 1,60)	0.206*	136 tender offers	CAPM (*m* = -72, -13) (*m* = +13, +72) (*m* = +13, +72)

Table 1.2. cont.

Study	Time Period (country)	Returns Prior to Merger Announcement, Acquiring Firms	Returns in Announcement Day (*d*) Month (*m*) Year (*y*) Acquiring Firms	Post-Merger Returns in Days (*d*), Month (*m*) Years (*y*) After Merger Acquiring Firms	Acquired Firms' Returns	Sample	Control Group
Kummer & Hoffmeister (1978)	1956-74 (USA)	0.170[b] (*m* = -40,-1)	0.052[b] (*m* = 0)	0.006[b] (*m* = 1,20)	0.187*	88 cash tender offers	Market portfolio
Langetieg (1978)	1929-69 (USA)	0.136* (*m* = -64 to -1)	-0.028 (*m* = 0 to +5)	-0.262 (*m* = +7 to 78)	0.128*	149 mergers of all kinds	Market portfolio and industry index
Bradley (1980)	1962-77 (USA)		0.04* (*d* = 0.5)	0.01[b] (*d* =6,40)	0.36* - 0.49*	161 tender offers	Market portfolio
Dodd (1980)	1971-77 (USA)		-0.011 (*d* = -1,0)	-0.072* (*d* = -10, 140)[f]	0.340*	71 mergers	Market portfolio
Kumps & Witterwulghe (1980)	1962-74 (Belgium)		-0.047 (*y* = 0)	-0.014 (*y* = 1,3)		26 mergers of all kinds	26 nonmerging firms matched by industry
Jenny & Weber (1980)	1962-72 (France)		0.116* (*y* = 0)	-0.095[b] (*y* = 1,3)		43 mergers of all kinds	43 nonmerging firms matched by size and industry
Ryden & Edberg (1980)	1962-76 (Sweden)		-0.040 (*y* = 0)	0.011[b] (*y* = 1,3)		23 mergers of all kinds	23 nonmerging firms
Cosh, Hughes &Singh (1980)	1967-69 (UK)	0.069* (*y* = -5,1)	0.187* (*y* = +1)	-0.169[b] (*y* = 1,5)		63 mergers of all kinds	63 nonmerging firms matched by size and industry
Mueller (1980)	1962-72 (USA)		0.088* (*y* = 0)	-0.084[b] (*y* = 1,3)		219 mergers of all kinds	219 nonmerging firms matched by size and industry
Firth (1980)	1969-75 (UK)	0.014[b] (*m* = 48, -1)	-0.063 (*m* = 0)	0.001[b] (*m* = 1,36)	0.363	434 mergers of all kinds	CAPM (*m* = -48, -13) (*m* = +13, +36)

Table 1.2. cont.

Study	Time Period (country)	Returns Prior to Merger Announcement, Acquiring Firms	Returns in Announcement Day (*d*) Month (*m*) Year (*y*) Acquiring Firms	Post-Merger Returns in Days (*d*), Month (*m*) Years (*y*) After Merger Acquiring Firms	Acquired Firms' Returns	Sample	Control Group
Asquith (1983)	1962-72 (USA)	0.132[b] (*d* = -480, -1)	0.002 (*m* = 0)	-0.072* (*d* = 1,240)	0.133*	196 mergers of all kinds	Market portfolio
Asquith Bruner & Multingo, Jr. (1983)	1963-79 (USA)		0.028* (m = 0)		0.175*	214 early mergers by firms beginnings merger programms after 1963	Market portfolio
Bradley, Desai & Kim (1983)	1962-80 (USA)		0.024* (*m* = 0)		0.318*	161 successful tender offers	Market portfolio
Malatesta (1983)	1969-74 (USA)	0.043* (*m* = -60,-1)	0.009 (*m* = 0)	-0.079* (*m* = 1,12)	0.168*	256 mergers of all kinds	CAPM (*m* = -62, -13) (*m* = 13,60)
Dodds & Quek (1985)	1974-76 (UK)		-0.002 (*m* = 0)	-0.068 (*m* -1,60)		70 mergers of all kinds	Market portfolio
Eckbo (1986)	1964-83 (Canada)	0.031* (*m* = -12, -1)	0.012 (*m* = 0)	0.006* (*m* = 1,12)	0.100*	413 targets of all kinds 1683 bidders	CAPM (m = -72, -13) (m = -72, -13) (m = +13, +72)
Varaiya (1986)	1975-83 (USA)		-0.036* (*d* = -20,0)	0.008 (*d* = 1,100)	0.411*	80 mergers and takeovers	CAPM (*t* = -300, -61)
Magenheim & Mueller (1987)	1976-81 (USA)	0.184* (*m* = -24, -4)	-0.003 (*m* = 0)	-0,422 (*m* = -3,36)		78 mergers of all kind	CAMP (*m* = -60, -25) (*m* = -36, -4) (*m* = -36, -4)

Table 1.2. cont.

Study	Time Period (country)	Returns Prior to Merger Announcement, Acquiring Firms	Returns in Announcement Day (*d*) Month (*m*) Year (*y*) Acquiring Firms	Post-Merger Returns in Days (*d*), Month (*m*) Years (*y*) After Merger Acquiring Firms	Acquired Firms' Returns	Sample	Control Group
Borg, Borg, and Leeth (1989)	1919-30 (USA)	0.169[b] (m = -60, -13)				134 mining and manufacturing mergers	Market portfolio
				-0.006 (m = 0)	-0.255 (m = 1,36)		CAPM (m = -60, -13)
Franks & Harris (1989)	1955-85 (UK)	0.570[b] (m = -71, -12)	0.010* (m = 0)	0.045 (m = 1,24)	0.297*	1814 targets 1048 bidders	Markets portfolio
			0.005[b] (m = 0)	-0.126 (m = 1,24)			CAPM (m = -71, -12)
Salinger (1992)	1976-78 (USA)	-0.015 (m = -4, -1)	-0.026* (m = 0)	-0.159 (m = 1,30)		40 mergers of all kind	CAPM (m = -64,-5)

* Returns are measured as differences between merging companies' returns and control group returns in all cases. In those studies in which the data were centered around the date of final consummation, the series were displaced backwards by 6 months to allow for the fact that announcements generally precede mergers by 6 months.

[a] Market portfolio implies the predicted performance given a firm's β *if* it performed as the market portfolio performs. CAPM predicts firm *i's* returns using the α and β from $R_{it} - R_{ft} = \alpha_i + \beta_i (R_{mt} - R_{ft}) + \mu_{it}$. If only one time interval was used to estimate all residual, only one is given. When 3 are given, the residuals prior to announcement are estimated from CAPM estimated over the first interval, the announcement residual from the second interval, and the post-announcement from the third.

[b] Reported data do not allow calculation of statistical significance.

[c] Month 0 in the Ellert study is the month in which a complaint is filed.

[d] Announcement of merger in Ellert study is measured as period from judicial complaint through settlement.

[e] Halpern's figures for acquiring firms are for largest of two companies involved in a merger. Acquired firms' figures are for the smallest of two merging firms.

[f] Dodd reports figure for 10 days before announcement until 10 days after merger is approved. Calculation based on assumption that there are on average 6 months (26 weeks times 5 working days) between a merger's announcement and its approval.

0, and a period after it (m = 13,72). The residuals from before the merger announcement are calculated from the estimates over the premerger period. Since the acquiring firms tend to be outperforming the market over substantial parts of the premerger period, the predicted performance for the firms is above that of the market. Thus, this technique underestimates the degree to which acquiring firms outperform the market in the premerger period. The excess returns of 11.7 percent for acquiring firms over the period m = -60,-1, would have been still greater had they been measured relative to the market portfolio.[14]

In stark contrast to the premerger period, acquiring firms are generally found to earn returns substantially *below* the market portfolio, or other control groups over the post-merger period. Of the 23 estimates of returns to acquiring company shareholders for at least 6 months after the announcement, the typical interval between announcement and consummation of a merger in the United States, 17 are negative with a median value of -6.8 percent. Once again those studies that calculate post-announcement residuals relative to the predicted returns from the CAPM over a post-merger period (e.g., Dodd and Ruback 1977, pp. 351-74) *underestimate* the extent to which these firms *underperform* the market over this period.

Thus, the typical pattern of share returns for acquiring companies is as follows: starting anywhere from two to five years prior to undertaking a merger the acquiring firm begins to outperform the market. Since it is inconceivable that the market is *reacting* to the effects of a merger several years down the road, one must assume that any causal linkage between these events runs from outperforming the market to undertaking an acquisition. As noted above, it is reasonable to assume that growth-oriented managers would choose to undertake unprofitable acquisitions more often when their company's profits are abnormally high and their shareholders have enjoyed substantial above market returns. The announcements of mergers, on the other hand, result in quite a mixed pattern of return estimates with the safest conclusion perhaps being "that for the stockholders of the acquiring firms, 'news' of an acquisition may not be worthwhile news" (Mandelker 1974, p. 321).[15] In the months that follow the shareholders of acquiring firms suffer relative declines in the returns on their shares, declines that continue in some cases for several years after the merger.

Several observers have interpreted the findings regarding returns to acquiring and acquired firm shareholders as (1) "consistent with value maximizing behavior on the part of bidding firms" (Halpern 1983, pp. 297-317) (2) "consistent with the operation of an efficient capital market" (Council of Economic Advisors 1985, p. 198), and (3) providing strong evidence "that take-overs generate aggregate net benefits to the economy" (Council of Economic Advisors 1985, p. 198). These conclusions reflect the following chain of reasoning. The negligible gains to acquiring firm shareholders at the time mergers are announced are a result of bidding between actual and potential acquirers in an efficient market that results in all of the gains from a change in control being bid away.[16] Since the capital market is efficient, the declines in returns to acquiring company shareholders over an extended period following merger announcements can be ignored. If these declines were related to the mergers, they would have occurred immediately upon the mergers' announcements under the capital market efficiency assumption. Since the acquired companies' shareholders are unquestionably better off as a result of the mergers, their gains represent a net increase in corporate wealth. Society is better off by this magnitude.

The logic underlying each of these arguments can be challenged. Those who believe that the evidence is consistent with value maximizing behavior tend to focus on the studies that find small positive gains to acquiring firm shareholders, e.g., the studies that focus only on hostile take-overs. But in all countries except the UK, hostile take-overs are a small fraction of all acquisitions. A full evaluation of the market for corporate control must take into account the effects of *all* transaction taking place in it.

The number of studies finding zero or negative gains at announcement is sufficiently large to warrant a no-appreciable-gain conclusion. Such an outcome is inconsistent with wealth maximizing behavior on the part of acquiring firm managers. Why do they invest their shareholders money in a market of high risk and zero expected gain?

The initial announcement of a merger seldom brings with it all of the information relevant for an evaluation of its consequences. Management changes, organizational reforms, spinoffs and antitrust challenges may all occur in the ensuing months and lead the market to reevaluate the future effects of a particular merger. The market efficiency hypothesis with respect to mergers presumes that the market has sufficient knowledge of the effects of past mergers to make an unbiased estimate of the effects of current mergers. But from whence does this knowledge spring? If corporate managers were to consult the writings of finance professors when forming this expectation, they might well expect mergers to be wealth creating, since most finance studies have drawn this conclusion, again in part because they ignore the decline in returns to acquiring firm shareholders that follow mergers.[17] Then too, there is the tendency to regard each new merger wave as different from the past, despite the consistency of the pattern of merger returns over the entire post-World War II period, and even for the merger wave of the '20s (Borg J. R., Borg M. O. and Leeth 1989, pp. 117-31). The coincidence of peaks in merger activity with stock market peaks, when optimism among investors is also at a peak, gives added reason to expect that managers, who undertake mergers, may ignore the evidence of merger failures in the past, and plunge ahead. Several studies of mergers have begun to question the assumption of market efficiency with respect to this activity (Jensen and Ruback 1983, p. 20; Salinger 1992, pp. 39-53; Magenheim and Mueller 1987, pp. 171-93; Agrawal, Jaffe and Mandelker 1992, pp. 1605-21).

The conclusion that mergers harm acquiring firm shareholders becomes stronger, when one estimates the *effect* of the merger as the *change* in performance of the acquiring firm's shares upon and following the merger announcements. Acquiring firms were outperforming the market prior to the mergers being announced. While it is unrealistic to assume that they would outperform the market indefinitely, it seems implausible also to assume that their performance would shift to being normal or subnormal just at the time the mergers are announced, *and that this shift is unrelated to the mergers.* If one were to assume that the firms would have had the same performance relative to the market portfolio after the merger announcement as before, the measured returns to acquiring firm shareholders would be much lower than those reported. For example, Franks and Harris (1989, pp. 225-49) report positive gains of 4.5 percent for acquiring firm shareholders in the UK over the 24 months after announcements relative to the market portfolio's performance over that period. But when they estimate returns over the same 24 months assuming that the acquiring firms would have performed relative to the market as they did over the premerger period (m = -71, -12), the acquiring firm shareholders are seen to have suffered a 12.6 percent *loss.*[18] In general merger and take-overs announcements come between two periods in which acquiring firms shift from substantially outperforming the market to underperforming it. To ignore this dramatic shift, and concentrate only upon the modest changes that occur right at the time of announcement seems questionable as a methodology for measuring the *effects* of the mergers.

The acid test of whether mergers create or destroy wealth is to add up the gains and losses on both sides and see what the total is. Since gains are generally measured as a percentage of market value, the results of this calculation are not apparent from the figures reported in Table 1.2. Acquiring firms are on average much larger than the companies that they acquire. In my 1980 study they were 10 times larger. With this difference in relative sizes the median gain of .196 for acquired firm shareholders is fully offset by a loss of only -.020 for the acquiring firm shareholders. If we combine the gains to acquiring firm shareholders at the time of announcement with those over the post-announcement period, the median wealth change for acquiring firm shareholders is -.029. Only four studies calculate the *net* wealth change from mergers. Two find it to be slightly negative (Firth 1980, pp. 315-47; Malatesta 1983, pp. 155-81), two slightly positive (Halpern 1973, pp. 554-75; Varaiya 1986, pp. 149-78).

VI. The Effects of Mergers on Concentration

The direct effects of horizontal mergers on industry concentration are obvious, and during waves of merger activity can be substantial. Markham (1955, p. 180) estimated that the first great merger wave in the United States created near monopolies in 71 industries. While the effects of horizontal merger waves on industry concentration in other countries have been less dramatic (Hannah 1974, pp. 1-20), they remain an important contributor to the maintenance and increases in industry concentration levels to today (Muller 1976, pp. 113-32).[19] The Celler-Kefauver Act of 1950 reduced the significance of horizontal merger activity significantly, until the 1980s when antitrust enforcement was relaxed. After 1950, therefore, attention in the US has shifted to the effects of mergers on aggregate concentration.

Changes in concentration are a function of three processes: the entry and exit of firms, the internal growth of existing firms, and the external growth through merger of existing firms. In a healthy economy the entry of new firms outstrips firm exits and would lead to substantial declines in concentration, if the other two processes were not in play. Philip Spilberg (1985) calculated that new entry would have reduced the fraction of assets held by the largest 200 corporations in the US from .373 in 1959 to .256 in 1978. Instead, the 200 largest owned .353 fraction of assets in 1978. Roughly, one third of the difference was attributable to the Gibrat effect of internal growth, two thirds to mergers. McGowan (1965, pp. 423-74) attributed all of the increase in aggregate concentration between 1950 and 1960 to mergers. Similar findings exist for the UK. Aaronovitch and Sawyer (1975, pp. 136-75) attribute more than 100 percent of the increase in concentration for the 25 largest firms between 1958 and 1967 to mergers, and estimate substantial fractions for other measures of concentration as well. Hannah and Kay (1977) attribute more than 100 percent of the increase in concentration between 1957 and 1969, by whatever measure, to mergers.

The first and second merger waves in the US raised industry and aggregate concentration levels substantially. Subsequent merger activity has tended to maintain aggregate concentration at these high levels. Those studies that have concluded that mergers do not have an important impact on aggregate concentration (Hay and Untiet 1981, pp. 163-91; White 1982, pp. 97-111) have emphasized that concentration has generally not risen much in periods of intense merger activity. But merger waves occur in times of prosperity when the net entry of firms is high. Were it not for these waves, concentration would be falling rapidly during times of prosperity.[20] The average size of firms today is far greater than it would be, if only the processes of entry, exit, and internal growth had affected it.

VII. Policy Implications

The most important economic development of the last century has been, perhaps, the emergence of the giant, diversified, hierarchical corporation as the "representative firm". Mergers have played a central role in this development. Scarcely a handful of the 200 largest corporations in the United States has not been significantly transformed at one point or another in its history by mergers. Although the effects of mergers on firm size and industry concentration are visible and often dramatic, their impact on social welfare is more subtle and controversial.

The standard approach to measuring the effects of mergers on social welfare is to assume that managers maximize profits, and thus that mergers must either increase market power, or economic efficiency, or both. If the former they are bad, and the extent of the welfare loss is measured by the lost consumers' surplus triangle that follows the exercise of the increase in market power. If only efficiency increases they are good, and the welfare gain is the increased consumers' and producers' surplus rectangles that ensue. If both effects are present, the net welfare change must be calculated. In a classic paper Williamson (1968, pp. 18-36) demonstrated that the rectangle gains will generally exceed the triangle losses.[21] Unless mergers only increase market power, the bias is in favor of mergers. This bias has governed US merger policy since 1980, and the merger policy in most other countries at all times.

There are at least two reasons to question this presumption in favor of mergers. First, there is a strong asymmetry in the intertemporal effects of mergers on market power and efficiency. In a growing economy a company eventually achieves the necessary size for economic efficiency through internal growth. With a 3 percent growth rate, only 5 years are needed to achieve a 16 percent size increase. Only in declining industries can time not achieve the same efficiency gains as mergers.[22] On the other hand, a market power increase, as measured by the change in market share, is not eliminated with time. The mergers that created the United States Steel company produced a firm that was arguably *less* efficient than its rivals as indicated by its continual decline in market share since its creation. Yet after nearly a century of decline, it continues to lead the remnants of the US steel industry.

A second reason to question a presumption in favor of allowing mergers to take place is because they may generate *neither* efficiency gains nor market power increases. Their only effects may be to *increase* company size and to *reduce* economic efficiency. A good deal of the evidence reviewed here suggests that on average this is the case.

Efficiency reducing mergers come about because managers have the discretion to invest corporate income in ways that reduce shareholder wealth. Whether this occurs because managers consciously realize that the mergers are likely to lose money, but undertake them anyway for the private gains they generate, or because they are swept away by the excitement of a booming stock market, the self-serving advice of an investment banker, or their own animal spirits and hubris is of no consequence for merger policy. If mergers lower economic efficiency, they harm society, and create a possible role for economic policy.

Although many mergers are a manifestation of managerial discretion, they are also a potential check on its abuse. In the '80s the corporate take-overs begin to fulfill this potential role, as first predicted by Marris (1963, pp. 185-209 and 1964) and Manne (1965, pp. 110-20). T. Boone Pickens, Carl Icahn, and compatriots emerged as Robin Hoods in the corporate forest taking money from corporate managers and returning it to their shareholders. The history of hostile take-overs and leveraged buyouts illustrates that mergers and take-overs can be both corporate wealth reducing and corporate wealth enhancing.[23] In a major study Bhagat, Shleifer, and Vishny (1990, pp. 1-84) analyzed 62 hostile take-overs between 1984 and 1986 to determine if they generated additional corporate wealth and efficiency, and if so, the source of these gains. Their major findings are as follows: (1) Measured at the time of announcement bidders lose money in a majority of cases. The average loss is relatively small (pp. 14-19). (2) The gains from laying off white (mostly) and blue collar workers vary considerably, accounting for some 10-20 percent of the premia paid on average (pp. 19-34). (3) Tax savings also vary a lot averaging less than the gains from layoffs (pp. 52-3). (4) On average 29.6 percent of the prices paid are recouped through the sale of parts of the acquired companies. In three cases a profit was made on resale alone (pp. 34-39). (5) The resold assets typically wind up being held by firms already in the same industry. The take-overs-spinoff process results ultimately in increases in industry concentration levels (pp. 40-4).

There are several observations to be made about these findings. First, that there are gains to be made from busting up existing firms, firms that often are the product of past mergers, suggests the misuse of managerial discretion by these target firm managers in undertaking mergers. That even hostile take-over bidders are not gaining on average suggests that some abuse of managerial discretion or hubris may even exist among hostile take-over bidders. Second, to the extent that the private gains from take-overs come from layoffs and wage reductions as reported by both Bhagatt, et al., and Lichtenberg and Siegel (1987, pp. 643-73; 1990, pp. 383-408), their social gains are likely to be less than the private gains. The take-overs in part are merely transferring rents from white and blue collar workers to shareholders. Although the elimination of the market power of these workers may generate triangle efficiency gains as well, these will as usual be dwarfed by the pure transfer rectangles. Third, the same conclusion holds without qualification for any transfers from taxpayers to shareholders. Finally, the ultimate judgment of the effect on social welfare of these take-overs must examine the impact on efficiency and market power of the essentially horizontal transfers of assets that the take-overs eventually produce, the tradeoff once again.

As in the analysis of the traditional profit-maximizing, market power-efficiency increasing mergers, the key policy issue regarding mergers, hostile take-overs, leveraged buyouts, and the like, is how to preserve the socially beneficial ones and prevent the rest. Neither a total ban on all mergers and take-overs, or a totally laissez faire policy is likely to be first best. Not surprisingly in a world of large corporations controlled by their managements, the policy thrust in the United States has been to prevent hostile take-overs, leveraged buyouts and the other actions that can curb managerial discretion, while allowing the friendly mergers which often are its most egregious manifestations. Space precludes a detailed analysis of the options, so I shall close with a mere listing of some possibilities.[24]

(1) Prohibit all devices, e.g., poison pills, by which management can protect itself from a hostile bid.

(2) Prohibit managers from holding voting shares, or at least from voting the shares they hold when a possible conflict between management and shareholders arises. Nonvoting shares held by management have an obvious positive incentive effect, and require no regulation.

(3) In the absence of (2), prohibit the issuance of multi-vote shares or their ownership by management.

(4) Require acquiring shareholder approval of all acquisitions above a certain size, perhaps by a supramajority (e.g., 3/4).

(5) Require that acquiring firms report income and balance sheet data on all acquisitions above a given size for a fixed time interval (e.g., 10 years) to allow shareholders and the market to evaluate these decisions more accurately.

(6) Repeal the Glass-Steagall Act to allow banks to hold shares in corporations and potentially play a role in monitoring them.

(7) Tax undistributed profits to encourage the complete payout of corporate earnings.

Notes

1. Mergers are defined as a "friendly" joining of two or more companies under one corporate roof and management team; take-overs as the unfriendly seizure of control of a company by one firm, or in some cases one individual, without the consent or over the protest of the acquired unit's management. The distinction can be arbitrary as some "friendly" mergers occur under the threat of a more hostile union. All of the companies embraced by Duke did not march happily to the alter (Tennant 1950, pp. 22-5). For much of this essay I shall use "mergers" or "acquisitions" to refer to both events, delineating take-overs only when I wish to focus on this form of combination. Overt take-overs were rare in the United States before the late 1960s.
2. Since the economy is much larger in 1990 than in 1890, the magnitudes of merger activity at these two points in time are not strictly comparable. In the peak year of merger activity during the first wave (1899), assets acquired equaled 12.9 percent of GNP. In 1988, they were 5 percent of GNP.
3. For the United Kingdom see Hannah (1974, pp. 1-20), Hughes (1989, pp. 30-98); for Belgium Kumps and Witterwulghe (1980, pp. 67-97); for Germany Cable, Palfrey, and Runge (1980, pp. 99-132); for France Jenny and Weber (1980, pp. 133-62); and for Sweden Ryden and Edberg (1980, pp. 193-226).
4. For a review of this literature see Jacquemin and Slade (1989, pp. 415-73).
5. See the discussion and examples in Steiner (1975, chs. 9, 10), and Scherer and Ross (1990, pp. 188-90).
6. The one exception to this generalization is the acquisition of a potential entrant, since entry is more likely in a boom than in a recession.
7. See the surveys by Steiner (1975), Mueller (1977, pp. 315-47), and Hughes, Mueller, and Singh (1980, pp. 1-26).
8. Boyle (1970, pp. 152-70); Conn (1973, pp. 154-9); Stevens (1973, pp. 149-58); Melicher and Rush (1974, pp. 141-49); Mueller (1980a, pp. 271-98); Harris, Stewart, and Carleton (1982, pp. 223-40); Rhoades (1987, pp. 277-92); Herman and Lowenstein (1988, pp. 211-40); and Alberts and Varaiya (1989, pp. 133-49). Schwartz (1982, pp. 391-8) and Amel and Rhoades (1989, pp. 17-27) found acquired industrial firms and banks, respectively, to be somewhat less profitable than similar units, although not so much to suggest impending bankruptcy. Ravenscraft and Scherer (1987) found acquired firms to be more profitable than nonacquired companies. In the UK acquired firms have tended to be slightly less profitable than one otherwise would expect, but not dramatically so (Singh 1971 and 1975, pp. 497-515; Kuehn 1975; Cosh, Hughes and Singh 1980, pp. 227-70). In other countries acquired companies are either as profitable or slightly less so than nonacquired units (see chapters in Mueller 1980a).
9. This managerial-life-cycle hypothesis of mergers resembles the capital-redeployment and defensive-diversification hypotheses put forward by Williamson (1970 and 1975) and Weston (1970, pp. 66-80), and with Mansinghka (1950, pp. 23-34). They differ mainly in that Williamson and Weston assume that the managers are profit maximizers, and that the mergers improve efficiency by creating an "internal capital market" and thus avoiding the inefficiencies of the external one.
10. Just how optimistic the managers of acquiring firms must be is illustrated in the study by Alberts and Varaiya (1989, pp. 133-49). They show that to justify the premia paid for companies in the 1970s and 1980s in the United States, managers of acquiring firms would have to anticipate improving the performance of an acquired unit from that of an average firm to one in the top decile of all companies. Gort and Hogarty (1970, pp. 167-84) conjectured that acquiring firm managers were overly optimistic in a much earlier study.
11. For surveys covering these early waves, see Markham (1955, pp. 141-82), Hogarty (1970, pp. 378-91), and Reid (1968).
12. Once the averaging effect of mergers was accounted for, I found that their "synergistic"

effect was negative. Reid (1970, pp. 937-46) and Melicher and Rush (1974, pp. 141-49) presented evidence indicating that the share- and bondholders of the Weston-Mansinghka conglomerates were not made better off as a result of the mergers.

13. Baldwin and Gorecki observe a high tendency for plants acquired from departing firms by firms not already in an industry, i.e. in complete nonhorizontal mergers, to exit the industry at a later date. This strikes me as an indication of an unsuccessful merger. They do not interpret these exits that way, however, but argue that merger is a form of entry and should be compared with "greenfield" entry (i.e., the entry of newly created firms), which is associated with very high exit rates. They find acquired firms exiting at the same rate as greenfield entrants later depart. But, in the absence of being acquired, an ongoing firm has a much higher probability of surviving than a greenfield entrant. If other, nonacquired existing plants are used as the control group, the high exit rate of acquired plants in Canada would make the Baldwin and Gorecki results more similar to mine for the United States.
14. For further discussion see Magenheim and Mueller (1987, pp. 171-93).
15. Several of the country studies in Mueller (1980a) report substantial gains to the shareholders of acquiring firms in the *year* of a merger. Since the stock price change over a year might include movement before the announcement, it is difficult to compare this result with the rest of the literature that uses a much narrower "window". The post-merger results for these studies do not suffer from this problem, and resemble those of the rest of the literature-continual relative declines in returns.
16. The more positive conclusions regarding the operation of the market for corporate control usually emphasize the results that find small positive gains to acquiring firm shareholders, particularly the studies that focus only on hostile take-overs. But a full appreciation of the impact of activity in the market for corporate control must take into account the returns to the far more numerous "friendly" mergers, as well, and the losses to acquiring firm shareholders that occur in the months that follow.
17. Caves (1989, pp. 151-74) emphasizes the sharp difference in the conclusions regarding mergers reached in the finance literature from those obtained by industrial organization economists examining actual ex post data.
18. Dodd and Ruback (1977, pp. 351-74) are often cited as evidence that shareholders of acquiring firms earn significantly higher returns as a result of take-overs. But they, unlike most other studies that calculate residuals from CAPM estimates, switch to *post*-event estimates of CAPM to measure "the effects" of the merger in the announcement month. Because bidder shareholders do significantly better by .028 in the announcement month than they will do in a still later period after the announcements - a period in which they will underperform the market - makes the tender offers wealth creating. Had they chosen to judge the *effects* of the tender offers relative to how the bidders were doing *before* the bid, a different conclusion might have been reached. See also Magenheim and Mueller (1977, pp. 315-47).
19. Weiss's (1965, pp. 172-81) study of horizontal mergers in the US between 1929 and 1958 would appear to contradict this conclusion, but he studied the 3 decades of the last century in which merger activity was the weakest.
20. Similarly, increases in concentration during steep economic declines when merger activity is lax, as occurred in the US in the '30s, do not imply that mergers do not affect aggregate concentration. Obviously, if they do not occur, they can have no effect. The increases in concentration that are sometimes observed in economic downturns are the result of exits far outweighing entry - the process that tends to reduce concentration in prosperity operating in reverse.
21. See, however, Ross (1968, pp. 1371-76) and DePrano and Nugent (1969, pp. 947-59), and Williamson's defense (1977).
22. We speak here of course of horizontal mergers only. But it is these where the tradeoff seems most likely to be at issue.

23. See Baker and Wruck (1989, pp. 163-90), Kaplan (1989e, pp. 191-212), and cases discussed by Adams and Brock (1989, ch. 8), Bhagat, et al. (1990, pp. 1-84).
24. For a fuller discussion see Adams and Brock (1989, ch. 15).

References

Aaronovitch, S. and Sawyer, M.C., 1975, "Mergers, growth and concentration", *Oxford Economic Papers*, 27, 136-55.

Adams, W. and Brock, J.W., 1989, *Dangerous Pursuits*, New York: Pantheon.

Agarwal, A., Jaffe, J.F. and Mandelker G.N., 1992, "The post-merger performance of acquiring firms: A re-examination of an anomaly", *Journal of Finance*, 47, 1605-71.

Alberts, W.W. and Varaiya, N.P., 1989, "Assessing the profitability of growth by acquisition: A 'premium recapture' approach", *International Journal of Industrial Organization*, 7, 133-49.

Amel, D.F. and Rhoades, S.A., 1989, "Empirical evidence on the motives for bank mergers", *Eastern Economic Journal*, 15, January 17-27.

Amihud, Y. and Baruch, L., 1981, "Risk reduction as a managerial motive for conglomerate mergers", *Bell Journal of Economics*, 12, 605-17.

Auerbach, A.J. and Reishuis, D., 1987, "Taxes and the merger decision", in John C. Coffee, Jr., Louis Lowenstein, and Susan Rose-Ackerman, eds., *Takeovers and Contexts for Corporate Control*, Oxford: Oxford University Press, 300-13.

Azzi, C., 1978, "Conglomerate mergers, default risk, and homemade mutual funds", *American Economic Review*, 68, 161-72.

Baldwin, J., 1991, *The dynamics of the competitive process*, mimeo, Queen's University, mimeo.

Baldwin, J. and Gorecki, P., 1990, "Mergers placed in the context of firm turnover", in *Bureau of the Census, 1990 Annual Research Conference, Proceedings*, Washington, D.C.: U.S. Department of Commerce, 53-73.

Baker, G.P. and Wruck, K.H., 1989, "Organizational changes and value creation in leveraged Buyouts", *Journal of Financial Economics*, 25, 163-90.

Bhagat, S., Shleifer, A. and Vishny, R.W., 1990, "Hostile take-overs in the 1980s: The return to corporate specialization", *Brookings Papers on Economic Activity*, 1-84.

Borg, J.R., Borg, M.O. and Leeth, J.D., 1989, "The success of mergers in the 1920s: A stock market appraisal of the second merger wave", *International Journal of Industrial Organization*, 7, 117-31.

Boyle, S.E., 1970, "Pre-merger growth and profit characteristics of large conglomerate mergers in the United States, 1948-68", *St. John's Law Review*, 44, Spring, special edition, 152-70.

Cable, J.R., Palfrey, P.R., and Runge, J.W., 1980, "Federal Republic of Germany, 1964-1974", in Mueller, ed., 1980a, 99-132.

Caves, R.E., 1989, "Mergers, take-overs and economic efficiency: Foresight vs. indsight", *International Journal of Industrial Organization*, 7, 151-74.

Caves, R.E. and Barton, D.R., 1990, *Efficiency in U.S. Manufacturing Industries*, Cambridge, Mass.: MIT Press.

Comanor, W.S., 1967, "Vertical mergers, market power, and the antitrust laws", *American Eco-*

nomic Review, 57, 254-65.

Conn, R.L., 1973, "Performance of conglomerate firms: Comment", *Journal of Finance*, 28, 154-9.

Cosh, A., Hughes, A. and Singh, A., 1980, "The causes and effects of take-overs in the United Kingdom: An empirical investigation for the late 1960s at the microeconomic level", in Mueller, ed., 227-70.

Council of Economic Advisors, 1985, *Annual Report*, Washington, D.C.: Government Printing Office.

Deneckere, R. and Davidson, C., 1985, "Incentives to form coalitions with Bertrand competition", *Rand Journal of Economics*, 16, 473-86.

DePrano, M.E. and Nugent, J.B., 1969, "Economies as an antitrust defense: Comment", *American Economic Review*, 59, Dec., 947-59.

Dodd, P. and Ruback, R., 1977, "Tender offers and stockholder returns: An empirical analysis", *Journal of Financial Economics*, 5, 351-74.

Dodds, J.C. and Quek, J.P., 1985, "Effect of mergers on the share price movement of the acquiring firms: A UK study", *Journal of Business Finance and Accounting*, 12, Summer, 285-96.

Dutz, M.A., 1989, "Horizontal mergers in declining industries", *International Journal of Industrial Organization*, 7, 11-33.

Eckbo, B.E., 1986, "Mergers and the market for corporate control: The Canadian evidence", *Canadian Journal of Economics*, 19, 236-60.

Evans, W.N. and Kessides, I.N, forthcoming, "Living by the 'golden rule': Multimarket contact in the U.S. airline industry", *Quarterly Journal of Economics*.

Firth, M., 1980, "Takeovers, shareholder returns, and the theory of the firm", *Quarterly Journal of Economics*, 94, 315-47.

Franks, J.R., Broyles, J.E. and Hecht, M.J., 1977, "An industry study of the profitability of mergers in the United Kingdom", *Journal of Finance*, 32, 1513-25.

Franks, J.R. and Harris, R.S., 1989, "Shareholder wealth effects of corporate take-overs", *Journal of Financial Economics*, 23, 225-49.

Geroski, P.A., 1984, "On the relationship between aggregate merger activity and the stock market", *European Economic Review*, 25, 223-33.

Gilson, R.J., Scholes, M.S. and Wolfson, M.A., 1987, "Taxation and the dynamics of corporate control: The uncertain case for tax-motivated acquisitions", in John C. Coffee, Jr., Louis Lowenstein, and Susan Rose-Ackerman, eds., *Takeovers and contexts for Corporate Control*, Oxford: Oxford University Press, 271-99.

Goldberg, L.G., 1973, "The effect of conglomerate mergers on competition", *Journal of Law and Economics*, 16, 137-58.

Gort, M., 1969, "An economic disturbance theory of mergers", *Quarterly Journal of Economics*, 83, 624-42.

Gort, M. and Hogarty, T.F., 1970, "New evidence on mergers", *Journal of Law and Economics*, 13, 167-84.

Halpern, P.J., 1973, "Empirical estimates of the amount and distribution of gains to companies in mergers", *Journal of Business*, 46, 554-75.

Halpern, P., 1983, "Corporate acquisitions: A theory of special cases? A review of event studies applied to acquisitions", *Journal of Finance*, 38, 297-317.

Hannah, L., 1974, "Mergers in British manufacturing industry, 1880-1918", *Oxford Economic Papers*, 26, 1-20.

Hannah, L. and Kay, J.A., 1977, *Concentration in modern industry*, Macmillan: London.

Harris, R.S., Stewart, J.F. and Carleton, W.T., 1982, "Financial characteristics of acquired firms", in M. Keenan and L.J. White, eds., *Mergers and acquisitions: Current problems in perspective*, Lexington, Mass.: Lexington Books, 223-40.

Hay, G. and Untiet, C., 1981, "Statistical measurement of the conglomerate problem", in Roger D. Blair and Robert F. Lanzillotti, eds., *The conglomerate corporation*, Cambridge, Mass.: Oelgeschlager, Gunn, and Hain, 163-91.

Herman, E.S. and Lowenstein, L., 1988, "The efficiency effects of hostile take-overs", in Coffee, J.C. Jr., Lowenstein, L., and Rose-Ackerman, S., eds., *Knights, raiders, and targets*, Oxford: Oxford University Press, 211-40.

Hogarty, T.F., 1970, "Profits from mergers: The evidence of fifty years", *St. John's Law Review*, 44, Spring, special edition, 378-91.

Hughes, A., 1989, "The impact of merger: A survey of empirical evidence for the UK", in Fairburn, James and Kay, John, eds., *Mergers and Merger Policy*, Oxford: Oxford University Press, 30-98.

Hughes, A. and Singh, A., 1980, "Mergers, concentration, and competition in advanced capitalist economies: An international comparison", in Mueller (1980a, pp. 1-26).

Ikeda, K. and Doi, N., 1983, "The performance of merging firms in Japanese manufacturing industry: 1964-75", *Journal of Industrial Economics*, 31, 257-66.

Jacquemin, A. and Slade, M.E., 1989, "Cartels, collusion, and horizontal merger", in Schmalensee, Richard and Willig, Robert, eds., *Handbook of industrial organization*, vol. 1, North Holland: Amsterdam, 415-73.

Jenny, F. and Weber, A.-P., 1980, "France, 1962-72", in Mueller, ed., 1980a, 133-62.

Jensen, M.C., 1986, "Agency costs of free cash flow, corporate finance and take-overs", *American Economic Review*, 76, 323-29.

Jensen, M.C. and Ruback, R.S., 1983, "The market for corporate control", *Journal of Financial Economics*, 11, 5-50.

Kaplan, S.N., 1989e, "Management buyouts: Evidence on taxes as a source of value", *Journal of Finance*, 44, 611-32.

Kaplan, S.N., 1989, "Campeau's Acquisition of Federated", *Journal of Financial Economics*, 25, 191-212.

Kuehn, D., 1975, *Takeovers and the theory of the firm*, London: Macmillan, 1975.

Kumps, A.-M. and Witterwulghe, R., 1980, "Belgium, 1962-74", in Mueller, ed., 1980a, 67-97.

Levy, H. and Sarnat, M., 1970, "Diversification, portfolio analysis and the uneasy case for conglomerate mergers", *Journal of Finance*, 25, 795-802.

Lichtenberg, F.R., 1992, "Industrial de-diversification and its consequences for productivity", *Journal of Economic Behavior and Organization*.

Lichtenberg, F.R. and Siegel, D., 1987, "Productivity and changes in ownership of manufacturing plants", *Brookings Papers on Economic Activity*, 643-73.

Lichtenberg, F.R. and Siegel, D., 1990, "The effect of ownership changes the employment and wages of central office and other personnel", *Journal of Law and Economics*, 33, 383-408.

Lichtenberg, F.R. and Siegel, D., 1990, "The effects of leveraged buyouts on productivity and related aspects of firm behavior", *Journal of Financial Economics*, 27, 165-94.

Lintner, J., 1971, "Expectations, mergers and equilibrium in purely competitive securities markets", *American Economic Review*, 61, 101-11.

Magenheim, E.B. and Mueller, D.C., 1987, "On measuring the effect of acquisitions on acquiring firm shareholders, or are acquiring firm shareholders better off after an acquisition than they were before?", in John C. Coffee, Jr., Louis Lowenstein, and Susan Rose-Ackerman, eds., *Take-overs and contexts for Corporate Control*, Oxford: Oxford University Press, 171-93.

Malatesta, P.H., 1983, "The wealth effect of merger activity and the objective functions of merging firms", *Journal of Financial Economics*, 11, 155-81.

Mandelker, G., 1974, "Risk and return: The case of merging firms", *Journal of Financial Economics*, 1, 303-35.

Manne, H.G., 1965, "Mergers and the market for corporate control", *Journal of Political Economy*, 73, 110-20.

Markham, J.W., 1955, "Survey of the evidence and findings on mergers", in *Business concentration and price policy*, New York: National Bureau of Economic Research, 141-82.

Marris, R., 1963, "A model of the 'managerial' enterprise", *Quarterly Journal of Economics*, 77, 185-209.

Marris, R., 1964, *The Economic Theory of Managerial Capitalism*, Glencoe: Free Press.

McDougall, F.M. and Round, D.K., 1986, *The Determinants and Effects of Corporate take-overs in Australia*, 1970-1981, Victoria: Australian Institute of Management.

McGowan, J.J., 1965, "The effect of alternative antimerger policies on the size distribution of firms", *Yale Economic Essays*, 5, 423-474.

Meeks, G., 1977, *Disappointing marriage: A study of the gains from merger*, Cambridge, England: Cambridge University Press.

Melicher, R.W. and Rush, D.F., 1974, "Evidence on the acquisition-related performance of conglomerate firms", *Journal of Finance*, 29, 141-49.

Melicher, R.W., Ledolter, J. and D'Antonio, L.J., 1983, "A time series analysis of aggregate merger activity", *Review of Economics and Statistics*, 65, 423-30.

Mueller, D.C., 1969, "A theory of conglomerate mergers", *Quarterly Journal of Economics*, 83, 643-659.

Mueller, D.C., 1972, "A life cycle theory of the firm", *Journal of Industrial Economics*, 20, 199-219.

Muller, J., 1976, "The impact of mergers on concentration: A study of eleven West German industries", *Journal of Industrial Economics*, 25, 113-32.

Mueller, D.C., 1977, "The effects of conglomerate mergers: A survey of the empirical evidence", *Journal of Banking and Finance*, 1, 315-47.

Mueller, D.C., 1980a, *The Determinants and Effects of Mergers: An International Comparison*, Cambridge, Mass.: Oelgeschlager, Gunn & Hain.

Mueller, D.C., 1980b, "A cross-national comparison of the results", in Mueller (1980a, pp. 299-314).

Mueller, D.C., 1980b, "The United States, 1962-1972", in Mueller (1980a, pp. 271-298).

Mueller, D.C., 1985, "Mergers and market share", *Review of Economics and Statistics*, 67, 259-67.

Mueller, D.C., 1986, *Profits in the Long Run*, Cambridge: Cambridge University Press.

Mueller, D.C., 1990, *The Dynamics of Company Profits*, Cambridge: Cambridge University Press.

Nelson, R.L., 1959, *Merger Movements in American Industry*, 1895-1956, Princeton: Princeton University Press.

Nelson, R.L., 1966, "Business cycle factors in the choice between internal and external growth", in W. Alberts and J. Segall, eds., *The Corporate Merger*, Chicago: University of Chicago Press.

Peer, H., 1980, "The Netherlands, 1962-1973", in Mueller, ed., 1980a, 163-91.

Perry, M.K., 1989, "Vertical integration: Determinants and effects", in Schmalensee, Richard and Willig, Robert, eds., *Handbook of Industrial Organization*, vol. 1, North-Holland: Amsterdam, 415-73.

Perry, M.K. and Porter, R.H., 1985, "Oligopoly and the incentive for horizontal merger", *American Economic Review*, 75, 19-27.

Ravenscraft, D.J. and Scherer, F.M., 1987, "Mergers and managerial performance", in John C. Coffee, Jr., Louis Lowenstein, and Susan Rose-Ackerman, eds., *Take-overs and contexts for Corporate Control*, Oxford: Oxford University Press, 1987.

Reid, S.R., 1968, *Mergers, Managers and the Economy*, New York: McGraw-Hill.

Reid, S.R., 1970, "A reply to the Weston/Mansinghka criticisms dealing with conglomerate mergers", *Journal of Finance*, 26, 937-46.

Rhoades, S.A., 1983, *Power, Empire Building, and Mergers*, Lexington, Mass.: Lexington Books.

Rhoades, S.A., 1987, "The operating performances of acquired firms in banking", in R.L. Wills, J.A. Caswell, and J.D. Culbertson, eds., *Issues after a century of federal competition policy*, Lexington, Mass.: Lexington Books, 277-92.

Roll, R., 1986, "The Hubris hypothesis of corporate take-overs", *Journal of Business*, 59, 197-216.

Roll, R., 1988, "Empirical evidence on take-over activity and shareholder wealth", in John C. Coffee, Jr., Louis Lowenstein, and Susan Rose-Ackerman, eds., *Take-overs and Contexts for Corporate Control*, Oxford: Oxford University Press, 241-52.

Ross, P., 1968, "Economies as an antitrust defense: Comment", *American Economic Review*, 58, 1371-76.

Ryden, B. and Edberg, J.-O., 1980, "Large mergers in Sweden, 1962-1976", in Mueller, ed., 1980a, 193-226.

Salant, S.W., Switzer, S. and Reynolds, R.J., 1983, "Losses from horizontal merger: The effects of an exogenous change in industry structure on Cournot-Nash equilibrium", *Quarterly Journal of Economics*, 98, 185-99.

Salinger, M., 1992, "Standard errors in event studies", *Journal of Financial and Quantitative Analysis*, 27, 39-53.

Scherer, F.M. and Ross, D., 1990, *Industrial market structure and economic Performance*, 3rd ed., Boston: Houghton Mifflin.

Scott, J.J., 1982, "Multimarket contact and economic performance", *Review of Economics and Statistics*, 64, 368-75.

Scott, J.J., 1989, "Purposive diversification as a motive for merger", *International Journal of Industrial Organization*, 7, 35-47.

Schumpeter, J.A., 1934, *The Theory of Economic Development*, Cambridge, Mass.: Harvard University Press.

Schwartz, S., 1982, "Factors affecting the probability of being acquired: Evidence for the United States", *Economic Journal*, 92, 391-8.

Shiller, R.J., 1981, "Do stock prices move too much to be justified by subsequent changes in dividends?", *American Economic Review*, 71, 421-36.

Shiller, R.J., 1984, "Stock prices and social dynamics", *Brookings Papers on Economic Activity*, 457-98.

Singh, A., 1971, *Take-overs: Their Relevance to the Stock Market and the Theory of the Firm*, Cambridge: Cambridge University Press.

Singh, A., 1975, "Takeovers economic natural selection, and the theory of the firm: Evidence from the post-war United Kingdom experience", *Economic Journal*, 85, 497-515.

Smith, V.L., 1970, "Corporate financial theory under uncertainty", *Quarterly Journal of Economics*, 84, August, 451-71.

Spilberg, P., 1985, *Mergers and aggregate concentration*, Ph.D. dissertation, University of Maryland, College Park.

Steiner, P.O., 1975, *Mergers: Motives, effects, policies*, Ann Arbor: University of Michigan Press.

Stevens, D.L., 1973, "Financial characteristics of merged firms - A multivariate analysis," *Journal of Financial and Quantitative Analysis*, 8, 149-58.

Stigler, G.J., 1950, "Monopoly and oligopoly by merger", *American Economic Review*, 23-34.

Tennant, R.B., 1950, *The American Cigarette Industry*, New Haven: Yale University Press.

Varaiya, N.P., 1986, "The returns to bidding firms and the gains from corporate take-overs: A reexamination", in A. Chen, ed., *Research in Finance*, 6, 149-78.

Weiss, L., 1965, "An evaluation of mergers in six industries", *The Review of Economics and Statistics*, 47, 172-81.

Weston, J.F., 1970, "The nature and significance of conglomerate firms", *St. John's Law Review*, 44, Spring, special edition, 66-80.

Weston, J.F. and Mansinghka, S.K., 1970, "Tests of the efficiency performance of conglomerate firms", *Journal of Finance*, 26, 919-36.

White, L.J., 1982, "Mergers and aggregate concentration", in Michael Keenan and Lawrence J. White, eds. *Mergers and Acquisitions*, Lexington, Mass.: Lexington Books, 97-111.

Williamson, O.E., 1968, "Economies as an anti-trust defense: The welfare trade-offs", *American Economic Review*, 58, 18-36 (rptd. with correction in C.K. Rowley, ed., *Readings in Industrial Economics*, London: Macmillan, 1972).

Williamson, O.E., 1970, *Corporate Control and Business Behavior: An Inquiry into the Effects of Organization form on Enterprise Behavior*, Englewood Cliffs, NJ: Prentice-Hall.

Williamson, O.E., 1975, *Markets and Hierarchies: Analysis and Antitrust Implications*, New York: Free Press.

Williamson, O.E., 1977, "Economies as an anti-trust defense revisited", in A.P. Jacquemin and H.W. de Jong, eds., *Welfare Aspects of Industrial Markets, Nijenrode Studies in Economics No. 2*, Leiden: Martinus Nijhoff.

Williamson, O.E., 1989, "Transaction cost economics", in Schmalensee, Richard and Willig, Robert, eds., *Handbook of Industrial Organization*, vol. 1, North-Holland: Amsterdam, 135-82.

2. Merger Activity and Antitrust Policy in the United States

ROBERT H. SMILEY

I. Introduction

The restructuring of the American corporation through mergers has been the single most significant financial activity in the U.S. in the 1980s. The numbers and amounts of assets involved in mergers each year is almost overwhelming; almost no large firms approach the end of the decade without having merged at least once or sold a division acquired in an earlier period. This restructuring, partly due to pressures to become more efficient, and partly due to purely financial motivations, will have a lasting impact on the organization of industry in the United States.

Why have there been so many mergers in this decade? Are the motivations efficiency based, such as the need to group together a more rational set of business units into the firm so as to compete internationally? Or are the motivations financial in nature, including defensive mergers to avoid being acquired by an unfriendly partner, or to reduce corporate income tax liabilities? Or are the managers involved merely seeking to direct larger and larger firms, and engaged in empire building as a result?

Whatever the cause, the ability of U.S. firms to merge at such a rapid pace in the 1980s was facilitated by U.S. antitrust policy. After developing an economics based, rational set of merger guidelines midway through its tenure, the Reagan administration proceeded to apply these guidelines in a manner that allowed many more firms to merge than was the case in prior administrations. Indeed, as the end of the Reagan administration approached, U.S. firms engaged in a virtual frenzy of merger activity - which continued even after it was apparent that another Republican would follow Reagan into the White House.

This paper is organized into three major sections. In Section II we review and document recent merger activity in the United States. Section III investigates the reasons behind this merger activity. After searching for an understanding of the cause behind aggregate or total merger activity - as it fluctuates through a business cycle - we then seek to determine which of several possible individual motivations is most likely to be responsible for most of the trend of merger activity in the recent past. Section IV begins by describing U.S. antitrust law, and the enforcement agencies which carry it out. We then explain the U.S. merger guidelines, which explain in some detail which mergers will be allowed to take place, and which mergers will be challenged. Finally in Section V, we review the enforcement activity of

G. Mussati (ed.), Mergers, Markets and Public Policy, 45–79.
© 1995 *Kluwer Academic Publishers.*

the Reagan administration and its use of these guidelines in the 1980s, and prospects for antitrust enforcement under President Clinton. The paper concludes, in Section VI, with a conclusions section.

II. Merger Activity in the United States

A casual reading of the American financial press indicates that mergers captivate the imagination of the American business public. Merger activity, or what the American academic community has begun to call "The Market for Corporate Control" affects a surprisingly large number of firms: in 1986 there were 4,323 mergers completed (a 28% increase from 1985), and they involved an acquisition of equity of more than 200 billion dollars (see Tables 2.1 and 2.2). In the 1970s there were between 926 and 1,529 mergers each year. In the 1980s, every year except 1980 has seen more than 2,000 mergers.

A merger is typically consummated through a tender offer; an offer to all or some of the shareholders to sell their shares to an acquiror. In order to motivate the shareholders to tender (offer for sale) their shares to the buyer, a premium must be paid. The average and median premium for these offers is shown in Table 2.3. Two things are striking about this table; first, the premiums are quite large. The simple average of the premiums paid from 1974 through 1987 is 43%. This indicates that the acquiror felt that the shares of the purchased firm were worth at least 43% more than the market value prior to the merger. Second, with the exception of 1974, both the average and the median premium show an increasing trend until 1979, followed by a decline in the premium paid through the 1980s.

Not all mergers are successful transactions, at least with hindsight. Indeed, Ravenscraft and Scherer (1987) argue that most mergers are disappointing to the acquiring firm, either because hoped for synergies or efficiencies did not meet their expectations, or because the acquired firm was poorly managed after the merger. Support for this view is found in Table 2.4, where it is shown that slightly less than 40% of all merger transactions in the 1980s involved the sale of previously acquired divisions to another firm.

As discussed in Section III, there are many reasons for undertaking a merger. Horizontal mergers are typically made for economies of scale or market power reasons. Horizontal mergers are approximately 40% of the total in recent years (see Table 2.5). Vertical mergers, which allow increased efficiency of processing activities and reduced risk of foreclosure, are approximately 12% of the total in recent years. The product extension mergers have risen to approximately 1/4 of the total, while pure conglomerate mergers are approximately 1/3 of the total number of mergers.

Table 2.1. Completed mergers, 1965-1984

Year	Number of Mergers	Year	Number of Mergers
1965	*1,893	1975	981
1966	*1,746	1976	1,145
1967	1,354	1977	1,209
1968	1,829	1978	1,452
1969	1,712	1979	1,527
1970	1,318	1980	1,568
1971	1,269	1981	2,326
1972	1,263	1982	2,295
1973	1,064	1983	2,344
1974	926	1984	2,999

*Merger and acquisition statistics were less systematically kept in the mid 1960s. The data for those years are Federal Trade Commission statistics for merger announcements (including those never executed) in mining and manufacturing. *Mergers & Acquisitions* began recording completed transactions in 1967 and data from 1967-84 are based on *M&A*'s count.
Source: *Mergers and Acquisitions*, 20, No. 3, p. 42, 1986.

Table 2.2. Ten-year merger completion record, 1978-1987

Year	No. of Transactions	% Change	Value $ mil	% Change
1978	1,452	—	*	—
1979	1,529	+ 5,3	34,197.2	—
1980	1,565	+ 2,4	32,958.9	- 3,6
1981	2,326	+48,6	67,263.6	+104,1
1982	2,296	- 1,3	60,398.4	- 10,2
1983	2,387	+ 4,0	52,579.7	- 12,9
1984	3,158	+32,3	125,986.3	+139.6
1985	3,428	+ 8,6	145,397.8	+ 15,4
1986	4,323	+28,1	204,438.9	+ 40,6
1987	3,701	-14,4	167,519.2	- 18,1

*Value data for this year are incomplete.
Source: *Mergers and Acquisitions*, 22, No. 6, p. 45, 1988.

Table 2.3. Percent premium paid over market price* 1968-1987

Year	Average	Median	Base *
1974	50.1	43.1	147
1975	41.4	30.1	129
1976	40.4	31.1	168
1977	40.9	36.2	218
1978	46.2	41.5	240
1979	49.9	47.6	229
1980	49.9	44.6	169
1981	48.0	41.9	166
1982	47.4	43.5	176
1983	37.7	34.0	168
1984	37.9	34.4	199
1985	37.1	27.7	331
1986	38.2	29.9	333
1987	38.3	30.8	237

*Base: the number of transactions where a premium over market was paid. Premiums can only be calculated on acquisitions of publicly traded companies.
Source: W.T. Grimm & Co., *Mergerstat Review*, p. 82, 1987.

Table 2.6 lists the ten most active industry areas for merger activity. Both manufacturing and service firms are well represented on this list, with chemicals and allied products being the largest merger value sector, while banking represents the largest number of mergers. In the case of chemicals and allied products, mergers are predominantly for the purpose of the rationalization of production, and the extension of the product lines of established multiproduct firms. The second, third and fourth ranking sector by value, and the largest by the number of mergers are all service sectors (retailing, banking and communication). Mergers in these sectors are predominantly for the purpose of network economies of scale. Mergers in banking and communications were profoundly affected by recent moves toward deregulation of these sectors by the government.

The countries most active in making acquisitions in the United States in 1987 are listed in Table 2.7. The most striking factor about this list is the fact that, with the exception of Japan, all of the leading firms in making transactions in the United States are English speaking. Indeed, all are members of the British Commonwealth.

When U.S. firms make acquisitions in other countries, however, language does not appear to be such an important barrier. But another pattern is apparent. With the exception of Canada, all five countries where U.S. firms make a large number of acquisitions are members of the European Community.

A discussion of the major changes in the market for corporate control would be incomplete if it did not include leveraged buyouts. A leveraged buyout is a transaction in which some individuals or a firm borrow some of the funds necessary to purchase the outstanding equity in an established firm. This borrowing of funds necessarily increases the leverage of the firm being acquired. These firms are then no longer traded on securities markets, but are held privately by the individuals who undertook the transaction. The number of leveraged buyouts and their volume is indicated in Table 2.8. From that table we can see that both the number of deals and the volume of the equity purchased has increased substantially since 1985. This increase in the volume of equity purchased has been made possible by the establishment of a major new financial instrument, the so called "junk bond". These are bonds which are of relatively high risk (because of the leverage involved), and relatively high yield. They are typically purchased by banks, insurance companies, pension funds and individuals.

Table 2.4. Divestitures, 1965-1987

Year	Number	Percent of all Transactions	Year	Number	Percent of all Transactions
1965	191	9 %	1976	1,204	53 %
1966	264	11 %	1977	1,002	45 %
1967	328	11 %	1978	820	39 %
1968	557	12 %	1979	752	35 %
1969	801	13 %	1980	666	35 %
1970	1,401	27 %	1981	830	35 %
1971	1,920	42 %	1982	875	37 %
1972	1,770	37 %	1983	932	37 %
1973	1,557	39 %	1984	900	36 %
1974	1,331	47 %	1985	1,218	41 %
1975	1,236	54 %	1986	1,259	38 %
			1987	807	40 %

Source: W.T. Grimm & Co., *Mergerstat Review*, p. 63, 1987.

Table 2.5. Distribution of manufacturing industry assets acquired by experience-oriented merger category, 1950-1977

Type of Merger	1950-55	1956-63	1964-72	1973-77	1950-77
			Percent of total*		
Horizontal	70.1	49.1	38.2	39.4	41.4
Vertical	12.3	15.8	9.0	11.6	10.9
Related business	19.1	26.9	23.7	26.5	24.8
Pure conglomerate	5.3	18.4	36.2	32.4	31.3

*Percentages do not sum to 100 because some horizontal mergers are also classified as vertical.
Source: Ravenscraft and Scherer (1987), p. 24.

Table 2.6. Most active industry areas by dollar volume, 1987

Rank Industry Area	Value $ mil *	No. of Mergers
1. Chemicals & Allied Products	16,638.4	148
2. Retailing	13,572.3	216
3. Banking	12,537.5	334
4. Communications	11,261.8	157
5. Nonelectrical Machinery	9,530.7	229
6. Mining, Oil & Gas	9,495.1	140
7. Petroleum Refining	9,088.4	12
8. Electrical & Electronic Machinery	7,132.7	205
9. Stone, Clay, Glass & Concrete	5,698.6	43
10. Business Services	5,103.1	185

*Based on 1,796 transactions in which price data were revealed.
Source: *Mergers and Acquisitions*, 22, No. 6, p. 46, 1988.

Table 2.7.1. Countries most active in making U.S. acquisitions, 1987

Countries	Transactions
United Kingdom	125
Canada	43
Australia	24
Japan	22
New Zealand	19

Source: *Mergers and Acquisitions*, 22, No. 6, p. 45, 1988.

Table 2.7.2. Countries attracting U.S. buyers, 1987

Countries	Transactions
United Kingdom	46
Canada	40
France	19
West Germany	12
Italy	10

Source: *Mergers and Acquisitions*, 22, No. 6, p. 45, 1988.

The types of leveraged buyouts for the year 1987 are also listed in Table 2.8. In terms of the volume of equity purchased, the major part of this activity was in "taking private" (removing from the stock exchange) a firm that was previously publicly traded. But a large proportion of the number of leveraged buyouts was for the purpose of divestiture, which typically involves the reversal of a previously effected merger.

Table 2.8.1. The leveraged buyout market, 1983-1987

Year	No. of Deals	Volume $ mil
1983	230	4,519.0
1984	253	18,807.3
1985	254	19,633.8
1986	331	46,428.9
1987	259	35,636.4

Table 2.8.2. Types of leveraged buyouts, 1987

Year	No. of Deals	Volume $ mil
Going Private	25	22,304.3
Divestitures	185	11,302.1
Private	49	2,029.9

Source: *Mergers and Acquisitions*, 22, No. 6, p. 59, 1988

III. Explanations of Merger Activity

The empirical literature on merger activity in the United States can be grouped into two parts; research which attempts to explain the aggregate level of merger activity, and research which attempts to differentiate between explanations for the motivations behind merger activity. Research on the explanations for aggregate merger activity is described in the following Section III. Attempts to discriminate between alternative theories of merger activity are presented in next one.

Aggregate merger activity

The earliest research on aggregate merger activity simply noted what appeared to be waves in the number of mergers and acquisitions. Stigler (1950) and Nelson (1959) are representative of these studies, which use little or no statistical methodology. Merger waves have been observed in the period around 1900 (Stigler's mergers for monopoly period), the period immediately before the depression (late 1920s, Stigler's mergers for oligopoly period), the late 1960s and early 1970s (conglomerate period), and the most recent few years. We should note that the overall importance of mergers, even when the number of mergers are simply counted rather than reflected in nominal (uncorrected for the inflation) dollars, can easily be overstated. If we normalize the number of mergers by some factor such as the level of real GNP, the results are rather different. The most recent periods of merger activity are much less important when one realizes that the GNP has grown very substantially. Furthermore, the merger spike which occurred at the turn of the century is seen to be quite remarkable using this methodology.

A recent paper by Shughart and Tollison (1984) has challenged the notion that merger activity has occurred in waves. Using annual data on U.S. mergers from 1895 to 1979, they are not able to reject the null hypothesis that merger levels are characterized by a white noise process or by a first order autoregressive scheme. They find that merger activity is best characterized as a random walk, and the presence of "merger waves" is doubtful. Golbe and White (1988) criticized this work because Shughart and Tollison never defined exactly what was meant by a merger wave, and thus did not formally test a wave hypothesis.

Other work has attempted to determine what factors cause aggregate merger activity. In a work based on the notion of Granger causality (Granger, 1969), Geroski (1984) attempts to determine whether the level of aggregate merger activity is related to the level of the stock market (the value of a stock market share price index). He finds that, at the very least, the correlation between aggregate merger activity and indices of share prices is unstable, and thus of little predictive value. In both the U.S. and U.K., using data over the period 1895 to 1979, he fails to reject the null hypothesis of no causality in both directions for subperiods.

In a much more detailed analysis, Melicher, Ledolter and D'Antonio (1983) investigate the causes of aggregate merger activity in the U.S. over the time period 1947-1977, using quarterly data. They found only a weak relationship between merger activity and economic conditions, and found that changes in industrial production and business failures lagged behind changes in merger activity. The relationships between aggregate merger activity and stock conditions were much stronger, however. Changes in stock prices (not the level of stock prices as investigated by Geroski) and interest rates were found to be good forecasters of merger activity. That is, increased merger activity tended to lag behind increased stock prices by one to two quarters.

Distinguishing between different merger theories

Why do firms merge? A number of possible explanations for merger activity will be discussed in this section. After a review of each possible motivation, the empirical research will be cited, if it exists. We caution the reader to keep in mind the "multiple cause" hypothesis of Peter Steiner (1975), namely that there are a number of different causes of mergers in any particular time period, and that the search for a dominant or primary cause may not be fruitful.

Mergers for market power

The leading paradigm in the field of industrial organization for the last 40 years has been the structure - conduct - performance model which originated in large part from Joe Bain's work. Because they can affect the structure of an industry, horizontal mergers can affect the conduct and thus the public (welfare) and private (profitability) performance of an industry. In particular, by eliminating a rival or by reducing the possibilities for free rider effects in collusion attempts, a merger can increase the market power (the ability of the surviving firm to raise price above the competitive level for a sustained period of time) of the combined firms. Indeed, as quoted by Scherer (1980), Thomas Edison had this to say about the formation of the General Electric Company in a time when managers were less concerned about antitrust violations,

> "Recently there has been sharp rivalry between [Thomson-Houston and Edison General Electric], and prices have been cut so that there has been little profit in the manufacture of electrical machinery for anybody. The consolidation of the companies . . . will do away with a competition which has become so sharp that the product of the factories has been worth little more than ordinary hardware."

The degree to which the market power motive has been operative for mergers in the United States in the recent past is affected by U.S. antitrust policy. Since antitrust policy in the United States was quite restrictive toward horizontal and vertical mergers over the period between the second world war and 1980, we would not expect to find a substantial number of mergers which have indeed increased market power, precisely because they would normally have been challenged and precluded by the U.S. antitrust authorities. Unfortunately, this is the period that provides the data most frequently used in studies of merger activity. So with an understanding that we are not likely to find a substantial number of mergers for market power, precisely because they were prevented by the legal statutes in the Unites States, we turn to the evidence.

In the most comprehensive empirical study of mergers and takeovers to date, Ravenscraft and Scherer (1987) examine 6,000 mergers and takeovers consummated between 1950 and 1976. Although the study is concerned primarily with the results (success) of mergers, the authors, in discussing motives for merger, conclude "The bulk of U.S. manufacturing company acquisitions made in the 1950-76 period were conglomerate, for which it is hard (but not impossible) to concoct convincing monopoly power scenarios. Most of the horizontal acquisitions involved market shares too small to confer much monopoly power, in part because larger horizontal acquisitions were under intense antitrust scrutiny."

In another study Mueller (1985) examines whether horizontal and conglomerate mergers have affected the market share of the merging firm. Whatever their motives, Mueller finds that mergers have not had a positive effect on market share, and so it is unlikely that they have augmented market power. He concludes "Companies acquired in a conglomerate merger and companies joining in horizontal mergers are both found to experience substantial losses in market shares relative to control group companies following the mergers."

An ingenious method for testing the effects of mergers was proposed by William F. Baxter, later to be Assistant Attorney General for antitrust enforcement in the Reagan administration. He argued "If the primary effect of the merger was attainment of efficiencies and more vigorous competition, securities prices of rival firms should fall; whereas the cartelization explanation should be revealed by increases" (Baxter 1980). His argument is that if the merger results in lower costs for the merged firms, they will have a competitive advantage over their rivals, and securities prices of their rivals (representing, as they do, the discounted future profits of the rivals) will fall as a result. Alternatively, if the merger is successful in increasing the market power of the merged firms, they will raise the prices of their products. Indeed, if the merger results in the clear cartelization of the industry, all firms in the industry will raise prices. In any case, the rivals should benefit from the acquired firms increased market power, since prices of one of their rivals will increase. This should lead to an increase in the share price of the rival. So the researcher can distinguish between the effects of a merger by observing the share prices of rivals.

To test the Baxter hypothesis requires the researcher to perform an event study, a common methodology in corporate finance. In an event study the returns to ownership of common stock in a merging company are compared with the returns to ownership of common stock in a matched nonmerging company (matched by industry, size, etc.), after correcting both for changes in the overall level of market returns and the relative risk of each of the companies. In a study of 65 horizontal and 11 vertical mergers, Eckbo (1983) splits his sample into those that were the subject of a legal challenge by the government (and thus had a substantial possibility of not being successful) and those that were unchallenged. He found that the rivals of firms in unchallenged mergers had no significant price effect; their share prices did not rise or fall, and thus *unchallenged* mergers do not appear to provide evidence of either market power or efficiency effects.

Challenged mergers, however, present a more interesting picture. First, "The rivals of the 65 horizontally challenged mergers in the data base on average earn significant positive abnormal returns at the time of the merger proposal announcement" (Eckbo, p. 269). This finding is consistent with market or monopoly power as the motive for merger. But, paradoxically, when a challenge is announced by the government, the rivals show a positive abnormal performance, rather than the decrease in share price that one would expect if a challenge would be expected to decrease the possibility of collusion.

In a more recent study of 627 corporate mergers, Cartwright, Kamerschen and Zieburtz (1987) find that in slightly over half of the cases, the rivals in horizontal mergers exhibited significantly positive abnormal returns, providing evidence of anti-competitive affect. In about 1/4 of the cases, the rivals had a negative price reaction to the proposed merger, which is consistent with a merger for efficiency reasons.

Finally, we can look at the effect of a particular merger on the price of the products sold. Barton and Sherman (1984) studied the merger between the Xidex corporation and its two major rivals for its two product lines, which occurred in 1976 and 1979. They found a significant price increase for each of the product lines after the acquisition occurred. The "price increase yielded substantial profit gains, in each case sufficient to recover the cost of the acquisition in about two years" (Barton and Sherman 1984, p. 176).

Efficiency motivations for mergers

Nearly all press announcements of mergers issued by the acquiring companies list the motivation as efficiencies, synergy, or some sort of cost reduction. This is, of course, to be expected since mergers for market power are illegal, and mergers for the reasons listed below (e.g. undervalued target firms) are usually unconvincing. But is increased efficiency the real motivation for mergers? And if so, do the merged firms indeed have lower costs?

How could a combination of two firms have lower costs than each of the firms operating separately? The simple economies of scale response is unconvincing, since most economies of scale occur within the plant, and a merger will not normally affect the operations at any single plant. Economies of scale, if in fact they are augmented by a merger, must be some sort of multiplant economies of scale (see Scherer, Beckenstein, Kaufer and Murphy, 1975). In addition, efficiencies could result from economies of scope made possible by a merger of firms in related industries. These economies of scope, or multiplant economies of scale, could result from combined research and development labs, management techniques, computer facilities, accounting procedures or any other operation which could be provided for both firms at less than the sum of the cost of providing it to the two individually. Similarly, product extension mergers can make better use of existing distribution networks, cooperative advertising, or retail outlets owned by the manufacturer.

Production rationalization could produce efficiencies in mergers. If, for example, two firms were producing similar products in distant locations, and each was shipping its product throughout the entire market at a high cost, a merger would allow each plant to specialize in the production of the product for a portion of the geographic territory. (I note that this merger may be in violation of the horizontal merger laws). Further, if each of two firms is producing a wide range of products, a merger may allow each to specialize in the production of a portion of the product line of the combined firm, thereby achieving economies of scale and of learning by doing through longer production runs.

Another way that a merger could reduce the total cost of the combined firms would be by displacing or removing the poor management of the target or acquired firm. This motivation for mergers, of course, is most common in hostile takeovers, and was first brought to the attention of the academic community by Manne (1965).

Finally, although not strictly an efficiency motive, the diversification reason for merger has received considerable attention. Although profits will not be increased, variability in returns or profits will be reduced if the cash flows or profits of the two merged firms are not perfectly correlated. Although popular as a motivation in the business community and the financial press, academics have tended to discount this motive as unconvincing since investors can achieve exactly the same diversification at the same cost or less by simply buying a diversified portfolio of securities. Since most investors hold diversified portfolios of common stocks in the United States, gains from diversification are likely to be ephemeral. The only possible gain would be a reduction in the probability of bankruptcy that would accrue to the combination.

How is one to determine empirically whether efficiencies are indeed the primary motivation for mergers? As stated above, efficiencies are clearly the most frequently cited motive for merger, and perhaps by this simple test we should accept the notion that they indeed *are* the primary motive. Short of some sort of survey of managers, which would have a great deal of difficulty gaining credibility, we should perhaps base our evaluation of the importance of merger *motives from* observing the *effects* of these mergers.

We have already described the work of Mueller (1980) who found that "Mergers led to a reduction in the profitability of the merging firms and a slowdown in their rate of growth of size." In a later study Mueller reached a similar conclusion, "no support was found for the hypothesis that mergers improve efficiency by consolidating the sales of the acquired companies on their most efficient product lines" (Mueller, 1985).

In their study of 6,000 mergers, Ravenscraft and Scherer find little evidence of efficiencies resulting from mergers "Our finding that, on average, profitability declines and efficiency losses resulted from mergers of the 1960s and early 1970s casts doubt on the widespread applicability of an efficiency theory of merger motives." (Ravenscraft and Scherer 1987, pp. 211-12). Indeed, the *only* evidence of efficiencies resulted from mergers when firms which had been acquired at an earlier date were subsequently sold off to either another firm in the same industry or to its own management. Because of the increased possibility of real economies of scale and scope resulting from a horizontal merger, and because of increased incentives for efficient operation that are present when the management of a firm buys it (such as a leveraged buyout), these are precisely the cases where we would expect the most impressive gains in efficiency through merger. But Ravenscraft and Scherer find overwhelming evidence of no efficiency gains in normal first-round acquisition. This, they believe, was primarily the result of a management failure, and was due to "the failure to manage acquired companies as well as they were managed before acquisition." (Ravenscraft & Scherer 1987, p. 212).

Whereas the studies of the largest number of mergers show little evidence of gains in efficiency, there is some evidence that, at the very least, managers did indeed *intend* to achieve efficiencies or some sort of synergy through merger. In a study of 83 mergers that occurred between 1970 and 1977, Stewart, Harris and Carleton (1984) find a significant correlation between the advertising to sales ratios of the acquired and the acquiring firms, and between the research and development expenditure to sales ratios of the acquired and the acquiring firms. They argue that these findings are consistent with two motivations; first that there will be economies of scope for firms that produce several products (after the merger), each of which is advertising intensive, and second, that managers tend to specialize in different types of industries or markets, and that they will therefore make acquisitions in like markets as their basic product - like with respect to advertising intensity, for example. They make similar arguments with respect to research and development intensity. Although far from convincing, this evidence is at least consistent with the possibility that economies of scope benefits may be present in mergers, and particular that savings (or a gain in expertise) in the advertising expenses of two combined firms, or the research and development expenses of two combined firms, may result.

Finally, there is a huge literature in the economics/finance area on the effects of mergers and takeovers on shareholders. These studies typically measure the effects on shareholders through the event study methodology described above, in which abnormal returns to ownership of stock are measured after controlling for the effects of overall stock market price movements, and the risk of the investments. Though we will not review the entire literature here (but see Jensen and Ruback 1983), we can summarize it briefly. First, there appear to be statistically significant and economically important gains to the shareholders of acquired firms. Second, acquiring firms either perform no better or worse than average, or show slight increases in value. The result, then, is that the combination of two firms results in an increase in the total value (acquiring and acquired firm together) of the firms' shares. Therefore, some argue that there must be some underlying reason for an increase in value of the two firms together, over what they were worth when valued by the market separately. But if the studies reviewed above are correct, namely that there are no increases in market power, nor are there any efficiencies that are gained through the merger, then what is the basis for this increase in value? First, although no "real efficiencies" result from the merger, the *financial* condition of the two firms combined are improved so that some gain in long term profitability will result. Second, perhaps the securities markets are wrong in evaluating the effects of the merger, and are wrong systematically. We will discuss these two hypotheses in turn below.

Tax related motives for merger

Returns to capital in the United States are treated differently, depending upon whether the capital provided by investors is debt capital or equity capital. Payment by the firm to providers of debt capital are not taxable to the firm (they are taxable to the individual). Equity returns are, however, the subject of a federal corporate income tax as well as a personal income tax on individuals who receive them - they are double taxed. For this reason, there is an argument for firms to have a high amount of debt in their capital structure, an argument that essentially amounts to the reduction of tax liabilities. Indeed, some would argue that there is a "optimal" capital structure, and that it is a function of the rate of taxation on equity income.

One dominant financial motive for merger in the 1980s deals directly with this "optimal" capital structure - proportion of debt and equity. If a firm has been financially conservatively managed, and thus has very little debt in its capital structure, the after tax flows to all holders of capital can be increased by a change in its capital structure toward more debt. Many takeovers in the 1980s have been as a result of this motivation. The overall transaction typically is one of the bidder purchasing the firm, issuing more debt (thus changing the capital structure), and using some of the proceeds of that newly issued debt to retire equity capital - purchase it in the marketplace. Indeed, frequently the bidder in a takeover will issue new debt as a means of raising the funds necessary to purchase the equity of the target firm.

Unfortunately, this phenomenon is too recent to be reflected in the academic press. However, a careful reading of the popular business press reveals that tax avoidance is the primary motive for merger in the late 1980s. Whether the "leveraging up" of the American business community is socially desirable from the perspective of the entire country, is quite another matter. Indeed, many economists (especially those at our central bank) are very concerned that a recession will bring forth a financial calamity and widespread bankruptcies, as firms find themselves unable to meet the very high debt payments resulting from this "leveraging up".

The "hubris" hypothesis, or management error

One possible motivation for merger that reconciles the fact that thousands of mergers occur each year even though little or no gain in value to the acquiring firm's shareholders is the hubris hypothesis. Hubris means pride or excessive confidence in oneself, and whereas a number of authors have discussed the possibility that managers are making systematic errors in undertaking mergers, the most sophisticated version of this discussion has been put forth by Richard Roll (1986).

According to Roll, one way to think of the valuation placed upon target firms by acquiring firms is as a random variable, which has as its mean the true underlying value of the target firm, (which is - realistically - best approximated by its current market price). The distribution of the "draws" of this random variable (or valuations of the target firm made by the acquiring firm) can best be approximated by some frequency distribution. Having valued the target firm, the acquiring firm must decide whether to proceed with a takeover bid - at some price below its estimated value (to allow for the recovery of transactions costs). Since a takeover bid with an announced price below the current market price will certainly fail, this valuation distribution will, in effect, be truncated at some point slightly above its mean. What we will observe then, is the upper tail of the distribution of draws or valuations. Since these valuations exceed the mean, they are likely to be too high, resulting in takeovers which cause the target firm to lose money on the total acquisition.

Roll considers whether "rational" managers would proceed in a market of this type. He notes that this phenomenon is essentially identical to the winner's curse phenomenon in auctions, and also notes that people do not adjust for the winner's curse in a manner that is rational. He argues that the rational managers should realize the underlying problem discussed in the paragraph above, and automatically adjust downward the valuation of the target firm - to correct for the winner's curse. Indeed, he argues that managers with the opportunity to make 20 or 30 takeover bids would probably learn about this bias, and would adjust downward their valuation of all target firms. But, he argues, individual managers make only one or two takeover bids during their managerial careers, and it is understandable that hubris or pride will cause them to believe that their valuation is correct, and even if they understand the bias discussed above, to assume that it will not apply to them.

The empirical evidence on this issue is mixed. The hubris hypothesis would predict that (A) the value of the bidding firm should decrease, (B) the value of the target firm should increase, and (C) that the combined value of the target and bidding firm should fall slightly (to account for transactions costs). The evidence on A and C is mixed; some studies have reported these values to increase, some to decrease, and all studies have reported that the change in value of acquiring firms and of the combined participants in the merger to be very small. The evidence on B is strongly positive - target firms gain in value during an acquisition.

In conclusion, the evidence on the hubris hypothesis is mixed. But we find it to be an extremely interesting hypothesis, though we are not quite ready to accept it as the "universal null hypothesis" that Roll argues for in his paper.

Growth maximizing or empire building motives for merger

Beginning with the work of Baumol (1959) and Maris (1964), economists became interested in the possibility that managers were pursuing other objectives than simply the maximization of the value of the firm. Different hypotheses argued that managers might be interested in maximizing the amount of sales made by the firms or the growth rate of sales, at the expense of lower profits. Economists proposing these theories based them on the fact that managers' objective functions might contain these elements directly (managers feel more powerful and prestigious if they are managing larger firms), or that managers' salaries might be higher if they were running larger firms - and this increase in salary from the size or growth rate of the firm would exceed the decrease in salary resulting from reduced profitability.

Rather than go into the empirical evidence on findings of this sort, we will merely note that the evidence uncovered and reviewed by Roll in his hubris hypothesis paper, described above, is consistent with these motivations. Mergers which allow for little or no increased value for the bidding firm's shareholders appear to be consistent with the hypothesis that the managers of these firms simply want to run larger units - build empires. In reviewing their own evidence, Ravenscraft and Scherer conclude "The most charitable, and probably also the most accurate, interpretation is that empire-building motives interacted with hubris. Merger-makers seriously overestimated their ability to integrate, motivate, and effectively control the companies they acquired, and as a result they underestimated the costs that came with formal control." Ravenscraft and Scherer (1987 p. 214).

The 1988 merger frenzy

The year 1988 appears on its way to set a new financial record in terms of mergers and leveraged buyouts. In the first three months of 1988, there were 15 mergers or leveraged buyouts involving a payment of more than $1 billion. The data is much too recent to analyze systematically and carefully, but a number of very recent motivations - nearly all financial in nature - appear to be operating currently.

Setting the stage for the merger activity in 1988 was the stock market decline in 1987. The value of the average share declined by 25% in October of 1987, and for a short period of time after that most financial entrepreneurs were in somewhat of a state of shock. But after adjusting to this shock, investment bankers and firms interested in making acquisitions quickly realized that the share prices of many firms had been reduced to the point where their purchase represented a very good - profitable - acquisition.

What also has begun to drive the number of acquisitions currently is the fact that the takeover or merger and acquisition process has become an industry by itself. There are approximately 50,000 investment analysts and entrepreneurs - primarily in New York - whose major line of work is to restructure corporations through mergers and leveraged buyouts. This is an increase from 10,000 approximately 5 years ago. These analysts are continually evaluating different firms, comparing the value placed by the analysts on the firm to the current market price, and approaching potential bidders with the results.

Driving this industry is the fact that there is a large amount of liquid capital available for the merger and acquisition business. Much of this capital has flowed into the United States from other countries as a result of the recent devaluation of the dollar. to quote the chairman of a prominent merger-prone firm - Sanford Sigoloff - Chairman of Wickes Companies, "The world is awash in cash". Indeed, the recent 25 billion dollar leveraged buyout of R.J.R. Incorporated was achieved by the firm of Kohlberg, Kravis, and Roberts owing to its ability to raise 20 billion dollars from institutional investors (banks, insurance companies, and mutual funds, in a matter of a day or so. This type of liquidity was unheard of in recent times especially for funds whose investors are willing to risk them for high yield, high risk lending.

Also fueling the recent increase in the number of mergers and leveraged buyouts is a basic restructuring of American industry. Many of the leveraged buyouts represent divisions of firms acquired in a recent merger, which simply did not fit with the total strategy of the acquiring firm. Another way to view this restructuring would be to ask what component parts of a business offer reasonable hope of economies of scale or scope. Those lines of business which are simply too distant from the basic thrust of the acquiring firm are frequently spun off - or sold to another bidder following a basic acquisition of a large firm. Indeed, the consulting firm McKinsey found, in an analysis of all 1986 acquisitions costing more than

100 million dollars, that within one year about 75% of the acquiring firms sold one or more divisions that they acquired during the basic merger. This restructuring is frequently rationalized or justified in terms of the necessity of American firms' movement toward a synergistic or logical structure, in order to compete in international markets. What appears to be the case, if the rhetoric is to be believed, is that firms are using the market for corporate control to achieve an internal structure that is designed to maximize the possibilities for economies of scale and scope. If there is no apparent reason for a division to be part of the firm, in these terms, that division will quickly be sold. Indeed, making mergers and acquisitions appears to be becoming part of the established way of doing business for many managers. "It is a way of life for most companies to look at 10 acquisition candidates a day. That's very different from a few years ago." A statement from John A. Morgan - managing director of an investment banking firm, quoted in *Business Week* (March 21, 1988, p. 124).

Finally, much of the merger activity may have also been driven by the possibility of a tightening of antitrust policy under a new president. As we note in the next section on antitrust policy, the Reagan administration has been characterized by an unprecedentedly relaxed attitude towards merger activity. Almost any likely new policy will be more strict, and challenge mergers that would have passed unchallenged in the Reagan administration. As a result, many firms are rushing to complete mergers before the January 20, 1989 change in administration.

IV. Public Policy towards Merger Activity

In this section we will review the United States public policy towards merger activity, both before the Reagan administration, and since 1980. We will first discuss the legal statutes governing merger activity, then turn to the enforcement policy of the Reagan administration, and finally we will discuss the future of United States policy toward merger activity.

The United States has a complicated, and perhaps peculiar system of government. There are basically three separate and relatively equal parts of the government. The U.S. Congress is made up of the House of Representatives and the Senate, and has as its basic responsibility the formulation of laws. The Executive Branch, headed by the President, and containing agencies such as the Department of Justice and the Federal Trade Commission, has as its responsibility the execution or enactment of these laws, including the prosecution of firms and individuals for violation of the laws. Finally, the courts interpret these laws and decide cases and operate at three levels - the U.S. District Court is the trial court and will reach the first level of decision; firms or individuals can then appeal through the Appellate Court, and the final appeal is the Supreme Court. The Supreme Court's basic function is to decide whether individuals or firms have violated laws, and whether laws passed by Congress are in conflict with the Constitution of the United States.

Public policy towards merger activity can be made in two ways. First, in the final analysis, it is the laws of the country - as passed by the Congress - that will determine what mergers are legal and illegal. Thus we should observe the legal statutes, and the cases that have been decided under these legal statutes, if we want to understand merger policy. This is the topic of Section 4.1. Second, the executive branch also makes merger policy by the cases it decides to prosecute. If a merger goes unchallenged by the Executive Branch, because the Department of Justice and the Federal Trade Commission have decided that they do not believe the merger is a sufficient problem to merit a legal challenge, then the courts will usually never have a chance to decide whether the merger is in violation of the legal statutes passed by the Congress. So in this sense, the Executive Branch also makes merger policy.

Laws governing mergers

Legal restrictions on merger activity have a more than one hundred year history in the United States. The decade of the 1880s saw the rise of the Standard Oil Company, which nearly monopolized world petroleum trade, and the rise of a political movement in the United States known for its position against bigness - in both government and (especially) in private enterprises. This political movement, known as populism, united the political power of a number of otherwise powerless groups, including farmers, small business, and labor. This movement resulted in the passage in 1890 of the Sherman Act, names for Senator John Sherman of Ohio. A major thrust of the Sherman Act is against monopoly, and many of the abuses which led to its passing had been carried out by firms which merged with many of their rivals to become monopolies.

Section II of the Sherman Act states

> "Every person who shall monopolize, or attempt to monopolize, or combine or conspire with any other person or persons, to monopolize any part of the trade or commerce among the several states, or with foreign nations, shall be deemed guilty of a felony...".

The first important legal case which used Section II of the Sherman Act was the U.S. vs. Northern Securities Company, a railroad formed by merger in 1901 which would have had a complete monopoly over all railroad service in the northwest quadrant of the United States. The Supreme Court declared the railroad to be in violation of the Sherman Act of 1904.

In 1911, within two weeks of each other, the Supreme Court struck down two other monopolies which had been formed through mergers around the turn of the century. The Court required the Standard Oil Company and the American Tobacco Company to be dissolved into component parts; Standard Oil into 33 geographically dispersed companies (one for each state), and American Tobacco into 16 different pieces, each representing a separate company. Among other violations, both the Standard Oil Company and the American Tobacco Company had been guilty of predatory pricing and abusive tactics towards firms they sought later to acquire through merger.

Although the second section of the Sherman Act has an effect on mergers *for the purpose of monopoly*, the major merger statute in the United States was passed in 1914, and is called the Clayton Act. This act, passed at the urging of President Woodrow Wilson, is designed to stop the formation of monopolies before they actually come into violation of the Sherman Act. As amended in 1950, Section 7 of the Clayton Act states

> "[t]hat no corporation engaged in commerce shall acquire, directly or indirectly, the whole or any part of the stock or other share capital and no corporation subject to the jurisdiction of the Federal Trade Commission shall acquire the whole or any part of the assets of another corporation engaged also in commerce, where in any line of commerce in any section of the country, *the effect of such acquisition may be substantially to lessen competition, or to tend to create a monopoly...*" (emphasis added).

As any reader can see, these two legal statutes are not terribly precise. Indeed, to understand the legal environment in which mergers occur in the United States, one must review the cases that have been decided by the Supreme Court. Although it might seem bizarre, it is traditional legal policy in the United Stated for the Congress to pass a rather general law, and then for the court system to define precisely what is meant by that law in its legal decisions and precedents. This is precisely what has happened in the area of merger policy.

The first major case under the revised (in 1950) Clayton Act was the government's challenge of a merger between two steel companies, Bethlehem Steel Corporation and Youngstown Sheet and Tube Company. Bethlehem was the nation's second largest steel producer (to United States Steel) with 16% of total U.S. ingot capacity, while Youngstown was the sixth largest and 4.6% of ingot capacity. The companies argued that they served different geographic markets, with Bethlehem serving the eastern United

States and Youngstown serving the midwest portion of the United States. The court was not convinced by this argument, as it observed that freight costs were falling, and barriers to the penetration of markets and different geographic areas were sufficiently low to view the geographic market as nationwide in scope. The courts struck down the merger, and Bethlehem Steel began a nationwide expansion program without the benefit of merger activity.

Most economists view the most extreme anti-merger decision in the United States to be that of the United States vs. Brown Shoe company. With 4% of national manufacturing output, the Brown Show Company had attempted to merge with the Kinney Shoe Company (0.5% of national output) in 1955. But the major reason for the disallowal of the merger was not manufacturing capacity, but retail sales. The court found that in 32 cities, the combined unit sales shares of the two firms exceeded 20%. The court viewed an individual city as the relevant geographic market (thus arguing that price increases in one city *would not* cause consumers to shift purchases to another city, *nor* cause entry from sellers in other cities into the original city). This impact on individual cities was sufficient, the court declared, to find a substantial lessening to competition under Section 7 of the Clayton Act.

The other major restrictive case was decided in 1966, when the Supreme Court struck down a merger between two Los Angeles retail grocery chain stores. The Von's Grocery Company was the third largest retail grocery chain in the Los Angeles area with a 4.7% of the market, and the Shopping Bag Food Stores was the 6th largest retailer with 2.8%. The combined firm would have a market share second only to the leading firm's, Safeway, which had 8% of the market. Again the court decided that the geographic market was an individual city, and after observing that the market share of the 20 top chains had risen from 44% in 1948 to 57% in 1958, the Supreme Court reversed a lower court decision which had favored the merger.

In the 1960s, horizontal merger policy in the United States thus became quite hostile. Unless one of the firms was otherwise going to fail, a merger between any two firms with a substantial market share in the same industry would be disallowed. This policy had several consequences; first, horizontal mergers between successful firms decreased substantially. If a firm felt it was too small to achieve economies of scale or scope, it would have to grow internally (perhaps at higher costs) in order to achieve those economies. Second, as described in Section III, there were still tax incentives and other reasons for merger to be a profitable avenue for growth. But since horizontal mergers were foreclosed by rigorous enforcement of the Clayton Act, firms chose to merge with firms in other industries, and the great conglomerate merger wave began in the mid 1960s. This merger wave was essentially caused by two factors; the tax and other advantages to merge, and the legal prohibitions against mergers with firms in the same industry.

Executive branch policies towards merger activity

Two agencies of the Executive Branch enforce merger policy in the United States. Within the Department of Justice, the Antitrust Division takes informal responsibility for one set of industries of the country. In addition, the Federal Trade Commission also enforces merger policy, and also takes informal responsibility for the remaining industries of the country.

Following the victory in the Brown Shoe and Vaughn's - Shopping Bag cases, it became apparent to the government that it would win nearly every merger case that it decided to prosecute. So the government began to be somewhat more careful in the cases it decided to bring, and in 1968 issued a set of merger guidelines which would inform firms about whether they could expect to be challenged if they chose to merge.

The 1968 Guidelines said that the Department of Justice would challenge mergers, in industries where the four-firm concentration ratio was greater than 75%, according to the following guidelines:

Acquiring firm	Acquired firm
4%	4% or more
10%	2% or more
15% or more	1% or more

If the four-firm concentration ratio was less than 75%, a merger would be challenged if the firms met the following criteria:

Acquiring firm	Acquired firm
5%	5% or more
10%	4% or more
15%	3% or more
20% or more	2% or more
25% or more	1% or more

These guidelines were in place until the Reagan administration came into office in 1981. As the reader can see, the small market shares necessary for a government challenge of a merger led to relatively few horizontal mergers being attempted in the period between 1968 and 1981.

Merger policy under the Reagan administration – The guidelines

The Reagan administration took an entirely different approach to merger policy. The effects of this policy can be seen in two ways: the mergers that the administration has not challenged; and the issuance of an entirely new set of Merger Guidelines, first released in 1982, and then revised in 1984. We will first discuss the merger guidelines in their final form - the 1984 version.

The approach to the decision of which merger to challenge and which not to challenge described in the merger guidelines is unique in several ways. First, the 1984 Guidelines are very careful in their description of how product and geographic markets are to be defined. Then, having defined the product and geographic market of the prospective merger partners, the 1984 Guidelines specify what mergers will and will not be challenged in terms of Hirschman - Herfindahl Indices (HHI) rather than concentration ratios. Third, a merger which otherwise might not be allowed to become effective will in fact be allowed if entry is free - if the market is contestable. Finally, even if the merger can be seen to result in a lessening of competition, it might be allowed if there are substantial efficiency gains. We now turn to a detailed discussion of the 1984 merger guidelines.

Although binding only on the U.S. Department of Justice, both the Federal Trade Commission and The Department of Justice have been guided by the guidelines in deciding which mergers to challenge. The main theme of the guidelines is to not allow a merger if it would create or enhance the market power of the surviving firm, where market power is defined as the ability of a single firm or group of firms to raise price above the competitive level for an extended period of time without experiencing entry.

The first step in determining whether a particular merger would enhance the market power of the participant is to define the product and geographic market in which the firms compete. The guidelines state that

> "A market is defined as a product or group of products and a geographic area in which it is sold such that a hypothetical, profit-maximizing firm, not subject to price regulation, that was the only present and future seller of those products in that area would impose a "small but significant and nontransitory" increase in price above prevailing or likely future levels. The group of products and geographic area that comprise a market will be referred to respectively as the "product market" and the

"geographic market".

> "Specifically, the Department will begin with each product (narrowly defined) produced or sold by each merging firm and ask what would happen if a hypothetical monopolist of that product imposed a "small but significant and nontransitory" increase in price. If the price increase would cause so many buyers to shift to other products that a hypothetical monopolist would not find it profitable to impose such an increase in price, then the Department will add to the product group the product that is the next-best substitute for the merging firm's product and ask the same question again. This process will continue until a group of products is identified for which a hypothetical monopolist could profitably impose a "small but significant and nontransitory" increase in price. The Department generally will consider the relevant product market to be the smallest group of products that satisfies this test."

Geographic markets are defined in a similar fashion. By a "small but significant and nontransitory" increase in price the Department will typically apply a 5% price increase over a period of one year as a test.

Once the Department has defined a product and geographic market, they will have grouped together a group of firms which clearly compete with each other, and whose cross-elasticity of demand for each other's products will be quite high. Once the scope of the market has been determined, the Department will then turn to the issue of whether the merger can be expected to lessen competition within that market substantially. Like the 1968 Guidelines, the 1984 Guidelines have a different policy toward mergers depending upon the *beginning* state of competition. Unlike the case in 1968, the 1984 Guidelines use the Hirschman - Herfindahl Index. The HHI is simply the sum of the square of the market shares of all of the firms competing in the relevant market.

If the HHI is below 1,000 after the merger, corresponding approximately to a concentration ration of 50%, the Department will not generally challenge mergers of firms in this market. It is interesting to note that under the Justice Department 1984 Merger Guidelines, neither the Brown Shoe nor the Von Grocery cases would have been initiated, since they fall into this category.

If the post merger HHI is between 1,000 and 1,800, corresponding roughly to a four firm concentration ratio range of 50 to 70%, the department is likely to challenge mergers that result in an *increase* in the HHI of more than 100 points. The increase in the HHI caused by a merger is twice the product of the individual market shares of the company. So if a market has a four firm concentration ratio of 60%, and an HHI after a merger of

1,500, then a merger between two firms with 7% market shares each would be on the borderline of being challenged and not being challenged.

The Department of Justice considers HHIs above 1,800 to represent markets that are highly concentrated. In these markets, corresponding roughly to markets with a four firm concentration ratio exceeding 70%, the Department will challenge mergers where the increase in the HHI is greater than 50 points. So if a market has a concentration ratio of 80%, the merger of two firms each of which have a 5% market share would be on the borderline of being challenged and not being challenged.

Having stated which mergers it would challenge, the Department of Justice then goes on to relax its standards in two cases. First,

> "if entry into a market is so easy that existing competitors could not succeed in raising price for any significant period of time, the Department is unlikely to challenge mergers in that market",

All mergers are thus permitted in contestable markets.

Business managers have always argued that the main purpose of mergers is efficiency gains, or synergies. Antitrust officials have usually responded that these efficiency gains are ephemeral, difficult to substantiate, and in any case can be gained through internal growth as well as through merger. So, not surprisingly, antitrust officials and the courts have looked rather negatively at the efficiency defense to a merger challenge. The 1984 Guidelines take a different stand, however. They explicitly state, for the first time in history, that an efficiency defense might succeed. In particular, they state

> "If the parties to the merger establish by clear and convincing evidence that a merger will achieve such efficiencies, the Department will consider those efficiencies in deciding whether to challenge the merger.

Cognizable efficiencies include, but are not limited to, achieving economies of scale, better integration of production facilities, plant specialization, lower transportation costs, and similar efficiencies relating to specific manufacturing, servicing, or distribution operations of the merging firms. The Department may also consider claimed efficiencies resulting from reductions in general selling, administrative, and overhead expenses, or that otherwise do not relate to specific manufacturing, servicing, or distribution operations of the merging firms... the Department will reject claims of efficiencies if equivalent or comparable savings can reasonably be achieved by the parties through other means. The parties must establish a greater level of expected net efficiencies the more significant are the competitive risks."

V. Enforcement of U.S. Merger Policy

In this section we attempt to characterize the rigor of enforcement of U.S. antitrust merger policy. While the statement of the Merger Guidelines in 1984 was probably the most important single tangible piece of evidence of the Reagan administration's merger policy, many other sections - including the cases it chose to prosecute also illustrate the tenor of merger policy. We review these trends in this section.

Probably the most important change in merger policy in the Reagan administration was the use of economic analysis in deciding which mergers to prosecute, and how to prosecute them. Nowhere is this more evident than in the Merger Guidelines, especially in the section on entry considerations. For the first time, the fact that a market might essentially be contestable was sufficient to allow firms within that market to merge, when they otherwise might have been prevented from doing so. Whether or not one agrees with this trend politically, it can be seen as a triumph of economic reasoning, especially if one believes that perfect contestability will indeed prevent firms from exercising market power in the long run.

Several other changes in merger policy in the Reagan administration make use of economic analysis more than in the past. For the first time, foreign competition (rather than just domestic competition) was given full weight in the analysis of market power. Provided that the firms designated as potential entrants were not limited in their response by domestic quotas, they would be treated as full potential entrants (thus making the market at least partially contestable), just as would any domestic firm.

Another change in emphasis in the Reagan administration's merger policy was the degree to which the administration was willing to make deals. Confident in their economic analysis and understanding of the relevant markets, economists and lawyers at the Justice Department and Federal Trade Commission were willing to strike bargains with firms that wished to merge, but which had (for example) geographic areas in which they overlapped as horizontal competitors. In cases such as Chevron Oil Company's acquisition of Gulf Oil, the Justice Department was willing to allow the merger after Chevron agreed to sell the retail outlets and some refineries, previously owned by Gulf, to Standard Oil of Ohio - a British Petroleum subsidiary. This change shows, on the one had, remarkable flexibility and leniency in the prosecution of antitrust cases, and on the other hand, substantial confidence in their own ability to craft competitive markets.

How have these changes affected the vigorousness of public policy toward merger activity? Unfortunately, it is probably impossible to measure - at least with a single number -the degree to which the Reagan administration has vigorously prosecuted mergers which are in violation of the law. If you ask a Reagan administration antitrust official, of course, they will argue that they have prosecuted *all* mergers which have the potential of "lessening" competition. On the other hand, mergers between very large firms - especially in the oil industry - leave the impression with members of the Democratic Party as well as *some* disinterested officials that the administration of the anti-merger statute has been rather lax.

Although very recent data is not available, Gallow, Craycraft and Bush (1985) present statistics for the period 1965 through 1979, contrasted with the period 1980 - 84. I should note that only 1981 through 1984 can be appropriately classified as "Reagan years," and given the length of time it takes to change administrations, perhaps even 1981 should be classified as a "Carter year." But in any case, we can contrast the number of *allegations of violations* of the Clayton Act over these two time periods. Taking the Justice Department and Federal Trade Commission together, there were 20 allegations per year of violation of the Clayton Act over the period 1965 through 1979, and 16.6 allegations of violations over the period 1980 through 1984. This is hardly an overwhelming difference, but we should note that these are allegations and not legal challenges.

Johnson and Smith (1987) allow us to compare horizontal merger cases filed by the United States Department of Justice. Over the period 1968 through 1980, 9.15 cases against horizontal mergers were filed each year. Over the period 1981 through 1984, 5.75 cases were filed each year. Even though cases filed is not a clear, appropriate measure of merger prosecution, since it does not measure how many cases "should" have been filed, this evidence indicates that 60% more cases were filed during the Nixon, Ford, and Carter years than during the first four years of the Reagan administration. This appears to be somewhat convincing evidence that, at least in terms of cases filed, the Reagan administration was less active in restricting mergers. This reinforces the popular belief that the Reagan administration was more lenient towards horizontal merger activity, and tends to support the popular press which reported that in the latter part of 1988 firms were rushing to complete horizontal mergers in advance of the new administration (even though it was a Republican administration) taking office.

Economic evidence and the Reagan merger policy

It is apparent from the discussion above that there was indeed a shift in merger policy in the Reagan administration. What caused this shift? Was it new economic learning? Or was it the manifestation of a probusiness, promerger administration searching the academic journals for any economic evidence that it could use in defense of its predetermined merger policy? We will discuss this question in this section.

Supporters of the Reagan administration antitrust policy, generally cite several factors as explanations of the shift to the new merger policy. The most important consideration would be a rethinking of a basic paradigm of industrial economics; the belief that an industry's *structure* will influence its *conduct* which will in turn determine its *performance*. This paradigm is due originally to Professor Joe Bain and others, and has been in place since the 1950s. The challenge to the paradigm begins from some early research by Harold Demsetz indicating that the structure of an industry can be affected by its performance, and in particular that concentrated industries may be so as the result of an economic competition in which relatively few, more efficient firms prospered and thus the industry became concentrated. Further evidence in support of this position is the fact that profitability is much more highly correlated with the market share of the two leading firms than it is with the overall industry concentration, a finding one would expect if those leading firms gained prominence because of efficiency advantages, rather than industry profitability being driven by collusion among the leading firms.

Supporters of the administration's antitrust policy also point to the fact that economic analysis is used far more than ever before. In particular, the emphasis upon the ease of entry (the contestibility of markets) results from the work of Baumol, Panzer and Willig (1982), and is a "reasonable" improvement upon prior merger enforcement practices, which basically ignored entry considerations. In addition, the possibility that efficiency gains might allow a merger which would otherwise be challenged, results from a reasonable comparison of costs and benefits, which is unprecedented.

We could summarize the position that the Reagan merger policy was driven by new learning and economic analysis by quoting the words of William F. Baxter, who was the antitrust chief under Reagan that settled the AT&T case and dismissed the IBM case on the same day. He wrote, in a private correspondence to the author,

> "I think the following are among the key attitudes that have driven the change. First, there has been an increasing perception, along the line of Williamson's work, that size and enterprise organization is itself driven by the market to a significant degree. Second, the intensification of international trade rivalry has caused higher value to be placed on the once ignored, or even negatively valued, factors of efficiency and rate of change of productivity. Third, a general perception of the instability of cartels has led to much greater skepticism that a tacit collusion is anywhere near as easy and as pervasive as was once supposed. Finally, I think there's a general recognition that the beneficiaries of the old populist antitrust were not in fact "the little guys" but somewhat smaller, less efficient

enterprises, often owned by very wealthy individuals."

There are others who believe that this "new learning" wasn't really new learning at all, and that the Reagan administration's merger policy was set in the minds of the politicians before reading any economic analysis. Probably the most vocal opponent of the current antitrust policy is Williard F. Mueller, a former director of the Bureau of Economics in the Federal Trade Commission, who argues that the "new learning" is based on research which is flawed and will lead to unprecedented concentration in markets in the United States (Mueller 1986).

A somewhat less severe critique of U.S. merger policy has been put forth by Dennis Mueller (1986) who is unrelated to Williard Mueller. Dennis Mueller takes issue with two empirical findings which provide the basis for much of the new antitrust policy; the relationship between concentration and profitability discussed immediately above, and the fact that mergers typically lead to large wealth gains for shareholders of target companies, and an overall gain for the combined shareholders, suggestive of possible gains in efficiency as a result of mergers. This latter critique has been discussed above.

Finally, there is the allegation that the Reagan administration has not even enforced its own merger guidelines. Even though the numerical criteria for a legal challenge to a merger are quite concrete, some authors such as Pitofsky (1988) argue that these numbers are not really utilized when the Department of Justice or Federal Trade Commission chooses which mergers to challenge, "for example, it now qualifies as an "open secret" that the DOJ usually defines relevant markets by asking whether a ten (not five) percent price rise would be profitable." ... "it appears that, in practice and until recently, the safe harbor HHI has been raised from the stated 1,000 to around 1,800, and mergers resulting in HHI increases in less than 250 have rarely if ever been challenged." ... "the threshold HHIs now apparently in force are so high that they appear to be a radical break from the past."

So the critique of the new merger policy comes essentially from two directions; first it is based on research which is flawed. And second, depending upon the particular research cited, the research had been in existence for a number of years prior to the point in time that the Reagan administration seized upon the research as "new learning". This lag seems suspiciously like the Reagan administration, having decided its merger policy from political reasoning and a comparison of votes to be gained and lost, then on earlier research seized as supportive of its view.

The 1992 Merger Guidelines

The U.S. Department of Justice and Federal Trade Commission share responsibility for antitrust policy in the United States. For the first time in history, the agencies jointly issued new Horizontal Merger Guidelines in 1992. These guidelines refined and expanded the 1984 Department of Justice Guidelines. The most significant changes to the earlier guidelines were to explain more clearly how horizontal mergers might lead to adverse competitive effects, and to provide more detail on how the departments would evaluate supply responses to mergers and new entry. These considerations are discussed in turn below.

In discussing the potential adverse competitive impacts of mergers, the 1992 Guidelines treat the issue of coordinated interaction between firms in great detail. They note that a reduced number of firms which would result from a horizontal merger will have an easier time, in general, reaching agreement on price. They point out that coordination will be easier the more homogeneous are the products, and will be easier, the more information is available about price and other terms of sale by the rival firms. They also point out that coordination and enforcement of restrictions against cutting price will be easier if buyers are large relative to the size of the market, and if sales are relatively infrequent and large.

The 1992 Guidelines also provide more detail about the government's likely treatment of possible supply responses to an increase in price following a merger, and new entry in the same circumstance. The guidelines discuss "uncommitted entrants", which are firms not currently producing or selling the relevant product, that would be likely to respond to a small and significant price increase. They also discuss firms which own productive and distributive assets which are currently in use in other markets, but which could be modified or redirected towards the market under study. With respect to the timeliness of entry, the guidelines only consider entry that will occur within a two-year period following a significant price increase. An entry must be likely if it is to be considered as an ameliorating factor to a merger, and will be determined to be likely if it would be profitable at premerger prices. In order to be likely, an entry must also be profitable with the share of the market available to a new entrant exceeding minimum viable scale. If minimum viable scale is very large relative to the portion of the market available to a new entrant, then entry will not be determined to be likely.

Prospects

In November of 1992, the United States of America elected a new president William Clinton. It is too early to predict the precise changes that President Clinton will make in these guidelines, or in the enforcement of antitrust policy in general, but some remarks can be ventured. To begin, Clinton is a more activist president who is more likely to examine and probably prevent some mergers that would have been allowed under Reagan and Bush. As a Democrat, his administration is perceived to be less pro-business than the preceding two, and early indications are that this perception is correct. While he is unlikely to abandon the trend towards greater use of economics in antitrust policy, he is more likely to apply the tests in a more stringent fashion.

VI. Conclusions

The subjects of this paper are merger activity in the United States, the reasons behind or causing the mergers observed in the recent past, and the antitrust law and policy which affects which mergers are to be challenged by the government, and which mergers are allowed to become effective.

Mergers and leveraged buyouts have captured the attention of the American business public. A reading of the *Financial Times* or the *Wall Street Journal* indicates that almost every day's news is dominated by mergers or leveraged buyouts by firms in the United States. The reason for this is not hard to understand. As we have documented, the number of mergers has followed an increasing trend, at least from its low point in the mid 70s. Over four thousand mergers were completed in 1986, with a combined market value of more than 200 billion dollars. The premium paid for the acquired firm, the difference between the purchase price and the market price of the shares immediately before the merger, has been declining throughout this period. Most recent mergers tend to be horizontal, with firms in the same industry combining, followed by mergers which are purely conglomerate, and mergers which are an extension of the line of business of the acquiring firm. The chemicals and allied products sector dominates the industries experiencing mergers, when they are measured by the market value. On the other hand, the mergers in the service sectors (retailing, banking, and communication) dominate merger activity when measured by the number of mergers effected. Foreign firms which make acquisitions within the U.S. are headquartered predominantly in English speaking countries, with the United Kingdom leading the group. On the other hand, when U.S. firms make acquisitions in other countries, they primarily look to the EEC. Finally, leveraged buyouts are an increasingly important phenomenon, with 331 leveraged buyouts occurring in 1986 with a combined market value of more than 46 billion dollars.

In Section III we considered different possible explanations for the level of merger activity. First we considered explanations for aggregate merger activity, and uncovered a good deal of disagreement in the literature. It is apparent that there is no simple relationship between the level of share prices, or economic activity (as measured by GNP) and aggregate merger activity. There does appear, however, to be a relationship between aggregate merger activity and changes in stock prices; increased merger activity lags behind increased stock prices.

We then turn to a discussion of other possible causes for merger activity in different sectors. Probably the leading explanation among economists for horizontal mergers is to increase the market power of the surviving firm, by decreasing the number of competitors and increasing the size of the surviving firm. Whether or not this is the *motive* behind a substantial number of mergers, economists who have investigated the effect of horizontal mergers on the market share of the surviving firm, or on stock prices have concluded that the *results* of horizontal mergers have generally not been to increase the market power of the surviving firms. The leading explanation for mergers by the participants (the managers involved) has been that mergers are efficiency increasing. The evidence indicates otherwise, however. Profitability and market share of the surviving firms typically decreases following a merger. We investigate several less widely accepted motives for merger, and reach mixed results. While the avoidance of income taxes appears to be an important motive in the most recent years, there is little evidence yet that it has been a dominant cause for merger activity. Other economists have argued that the managers involved are simply building empires or maximizing growth, or that they are systematically making errors when they acquire firms at prices above the market level (with a positive premium). The evidence on these two hypotheses is mixed. Finally, merger activity in the last few years of the Reagan administration appears (at least from reading the financial press) to be driven by a fear that the relaxed antitrust attitude of the Reagan administration will be replaced by a more stringent enforcement of antitrust laws.

Public policy toward merger activity is driven by the Clayton Act of 1914, which states that a merger shall be illegal if "the effect of such acquisition may be substantially to lessen competition, or to tend to create a monopoly." The enforcement of this legal statute is in the hands of the executive branch of the government, and has changed rather dramatically in the last 10 years. In 1984, the government issued a revised set of merger guidelines, which used (more than ever before) economic analysis in deciding which mergers to challenge, and which mergers to allow. The guidelines are very careful in defining product and geographic markets, and in measuring the impact of mergers on concentration in these markets. For the first time, the government has allowed an efficiency defense to outweigh or overcome the possible anticompetitive effects of a merger, and has also specified rather carefully what conditions of entry (contestable markets) are necessary before the merger will be allowed.

Although the Reagan administration was very careful in writing and thinking through these merger guidelines, there is a great deal of debate about whether the Reagan administration has vigorously enforced them. There is some evidence that there have been fewer cases filed by the Justice Department and Federal Trade Commission, and some anecdotal evidence that the Reagan administration does not really use its own concentration thresholds in deciding which mergers to challenge.

The future of U.S. merger policy, now that another Republican has been elected, would appear to focus on the merger guidelines, and whether or not these merger guidelines will be enforced strictly. A reasonable prediction is that the new Bush administration will be somewhat more true to the merger guidelines, and will challenge some mergers which the Reagan administration would not have challenged.

References

Baumol, W.J., 1959, *Business Behavior, Value, and Growth*, Macmillan, New York, Chs. 5-10.

Baumol, W.J., Panzar, J.C. and Willig, R.D., 1982, *Contestable Markets and The Theory of Industry Structure*,, New York, NY, Harcourt Brace Jovanovich.

Barton, D.M. and Sherman, R., 1984, "The Price and Profit Effects of Horizontal Merger: A Case Study", *The Journal of Industrial Economics*, 33:2, 165-177.

Baxter, W., 1980, *The Political Economy of Antitrust*, Lexington Books: Lexington Ma., *Business Week*, 1988, March 21st.

Cartwright, P.A., Kamerschen, D.R. and Zieburtz, W.B., Jr., 1987, "The Competitive Impact of Mergers, 1930-1979", *American Business Law Journal*, 34-62.

Demsetz, H., 1973, "Industry Structure, Market Rivalry, and Public Policy", *Journal of Law & Economics*, 16, 1-10.

Gallo, J.C., Craycraft, J.L. and Bush, S.C., 1985, "Guess Who Came to Dinner: An Empirical Study of Federal Antitrust Enforcement for the Period 1963-1984", *Review of Industrial Organization*, 2, 106-131.

Geroski, P.A., 1984, "On the Relationship Between Aggregate Merger Activity and the Stock Market", *European Economic Review*, 25, 223-233.

Golbe, D.L. and White, L.J., 1988, "Mergers and Acquisitions in the U.S. Economy: An Aggregate and Historical Overview", in *Mergers and Acquisitions*, A.J. Auerbach ed., The University of Chicago Press, Chicago, 25-47.

Granger, C., 1969, "Investigating Causal Relations by Econometric Models and Cross-Spectral Methods", *Econometrica*, 37, 424-438.

Grimm, W.T. & Co., 1987, *Mergerstat Review*.

Jensen, M.C. and Ruback R.S., 1983, "The Market for Corporate Control", *Journal of Financial Economics*, 11, 5-50.

Johnson, R.L. and Smith, D.D., 1987, "Antitrust Division Merger Procedures and Policy, 1968-1984", *The Antitrust Bulletin*, 967-988.

Manne, H.G., 1965, "Mergers and the Market for Corporate Control", *The Journal of Political Economy*, 73, 110-20.

Marris, 1964, *The Economic Theory of "Managerial" Capitalism*, Free Press of Glencoe, New York.

Melicher, R., Ledolter, J. and D'Antonio, L., 1983, "A Time Series Analysis of Aggregate Merger Activity", *Review of Economics and Statistics*, 65, 423-429.

Mergers and Acquisitions, 20, No. 3, 1986.

Mergers and Acquisitions, 22, No. 6, 1988.

Mueller, D.C., 1980, "The United States, 1962-1972", in *The Determininants and Effects of Mergers: An International Comparison*, D.C. Mueller ed., Oelgeschlager, Gunn & Hain, Publishers, Inc., Cambridge, MA., Ch. 9.

Mueller, D.C., 1985, "Mergers and Market Share", *Review of Economics and Statistics*, 67, 259-267.

Mueller, D.C., 1986, "United States' Antitrust: At the Crossroads", in *Mainstreams in Industrial Organization*, de Jong, H.W., Shepherd, W.G. eds., Martinus Nijhoff Publishers, The Netherlands, Ch. 9.

Mueller, W.F., 1986, "A New Attack on Antitrust: The Chicago Case", *Antitrust Law and Economics Review*, 29-66.

Nelson, R., 1959, *Merger Movements in American Industry: 1895 – 1956*, Princeton University Press, Cambridge, MA.

Pitosfky, R., 1988, "Antitrust in the Decade Ahead: Some Predictions About Merger Enforcement", *Antitrust Law Journal*, 57:1, 65-73.

Ravenscraft, D.J. and Scherer, F.M., 1987, *Mergers, Sell-offs, and Economic Efficiency*, The Brookings Institution, Washington, D.C.

Roll, R., 1986, "The Hubris Hypothesis of Corporate Takeovers", *Journal of Business*, 59:2, 197-216.

Scherer, F.M., 1980, *Industrial Market Structure and Economic Performance*, 2nd ed., Rand McNally College Publishing Company, Chicago, IL.

Scherer, F.M., Beckenstein, A., Kaufer, E. and Murphy, R.D., 1975, *The Economics of Multi-Plant Operation: An International Comparisons Study*, Harvard University Press, Cambridge, MA.

Shughart, W.F., II and Tollison, R.D., 1984, "The Random Character of Merger Activity", *The Rand Journal of Economics*, 15:4, 500-509.

Steiner, P.,1975, *Mergers: Motives, Effects, Policies*, University of Michigan Press, Ann Arbor, MI.

Stewart, J.F., Harris, R.S. and Carleton, Willard T., 1984, "The Role of Market Structure in Merger Behavior", *The Journal of Industrial Economics*, 32:3, 293-312.

Stigler, G., 1950, "Monopoly and Oligopoly by Merger", *American Economic Review, Papers and Proceedings*, 40, 23-24.

U.S. Department of Justice, 1986, *Merger Guidelines.*

U.S. Department of Justice, 1982, *Merger Guidelines.*

U.S. Department of Justice, 1984, *Merger Guidelines.*

U.S. Department of Justice and Federal Trade Commission, 1992, *Merger Guidelines.*

3. Horizontal Concentration and European Merger Policy*

ALEXIS JACQUEMIN

I. Introduction

In the second section of this policy paper, the main theoretical arguments concerning the costs and benefits of horizontal mergers as a way of modifying market conditions are identified, as well as the exploration of some indicators that could be used to evaluate the probability of these costs and benefits in a European context.

The third section will examine the European merger control regulation based on the dual view that restructuring required by the completion of the European Community's internal market should lead in certain areas, to beneficial concentration operations but, simultaneously, these operations may also create harmful dominant positions.

II. Costs and Benefits of Mergers in the European Context

A sequence of questions can be asked about the effects of horizontal mergers and take-overs. First, what are the theoretical bases for efficiency gains from mergers, and what is the evidence from empirical studies. Second, to the extent that there is a net positive contribution to resource productivity, what are the key elements for examining the possible tradeoff between the benefits of these mergers and the consequences of enhanced market power.

Expected effects

Two main types of benefits can be attributed to mergers: a reduction in production and transaction costs, an improvement in the efficiency of management. But against these potential benefits can also be set possible inefficiencies resulting from mergers.

The role of economies of scale in production is well known. These cost savings can accrue from a better division of labour within the production unit, the spreading of fixed costs, and longer production runs. Mergers which lead to reorganization may help firms to realize these economies and to attain the optimum efficient scale. The size of economies achieved will depend on the slope of the average cost curve for output below the optimum scale. There can also be scale economies in functions such as

G. Mussati (ed.), Mergers, Markets and Public Policy, 81–94.
© 1995 *Kluwer Academic Publishers.*

transport, distribution and research. Besides these static scale economies there is the phenomenon of learning effects associated with the increasing experience of production of a good or service. These mean that the cost of producing each extra unit decreases as the cumulative previous output increases. Finally, mention should be made of the role of "scope economies", whereby the sum of the costs of producing two products separately may be higher than the cost of producing them together. These various phenomena have led many authors (see for example Demsetz, 1974) to conclude that high concentration - chiefly brought about by mergers - and large market shares are a sign of efficiency because they show that firms with low costs have increased their market shares at the expense of the less efficient firms. The low costs lead in the short run to higher profitability.

All these phenomena are thus prompted by the search for efficiency.

But for an organization to be able to benefit from the market advantageously and for such mergers to yield real synergies, machinery within the new entity needs to be set up to make its internal operation efficient. Yet the pitfalls awaiting the large merged organization are legendary: poor communications, sour industrial relations climate, corporate culture clashes, failure to cut out costly duplication, insufficient coordination, and finally lack of flexibility.

In recent years, the question of firms' flexibility in an increasingly uncertain world has become more and more important. Some of the difficulties large firms have in adapting to their changing environment may be due to the over rigid organization imposed in the course of increasing concentration.

A second possible benefit of mergers arises from the take-over process. The various forms of take-over can be just as effective a means of transferring control of one company's assets to another as a full legal merger, and the replacement of the acquired company's management can likewise lead to better exploitation of its resources. This "market for corporate control" also reduces the dangers of conflicts of goals between the owners and managers of companies. To the extent that managers have different preferences from shareholders, in terms of profits, sales or degree of risk aversion, the take-over mechanism helps reduce the associated distortions.

The mere threat of take-over is an incentive for management or the controlling shareholder to run the business in the best interests of the company. Conversely, many of the defense tactics used against hostile take-overs may be damaging to the interests of the shareholders of the target company and serve only those of its management. A very strict regulation of take-overs might therefore have undesirable consequences.

On the other hand, a basic assumption behind the favourable view of hostile take-overs is that the stock market correctly reflects the value of the acquired and acquiring firms. This is not necessarily the case. The expected benefits may not be realized, with the take-over failing to improve performance but only redistributing profits from the managers to the owners. Moreover, the management of the predator company may be guided by motives other than profit maximization, motives which reflect their own interests and cause them to pay too high a price for the acquisition.

Added to this are various considerations concerning the perverse effects that take-over activity can have on the actual management of companies. Take-overs may absorb a large proportion of management time and induce some managers to give more attention to financial transactions than to productivity and competitiveness. The threat of take-over encourages the maintenance of excessive liquidity and the pursuit of a short term profit, at the expense of strategic investment that would yield a high return only in the long term. There are also dangers in firms taking on increasing debts either to finance or ward off take-overs. In some cases, key assets needed for an industrial growth or diversification strategy are sold off to finance or prevent a take-over. Finally, frequent changes in the controlling shareholders, decision centres and headquarters of companies are apt to affect the ability of management to enter into lasting commitments in relation to specific human capital and their loyalty to the company.

Empirical studies

The theoretical arguments about the contribution of mergers to the productivity of the business assets do not yield a general presumption in their favour. It is therefore useful to look at the results of empirical research into the effects of mergers.

As for the effects in terms of profitability and growth, many studies point to the absence of substantial efficiency gains. A comparative study, directed by Mueller (1980), of results from various EC countries concerning full legal mergers concluded that the chances of success are limited and that the costs of the changes in organization (difficulty of "digesting" the acquisition, diseconomies of large organizations) are often greater than the benefits claimed by the promoters.

Studies by management consultants come to similar conclusions. Coley and Reinton (1988) looked at U.S. and British companies in the *Fortune* 250 list and the *Financial Times* 500 which in the past had made acquisitions to enter new markets. They conclude that only 23% of the 116 firms analysed were able to recover the cost of their capital or, better still, the funds invested in the acquisition programme. It also appears that the higher the degree of diversification, the smaller is the likelihood of success. For horizontal mergers in which the acquired firm is not large, however, the success rate is around 45%. The main reasons for failure appear to be: too high a price paid for the acquisition, overestimation of the potential of the acquired business in terms of synergies and market position, and inadequate management of the process of integration after the acquisition.

More generally, there is a striking contrast between ex ante event studies of the corporate mergers' potential gains and the ex post evaluations of the effective results. In his introduction to a special issue on "mergers", Mueller (1989) concludes that prior to the mergers the shares of acquiring firms tend to outperform the market. At the time of the announcement, there is little change in the acquiring firm's share price. The postacquisition performance of acquiring company share prices is below their premerger performance, and in many studies below that of the market. This postmerger performance matches the constant or declining performance of the acquired units measured in profitability, market shares or productivity. "This pattern appears to be characteristic of mergers in the United States over at least the last 60 years, and probably the last century. It also appears characteristic of mergers in Europe and Japan".

Trade-off issues in a European perspective

Given these results, one can conclude that in many cases, there is no real trade-off between efficiency gains from mergers, notably in the form of cost reductions, and an increase in monopoly power, because in the first place net efficiency gains are simply not there. Still there are situations where the trade-off can be relevant.

A horizontal merger reducing the number of independent firms permits coordinated use of previously independent productive assets (capital, patents, trademarks...) and increases concentration in the relevant market. This increase can lead to higher prices and facilitate collusion. It is then necessary to compare these risks to competition with the potential efficiency gains.

A wellknown paper by Williamson (1968) has proposed a partial equilibrium formula for measuring the respective sizes of cost savings and surplus reductions due to a restriction of output, that a horizontal merger could induce.

However, this *naive* trade-off analysis requires a number of qualifications including matters of timing and uncertainty, nonprice competition and variety of products, x-inefficiency, income distribution effects and so on.[1] Three aspects are especially relevant in the European context: first consideration of the new industry structure following mergers, second the international trade dimension, within the Common Market and with the rest of the world, third the role of mergers in high technology activities.

Concerning the first aspect, it is necessary to have a model of industry's behaviour explaining the adjustments of prices and quantities in response to a merger. Farrell and Shapiro (1990) provide such a model for the Cournot case. A crucial result of their analysis is the role of the response of non participant firms to any output reduction by the merging parties. If nonparticipant firms reduce their outputs, the merger may well lower welfare even though it is profitable. The case is most relevant if the merger makes collusion more likely, or if the oligopolists compete in price among differentiated products.[2] It is also more probable, the larger the combined market share of the merging firms relative to the (weighted) share of the outsiders. On the contrary, if non participant firms with large mark-ups expand their outputs noticeably in response to the merger, a significant welfare gain can be provided.[3]

In the European market context, this leads to the consideration of several phenomena. The suppression of nontariff barriers, by making easier arbitrage for buyers and intermediaries, leads to an expanding market and a larger potential demand, so that there is a high probability that firms not participating in a merger will be very responsive to price increases and will tend to expand their outputs. This conjecture is reinforced in expanding industries, given that a growing market attracts entries; these entries are relatively easy because incumbent firms have less advantages in terms of cost, experience and reputation, than when established in mature or declining industries. Furthermore many mergers and take-overs in the EC correspond to a twofold strategy : firms acquire assets in the activities they are best at and sell assets related to activities in which their competitive position is weak; they extend their geographical sphere of operation by buying up firms in other Member States in their core business. This trend according to which firms prefer to concentrate on their top grade products, and increase their geographical diversification, as an alternative to product diversification in a limited geographical area, is compatible with an industry structure favourable to output expansion (Buigues and Jacquemin, 1989).

On the other hand, existing data suggest that the total number of mergers and acquisitions involving at least one of the top 1000 EC firms has been steadily increasing, from 185 in 1984/85 to 343 in 1991/92. The breakdown by combined turnover of the firms concerned confirms the trend towards an increase in large scale operations. In 1992, one operation in four had a combined turnover exceeding ECU 10.000 million, and two third ECU 5.000 million. This trend can be dangerous to the extent that positive welfare effects are less probable if the market share of the merging firms is large relative to that of the non participant firms and to the extent that the more power the merging firms hold premerger, the larger the cost reduction has to be in order for the postmerger price to fall.

The *international dimension* is another crucial factor for evaluating the impact of European mergers. It is well known that competition from imports considerably limits the market power of domestic producers. An econometric study (Jacquemin and Sapir, 1991) using a sample of over one hundred, three digit European manufacturing sectors confirms that imports from intra and extra EC origins exert a significant disciplinary effect on price-cost margins, but mainly played by extra EC imports. Furthermore, the potential pressure of imports measured by the height of existing trade barriers as well as actual import competition, has a significant impact. All other things being equal it is therefore probable that mergers in industries relatively open to international trade, from within or outside the Community, are less dangerous for competition than mergers in relatively closed industries. This presumption has been analysed in a series of recent studies. Ross (1988), for instance, shows that the lowering of tariff barriers is more effective in limiting price increasing effects of a merger, the larger the number of foreign firms. However, foreign competition is far from being a perfect substitute for domestic competition in that it is subject to extra uncertainties that do not affect domestic production. Ordover and Willig (1988) have put forward a model which suggests that the effectiveness of competition policy depends on the protectionism of trade policy, via tariffs and quotas. Macroeconomic policy also plays a role: the effect of a reduction in the number of domestic producers is very sensitive not only to the number of foreign firms, but also to the level and variability of the exchange rate. If the main protection against domestic monopoly power is imports, exchange rate volatility will lessen this protection. From this point of view, the European Monetary System indirectly could have a beneficial impact on competition in the common market.

An inverse problem is the monopoly power effect of EC mergers on the rest of the world. If we assume a selfish policy maximising domestic social welfare and ignoring the perverse effects on the rest of the world, the only losses that need be considered by an European merger policy, are the reductions in the European consumer surplus, and the only gains the increase in the profits of European producers. All things been equal, the net European gain in welfare resulting from a merger would be the greater, the larger the degree of European involvement in the merger and the lower the proportion of the output consumed in Europe.

A third aspect especially relevant in the European context is the role of *mergers in high-technology industries*. Over the recent years, the Community has lost world market shares in several of these sectors (electrical and electronic equipment, information technology...). These industries are highly R&D intensive. This is because of the indivisibilities in R&D up to certain thresholds and because firms require a sufficient scale of operation in order to undertake research programmes. There are many other economic reasons why linkups between European firms in such industries are justified. They allow an exploitation of network externalities. They increase the resources available and so encourage the undertaking of more ambitious and risky projects which single firms cannot afford. They also help cut out duplication and may encourage transfers of technology, thus speeding up the dissemination of innovation. Ordover and Baumol (1988), in their analysis of mergers in hightechnology industries, conclude that mergers in hightechnology industries, in which technologies and products are shortlived, should raise fewer concerns than would similar mergers in industries which have entered their stable phase. This suggestion holds as long as hightechnology mergers do not combine firms with large shares of substitute R&D assets that also require large shares of market specific assets for their effective exploitation. On the whole the message here is that when there is a tradeoff between static and dynamic efficiency, it is wise to favour the longrun dynamic performance that is expected to ultimately overcome any static loss.

Still, the existence of such a tradeoff can be questioned in most industries. In fact, some evidence suggests that R&D is not characterised by substantial economies of scale and that monopoly power can be expected to inhibit R&D and technological advance in the long run.[4] Furthermore avoiding wasteful duplication, internalising external effects and insuring a large dissemination of knowledge could be obtained through less dangerous devices than full mergers, such as R&D cooperation at the "precompetitive stage". What can be effectively argued is that in industries characterised by shortlived hightechnology and rapidly expanding demand, all other things being equal, the prospect of efficiency gains is enhanced and the danger of monopoly power is limited. In the European context however, we observe that the number of mergers and acquisitions involving firms in the top 1000 has risen significantly less rapidly in the highgrowth, hightechnology sectors than in the rest of industry.

Table 3.1. Illustration of an industrial classification according to the expected effects of a merger on competition and efficiency.

	Prospects of efficiency gains (scale economies and technological content)	
Danger of reduction of competition (degree of trade openness and growth rate of demand)		
	Weak	Strong
Strong	Examples	Examples
	Tobacco products Metal goods	Electrical plant and machinery Railway rolling stock
Weak	Examples	Examples
	Textile and clothing Leather goods	Telecommunications Computers

On the basis of the previous discussion, it is tempting to use some basic criteria to classify, on a prima facie basis, industries, according to the expected effects on competition and efficiency. An illustration of this approach is given in Table 3.1, elaborated for a first screening of European merger proposals. Four indicators among many others have been used: prospects of efficiency gains are based on the relative importance of economies of scale and of technological content, dangers of reduced competition rely on the degree of trade openness and the growth rate of market demand. An application of this type of classification to the 120 European manufacturing industries at the three-digit NACE level has been made in Jacquemin, Buigues and Ilzkovitz (1989).

III. European Policy Toward Mergers

The European regulation

There is no article in the Treaty of Rome which specifically deals with mergers and acquisitions. However the Commission and the European Court of Justice have interpreted Articles 85 and 86, the two pillars of EC-Competition policy, in such a way as to make them partly applicable to mergers.

But this power is limited and not very effective. With Article 86, the control only concerns firms already dominant and in principle is made after it has occurred. But the economic, financial and social costs of an eventual dismemberment after the operation has been fulfilled would be generally prohibitive. Furthermore, the absence of clear rules in terms of competence and procedures create legal uncertainty for firms, including possible conflicts of jurisdiction. Article 85 has a very limited domain of application as it requires an agreement and excludes a case of full control.

This explains why the Commission proposed, as far back as in 1973, a specific regulation on Community merger control. Such a Regulation has been adopted in 1990 and is implemented since 1991.

The new Regulation is founded upon two main points:

a) The regime is applicable to major mergers which have a truly European dimension, linked to transnational externalities. The aim should be to prevent both the creation and the enlargement of dominant market positions.
b) The Regulation does not provide for authorization in derogation from the prohibition, on the basis of the efficiency effects of the merger, but ef-

ficiency becomes one element in the overall appraisal.

Each of them corresponds to delicate economic problems.

Criteria for identifying a dominant position

In the Regulation, the first two articles state that the mergers covered by the Regulation are those which have a Community dimension; among them, mergers which create or strengthen a dominant position in the Common Market or a substantial part of it are to be condemned. As far as the definition of operation of a Community dimension is concerned a criterion based on turnover is used. A merger operation is considered to be of a Community dimension and thus subject to regulation "when the total worldwide turnover of the total number of firms concerned represents a sum in excess of 5 billion ECU, and the total turnover realised within the Community by at least two of the firms involved represents a figure in excess of 250 million ECU".

Recourse to such thresholds is guided by a concern to achieve the maximum reduction in the legal insecurity relating to the applicability of the ruling since the calculation of turnover is much more direct than of market shares, and by the desire to limit to an operational level the number of cases to be examined. Whatever the precise numerical values of these thresholds, this choice calls for important caveat. First the use of firm size is clearly suspect both on economic and legal grounds. Size has indeed to be viewed within the context of the relevant market. Second, even for sectors aggregated at a three-digit level, this threshold is sometimes quite high in relation to the amount of economic activity concerned, so that a complete monopolisation would not fall within the scope of application; for other sectors the figure is low when compared with the total value of Community production.

Among the criteria which assist the process of deciding whether or not there exists the creation or the reinforcement of a dominant position are the following:

- market position and economic and financial power of the firms concerned;
- the possibility of choosing suppliers and consumers;
- access to suppliers or to markets;
- the structure of the markets affected taking into account international competition;
- barriers to entry (legal or de facto);
- supply and demand trends for the goods or services concerned.

It is to be noted that, in contrast with the U.S. approach, there is no use of numerical guidelines such as a certain change in the Herfindahl index, which in the light of the recent literature could be wiser. Some other criteria are mentioned, such as "market position", "economic and financial power of the firms concerned" and "structure of the markets affected". These factors are at best ambiguous indicators without clear economic content.

Market position, for example, can only be determined by reference to a number of structural features. Market structure itself encompasses the distribution of market shares and entry barriers which are mentioned separately. As for economic and financial power, this probably cannot be equated with a size or performance criterion, since the Court of Justice has explicitly rejected the relevance of these two factors for establishing the existence of a dominant position.

That leaves four criteria that correspond to the first two theoretical aspects discussed in the previous section. The "possibilities of choice of suppliers and consumers", "access to supplies or markets", "the existence of legal or de facto barriers to entry" and "the trend of supply and demand for the goods or services concerned", are important indicators of the new industry structure following a merger. "International competition", must be taken into account in defining the relevant market, in measuring market shares and in evaluating entry barriers.

However, the overall impression is that the list of criteria for identifying the creation or the reinforcement of a dominant position is unsystematic. Happily, they have been fleshed out by guidelines elucidating their content and their use.

Efficiency considerations

As also seen in the previous section, some efficiency gains can be expected from mergers, especially in hightechnology industries On the other hand, empirical evidence on past experience does not justify a general presumption in favour of mergers as a very effective way to achieve the objective of improving the productivity of business assets. It is in this context that the approach adopted in the Regulation must be considered.

The rule for determining whether a merger creates or strengthens a dominant position is that the Commission will take into account "the development of technical and economic progress provided that it is to the consumers' advantage and does not form an obstacle to competition". This raises a central question. The wording suggests that the regulation contains no "efficiency defence" at all, such as the one stated in Article 85 par. 3 for cartels, and that effective competition is the only reference. Indeed, given that the criterion of technical and economic progress can be used only if it is perfectly compatible with competition and consumers' interests, it is difficult to see how an operation which creates or reinforces a dominant position could be accepted because the negative, anticompetitive effects outweigh the positive effects of such a progress. The wording also implies that only consumers' surplus, and not producers' surplus, is retained: apparently some sacrifice of consumer interest for the sake of higher profits is not accepted. If this is so, the role of efficiency criteria in the regulation is empty.

It is hard to believe that in practice such a strict policy will be fully implemented and that the role of potential dynamic efficiency gains will be ignored. It must be underlined that, contrary to recent trends characterizing other legislations, especially in Canada, the new European regulation on mergers shows that the goal of preserving an open competition system in the European market remains a central concern. However, a danger is that instead of an explicit cost-benefit analysis, surreptitious compromises would be sought within the Commission.

The first applications

During 1991, the first year it held the power to vet large concentrations, the Commission received 63 notifications. In six decisions, it found that there were doubts; in three cases it declared the concentration compatible with the common market subject to certain conditions and obligations, mainly demanding some divestments or restructuring (Alcatel/Telettra, Magneti Marelli/CEA and Bosch/Varta). In one case, it declared incompatibility and prohibited the concentration: the acquisition of de Havilland, a Canadian subsidiary of Boeing, by Aérospatiale of France and Alenia of Italy. The Commission argued mainly that the merger would have given de Havilland and ATR (the Franco-Italian joint venture) 50 percent of the world market and 67 percent of the EC market for commuter aircraft with 20 to 70 seats. This would have created a dominant position, affecting even the largest producers (such as British Aerospace and Fokker), with no competition from the United States or Japan. Whatever its specific merits and problems (especially the definition of the relevant market), it can be argued that this first negative decision by the Commission is important : even in a "special" sector such as aerospace, the Commission seems to stuck to the principle that mergers and take-overs should be judged purely on competitive grounds.

However, there are still some ambiguities about the role of economies in the decision. Having established that the ATR/de Havilland merger would led to reduce competition, the Commission states: "without prejudice as to whether cost saving consideration are relevant for the assessments under Article 2 of the Merger regulation, such cost savings would have a negligible impact on the overall operations of the ATR/de Havilland, amounting to around 0.5% of the combined turnover". According to Jenny (1992),

> "this decision offers some solace to the economists in that, although the Commission refuses to say explicitly whether productive efficiency gains are relevant for considering whether or not a merger is compatible with the common market, it nevertheless does discuss the importance of the manufacturing cost reductions alleged by the parties in a way that, at least implicitly, suggests that productive efficiency gains must be compared to the potential losses of consumer surplus due to the increase in concentration brought about by the merger" (p. 95).

In another decision on the acquisition of NCR (a computer manufacturer) by ATT (January 1991), the Commission seems to go further and to argue that the merger could have been illegal because it would yield economies, and hence create or strengthen a dominant position. Its conclusion was that the potential advantages which ATT hopes to gain from this concentration are for the moment theoretical and have yet to be proved in a future market place. This could suggest that had the Commission believed that the merger was likely to contribute to economic progress, it would have considered opposing it.

In spite of these ambiguities, it is fair to say that until now the new merger control rules are being incorporated into the Community's legal system in a satisfactory manner. Firms seem pleased to have only a single Commission procedure to deal with, a procedure which, though new, has the advantage of replacing the large number of procedures which, before the Regulation was implemented, had to be gone through with various national authorities. Also firms accept on the whole the Commission's requirements regarding the information that has to be supplied in the notification form, such acceptance being facilitated by the Commission's practice of holding pre notification meetings between the Directorate General for Competition and the representatives of the firms involved in the merger.

IV. Conclusion

The 1992 program has marked a new stage in the European competitive environment and is leading to new challenges for corporate strategies. The observed restructuring taking place is being made through internal and external operations that differ substantially among industries leading to relocation and geographical expansion, new product line selections, better exploitation of scale and scope economies, coordination and concentration of dispersed activities. Mergers and take-overs are one of the possible routes for such a restructuring, but neither theory nor empirical work provides any castiron arguments in favour of a presumption that these operations are generally efficient. Furthermore, even when they can be efficient, the corresponding gains must be compared with the effects of a possible increase in monopoly power. This could lead to complex trade-offs where the expected new industry structure following the merger, the degree of openness to international trade and the long-run dynamic performance linked with learning and technical change, are especially relevant aspects in the European context. On one hand, such complexity suggests that it would be presumptuous to advocate 'finetuned' optimal merger policy. On the other hand, the strict approach adopted in the new Regulation still requires more precisions which strongly conditions the quality of its implementation.

Notes

* The views set out in this paper are expressed in a personal capacity. It is mainly based on an article published in the *European Economic Review*, vol. 34, n° 2/3, May 1990.

1. For a brief review of these aspects, see A. Jacquemin and M. Slade (1989).
2. For the case of differentiated products, R. Deneckere and C. Davidson (1985) show that when the merging firms raise their prices, non-participant firms will do the same since price-reaction schedules slope upward. Mergers will then not increase social welfare. Indeed the merger permits the two combined price-competing firms to raise their price and induce non-participant firms to raise the price of competing substitutes.
3. Let us recall that in a Cournot equilibrium, large markups are associated with large market shares and large firms have lower marginal costs.
4. M. Neumann,, I. Böbel, and Haid, A. (1982). See also P. Geroski, (1987).

References

Coley, S. and S. Reinton, 1988, "The hunt of value", *The McKinsey Quarterly*, Spring.

d'Aspremont, Cl. and A. Jacquemin, 1988, "Cooperative and non-cooperative R&D in duopoly with spillovers", *American Economic Review*, 5.

Demsetz, H., 1974, "Two systems of belief about monopoly", in D. Goldschmid, H. Mann and J. Weston, eds., *Industrial Concentration: The New Learning*, Little Brown, Boston, MA.

Deneckere, R. and C. Davidson, 1985, "Incentives to form coalitions with Bertrand competition", *Rand Journal of Economics*, 16.

Farrell, J. and C. Shapiro, 1990, "Horizontal mergers: An equilibrium analysis", *American Economic Review*, March.

Geroski, P., 1987, *Competition and Innovation, Report prepared for the EC Commission*, Brussels.

Jacquemin, A., P. Buigues and F. Ilzkovitz, 1989, "Horizontal mergers and competition policy in the European Community", *European Economy*, 40, May.

Jacquemin, A. and A. Sapir, 1991, "Competition and imports in the European market", in A. Winters and A. Venables (eds.), *European Integration: trade and industry*, Cambridge University Press.

Jacquemin, A. and M. Slade, 1989, "Cartels, collusion and horizontal mergers", in R. Schmalensee and R. Willig, eds., *Handbook in Industrial Organization*, North Holland, Amsterdam.

Jenny, F., 1992, "Competition and competition policy", in W.J. Adams, ed., *Singular Europe*, The University of Michigan Press, Ann Arbor.

Mueller, D., 1980, *The Determinants and Effects of Mergers, an International Comparison*, Oelgeschlager, Gum and Marin, Cambridge.

Mueller, D,. 1989, "Mergers, causes, effects and policies", *International Journal of Industrial Organization*.

Ordover, J. and W. Baumol, 1988, "Antitrust policy and high technology industries", *Oxford Review of Economic Policy*, 4.

Ordover, J. and R. Willig, 1985, "Perspectives on mergers and world competition", Discussion paper, 88, Princeton.

Ross, T., 1988, "On the price effects of mergers in the freer trade", *International Journal of Industrial Organization*, 2.

Williamson, O., 1968, "Economics as an antitrust defense: The welfare trade-offs", *American Economic Review*, 58.

4. Competition Policy in the Federal Republic of Germany

MANFRED NEUMANN

I. Introduction

This paper will provide a review of the development of, and the experience with, competition policy in West Germany and will conclude with discussing some current problems. Competition policy in West Germany did not come about all at one time. Its origins must be traced back to the experience with the proliferation of cartels after the turn of the century and the interventionistic stance of economic policy during the interwar period. Competition policy then evolved step by step guided both by experience and shaped by changing political majorities.

The cornerstone of competition policy is embodied in the "Law Against Restraints of Competition" (Gesetz gegen Wettbewerbsbeschränkungen), henceforth abbreviated GWB, which was enacted in 1957 and which has been amended several times. Competition policy, however is in no way confined to the GWB. Various other regulations must be considered as part of competition policy as well, such as those pertaining to prohibiting unfair trading, to taxation and subsidies, regulation of banking and insurance, of traffic, public utilities and the organization of the stock exchange. A substantial influence on competition is exercised by the stance of policy regarding foreign trade and the movement of capital across the national borders. In short, the social framework has a substantial bearing on the degree of competition prevailing in the economy. These influences must be taken into account when it comes to evaluating the impact of the exercise of competition policy as based on the GWB.

The rest of the paper is organized as follows. In the first part, I will review the historical background and some fundamental issues governing competition policy in Germany. The second part is devoted to discussing the major regulations contained in the Act Against Restraints of Competition (GWB) and their enforcement by government agencies, in particular the Federal Cartel Office (Bundeskartellamt) and the courts. The third part provides an assessment of the impact of competition policy on the structure and performance of German industry. In this part, I will also discuss the side effects of the social framework on the efficacy of competition policy and some current problems.

G. Mussati (ed.), Mergers, Markets and Public Policy, 95–131.
© 1995 *Kluwer Academic Publishers.*

II. Competition Policy in Historical Perspective

Upon an accelerated increase in the number of cartels during the later decades of the 19th century the Court of Justice of the German Empire (Reichsgericht) ruled in 1897 that cartels are principally legal since freedom of business activity, according to the view of the Court, is deemed to encompass freedom to enter contracts which regulate prices in a particular industry. According to later critics (Böhm 1948, Möschel 1972), the legal reasoning of the Court is somewhat questionable. Still, the ruling itself was in accord with the opinion of a large majority of economists of the late 19th century. Some of them refused to consider cartels as organizations exploiting consumers but viewed them in a romantic light as being regulators of an otherwise chaotic environment. The leading German socialist of that time, August Bebel, in a parliamentary debate alluded to the emergence of cartels as a welcome step towards socialism (Möschel 1972, p. 15). Thus, for different reasons, cartels were welcomed by a majority of economists and politicians.

Actually, the number of cartels in existence in 1897 exceeded 250. After the Court had put aside all remaining legal obstacles cartels proliferated tremendously. Just before World War I the number of cartels exceeded 600, in 1922 it outnumbered 1000, and in 1925 the number of cartels was estimated as lying between 2000 and 2500 (Fischer 1954, p. 443). So Germany became the country of cartels. Eventually, the Nazi regime after 1933 found it expedient to declare membership in a cartel as mandatory, and finally, ten years later, the cartels were simply changed into government agencies of the centrally planned war economy.

In 1923, towards the very end of the hyperinflation, a law against the abuses of cartels was enacted. It was motivated, first, by the obviously erroneous notion that the tremendous price increases had to be attributed to the cartels and that cartels should be forbidden to raise prices unreasonably. Not unexpectedly, this part of the provision remained completely ineffective. The second aim of the act was to inhibit undue restrictions of freedom of cartel members.

After World War II cartels were declared illegal by the Allied Military Government the legislation of which was guided by the principles of U.S.Antitrust policy. This legislation remained valid until in 1957 it was replaced by the Act Against Restraints of Competition.

In the meantime, however, a group of German economists and lawyers, which became to be known as the Ordo-liberal School, during the war and immediately after the war, had developed principles of economic policy which were to become decisive after the foundation of the Federal Republic of Germany in 1949. The most prominent persons were Walter Eucken, an economist, and Franz Böhm, a lawyer, respectively. The principles developed by these people, later on, were politically sold under the label of "Social Market Economy" (Soziale Marktwirtschaft), a term coined by Alfred Müller-Armack, and implemented under the leadership of Ludwig Erhard, the first Minister of Economics of the Federal Republic of Germany.

To understand competition as conceived within the notion of Social Market Economy it is useful to start with an outline of two opposing views, i.e., the concept of a spontaneous order which is closely related to the ideas of the libertarian tradition grown up in Chicago on one hand and competition policy as a part of industrial policy guided by welfare economics on the other hand. A discussion of these opposing views will also enhance the understanding of German competition policy vis-à-vis the socalled Chicago School.

Spontaneous order

According to Hayek (1973) freedom of action will bring about what he called a spontaneous order the emergence of which is beyond being fully understood. In the words of Hayek (p. 41)

> "Since a spontaneous order results from the individual elements adapting themselves to circumstances which directly affect only some of them, and which in their totality need not be known to anyone, it may extend to circumstances so complex that no mind can comprehend them all."

The underlying idea is that by the interaction of individuals, particularly in the market place, informations are utilized and brought to fruitful application which are beyond the command of any single individual. That is of course the same idea which originally Adam Smith put forward by suggesting that individual self-regard is conducive to fostering the public interest. Although each individual intends only his own gain, he is "led by an invisible hand to promote an end which was no part of his intention" (Smith, p. 477). The validity of the invisible hand theorem of course is predicated on the existence of competition. The notion of a spontaneous order implies that freedom alone will guarantee competition. Thus, according to this view, no further provision need be taken except those to ensure freedom of action. Any specific organizational safeguards to foster competition or any regulations against restraints of competition thus appear to be superfluous. Any restraints of trade set up by private contract are deemed to be swept away by the forces of competition arising from individual freedom.

Yet the experience with the development of cartels in Germany after the turn of the century offers a telling counterexample which, to my mind, convincingly refutes the validity of the claim that freedom alone will suffice to establish a competitive order which gives room to the working of the invisible hand. This conclusion has also been drawn by the economists and lawyers of the Ordo-liberal School. They therefore attempted to conceptualize an economic order sufficient to inhibit restraints of competition. In doing so they also had to avoid falling victim to the opposite fallacy of competition policy as conceived of as a branch of applied welfare economies.

Competition policy as a branch of applied welfare economics

Since a desirable performance of the economy can hardly be achieved by exercising direct influence on the behaviour of firms and private households without interfering with individual freedom competition policy, conceived of as a branch of welfare economics, seeks to set up and maintain market structures which are deemed to be conducive to the enhancement of economic welfare.

To define an appropriate market structure one must have recourse to economic theory which, even at an abstract level, abounds with controversies with regard to the structure-performance relationship. Furthermore, the main body of traditional welfare economics is a static theory. Actually, however, competition does not exhaust itself in a static environment to give rise to a set of prices which yield an efficient allocation of given resources. Competition in the real world is a dynamic process generating innovations, i.e., new products, new processes, and new organizational forms. Schumpeter therefore aptly characterized it as a process of creative destruction. If that is so, an optimal market structure turns out to be a highly elusive concept. What is the appropriate time horizon? Whose welfare does count more, the welfare of innovators or the welfare of those who find themselves on the losing side? If the desirable market structures is to be defined by the political process decision makers will be subject to pressures from all kinds of interest groups. It can in particular be expected that the short run perspective dominates. Those who are losing can easily be identified whereas the benefits of innovations are mostly of a dispersed nature and frequently not immediately obvious. Therefore, the representatives of those sectors which are endangered by innovations usually have a more compelling case and will easily find political support. Hence competition policy degenerates into an industrial policy which falls victim to demands of vociferous interest groups. That will exert a retarding influence on innovations and thus on economic welfare as seen from a long run perspective.

Competition policy in the framework of a social market economy

Competition policy must steer a course between the Scylla and Charybdis of either giving leeway to a proliferation of restraints of competition of or falling victim to the pressures of various interest groups.

The guiding principle of German competition policy is twofold. Maintenance of competition is considered to be the only way to safeguard individual freedom of economic activity and, simultaneously, to harness self-interest for serving the public interest. It is presumed to do so, first, by enhancing efficiency in production and distribution of commodities and services, and, second, by being an extremely powerful method to discover new ways and means of economic activity. In fact, as has been suggested by Hayek (1968), competition is the most effective method of discovery because it utilizes scattered knowledge of a multitude of individuals which cannot be put to use by any other method of coordinating individual activities.

From this point of view a competitive order appears to be a public good to be maintained by appropriate government action. This statement, since it embodies the logical basis for competition policy, requires some elaboration. It is useful to recall that competition which really counts is competition by introducing new products and processes. It is not price competition, as traditionally depicted in the textbooks. That is not to deny the importance of prices. Changes in relative prices, however, are mostly driven by innovations. In comparison to changes in technologies by innovations prices are ephemeral.

The overriding importance of technology and technological change was clearly recognized by Mr. Justice Stone in the Trenton Pottery case in the U.S.A. which became leading for the law against price fixing.

> "The power to fix prices, whether reasonably exercised or not involves power to control the market and to fix arbitrary and unreasonable prices. The reasonable price of today may through economic business changes become the unreasonable price of tomorrow. Once established, it may be maintained unchanged because of the absence of competition" (cited in Neale 1966, p. 36).

Competition which generates innovations is a public good because the social benefits of a particular innovation usually exceeds the gains the innovator himself can draw from it. Innovations provide informations about new ways of doing things which are disseminated by signals of the market and thus become available to everybody. They thus pave the way of subsequent innovations that engender gains which were not part of the intentions of the prior innovator. In this way innovations give rise to external economies. Moreover, as suggested by Arrow (1962) an incumbent may suffer losses from adopting a new technique. Therefore, given sunk costs, his net gain is below the gain to be expected by a newcomer to the industry.

A newcomer may thus be more eager to adopt an innovation and thus induce subsequent innovations which would be retarded by the reluctance of an incumbent to innovate. Hence competition by newcomers is socially desirable although it frequently engenders losses to incumbents.

Incumbents therefore can be expected to seek protection for their sunk investments. First, they may try to persuade the government to provide protection from competition. Second, they may undertake mergers in order to gain market control which offers scope for strategic moves aiming at entry deterrence. The immediate effect of a merger is an increase in horizontal concentration provided entry can be forestalled. That gives rise to higher profits even if collusion does not obtain. Greater ease of setting up and maintaining collusive agreements after merger has occurred gives an extra motivation to merge. Therefore, subsequent upon a merger, prices are likely to rise. This tendency may be fully or partially offset by decreasing average costs due to economies of scale or economies of scope. These economies, however, are of a static nature and will, therefore, after some time be exhausted.

Since market power is being undermined by entry of new competitors the thrust of competition policy should be directed at keeping markets open for newcomers. Entry may be blocked by predatory practices, however. Such strategies are most likely to be adopted if incumbents enjoy market control (Mestmäcker 1984, pp. 201 ff.). The denial of predatory price-cutting as a rational device by McGee (1958, 1985) has been convincingly refuted by Burns (1986). In a study concerning the practices of the American Tobacco Trust he demonstrated that the Trust, by setting up bogus independent companies for price-cutting, achieved a reduction of the purchase price of smaller rival firms which could then be cheaply acquired. This practices also created a reputation of the incumbent that discouraged potential entry. Predatory conduct has in the past also been observed to be exercised by cartels to discipline outsiders.

From these observations it follows that in order to safeguard freedom of entry, first, cartels and similar contractual restraints should be illegal. Second, predatory conduct of dominant firms should be prevented by both surveillance of those firms and prohibition of mergers which are likely to engender entry deterrent strategies.

These are the principles which are at the bottom of German competition policy. Yet, the application of these principles is somewhat attenuated by the intrusion of constructivism as derived from welfare economics.

The Federal Government, upon submitting the bill that later became the Act Against Restraints of Competition (GWB) to parliament, stated as an aim to be pursued that by providing for the existence of a multitude of enterprises a decentralized structure of the economy should be maintained.

The meaning of this aim is ambiguous. It can be justified on the ground that a decentralized structure provides for a great number of independent search processes to take place such that the probability of success is augmented. On the other hand, the promise to maintain a decentralized structure can be, and has been, interpreted by a particular industry concerned that some protection from inroads of competition which might upset the prevailing structure should be provided by the government.

The legislation of 1957 which took effect in 1958 contained two elements. First, it established a per se rule against cartels and outlawed vertical agreements if they unreasonably restrict the freedom of the parties to the contract. The rule against cartels is attenuated by a number of exemptions to be discussed in detail below. Second, the GWB provided for dominant firms and permitted cartels to be subject to supervision with regard to abusive exercise of market power. The administration of the GWB has been assigned to a Federal authority, i.e. the Federal Cartel Office, and appropriate authorities of the Federal States (Länder) as far as local violations of the law are concerned.

The original bill, as drafted by the Federal Government, also contained provisions for merger control. These were however dropped upon objections raised by interest groups arguing that a prohibition of mergers would be harmful since benefits to be enjoyed by exploiting economies of scale had to be sacrificed. So a typical trade-off argument of industrial policy was used by pressure groups to talk the parliament out of passing a provision for merger control. Hence the Act, as eventually passed by parliament, fell substantially short of what the proponents of a competitive order had originally envisaged. The insight derived therefrom that economic power could not be completely excluded later on lent support to demands for codetermination by employees and trade unions in business enterprises which were passed into law after the parliamentary majority had changed.

An amendment providing for merger control was only passed in 1973 after the conservative coalition of the first two decades of the Federal Republic of Germany had been replaced by a coalition of Social Democrats (SPD) and the Free Democrats (FDP). Upon this change of majorities the stance of competition policy shifted somewhat into the direction of industrial policy in that merger control was conceived of as a chance to actively shape industrial structure. That gave rise to a heated debate about the proper use of merger control the impact of which on the enforcement of merger control will be discussed below in more detail.

Competition implies that those firms which are unable to keep up with their more successful rivals are displaced. This kind of selection is a constitutive property of the competitive process which has never come under dispute. Yet, the contest in the market place should be carried out with fairness. Unfair methods, such as fraud, slander, blackmail and boycotts must not be employed. Businessmen can seek protection from this kind of unfair competition by having recourse to the remedies provided by the Act Against Unfair Competition (Gesetz gegen den unlauteren Wettbewerb). They may sue violators for damages.

From the very beginning of the implementation of a Social Market Economy it has been undisputed that a competitive order must be supplemented by a social welfare policy which should come in two parts. First, individuals should be aided to become fit for joining the competitive game. Second, those who find themselves on the losing side should be supported to either become capable to rejoin the game after retraining and search or they should be provided with the means for a decent life if they are sick or too old to find an equivalent employment again. The attitudes towards the desirable extent of aids naturally differ as between followers of the various political colours.

A final element of a Social Market Economy deserves particular notice. That is monetary stability. The reliability of price signals disseminated by the market is seriously vitiated by inflation. Experience shows that inflation has never occurred at a constant rate which might be expected with certainty and thus enters all contracts without creating distortions. Since inflation occurs at changing rates price signals become ambiguous. Ascertaining whether the increase in a particular price signals a change in relative prices or just a loss of purchasing power of money is only possible ex post. Thus under inflationary conditions the proper functioning of markets is impaired. Therefore the architects of the notion of a Social Market Economy emphasized the importance of monetary stability the pursuit of which by an independent monetary authority has been a constitutive part of a competitive order and a necessary companion of competition policy.

III. The Act Against Restraints of Competition and its Enforcement

In the sequel an outline of the provisions of the Act Against Restraints of Competition (GWB) will be given. Some leading cases tried in the courts will briefly be discussed. For reasons of space it is not possible to take up each detail of the law. Hence the presentation of the law and its discussion will necessarily be somewhat cursory.

Contractual restraints

Horizontal contracts of private or public enterprises aiming at restraining competition, i.e., cartels, are disallowed (Section 1 of GWB). Those contracts are null and void and participants in such agreement are subject to be fined (Section 38 of GWB).

This rule against cartels also applies to contracts which only indirectly influence market behaviour of firms. A conspicuous example is an open price system where informations about the terms of past transactions are disseminated to sellers only. Such an arrangement is deemed to create mutual trust among competing firms. It is thus conducive to collusive behaviour.

Originally only explicit contracts aiming at influencing the terms of market transactions were illegal. Only after the Federal Cartel Office failed to successfully prosecute dyestuff producers for tacit collusion an amendment to the Act Against Restraints of Competition was enacted in 1973 which outlawed tacit collusion as well (Section 25 subparagraph 1 of GWB). This amendment put the German regulation for domestic cartels on an equal footing with the rules laid down in Article 85 of the Treaty of Rome.

Vertical restraints, such as agreements about exclusive dealing and territorial restraints, are banned subject to a rule of reason. A franchising contract, for example, is generally permitted unless it is abused as a pretext for the maintenance of horizontal agreements or any unreasonable restraint of the freedom of participants. The same applies to licensing of patent rights in so far as the restraints agreed upon in the contract exceed the contents of the patent right.

Resale price maintenance which originally was generally allowed for branded commodities, provided competition prevailed among producers, became to be banned in 1973 except for products of publishers, such as books, journals and newspapers. Since 1973 producers may recommend prices for resale the observation of which is not obligatory. Both resale price maintenance and non obligatory price recommendations are subject to supervision by the Federal Cartel Office. Both can be interdicted if abusively exercised. An abuse consists, for example, in recommending resale prices which substantial exceed those prices which actually obtain in the market place.

Disallowing resale price maintenance in 1973 was principally motivated by the fact that its exercise appeared to be increasingly abusive. With the rise of large discounters producers of branded commodities were no longer able to secure the actual prices at the stores to be in line with the resale prices set by the producers. More and more branded commodities were used to attract customers to the stores by selling them at lower prices. Since large discounters command some buying power most producers were unable to stop them from underselling their products. That of course entailed an advantage of large retailers over smaller ones who could more easily be forced by legal means to maintain resale prices as set by the producers.

Furthermore, resale price maintenance was prohibited because it became to be considered as a cartel among retailers. The justification for resale price maintenance usually given by spokesmen of industry that it would guarantee a fee for the retailer to provide services in favour of the producer became to be considered as a pretext. Why should the customer be charged with a higher price regardless of whether he wants such a service or not? The subsequent development of retailing in Germany overwhelmingly led to lower prices without a significant deterioration of quality. Thus the old arguments in favour of resale price maintenance which more recently have been excavated by adherents of the so-called Chicago School (Bittlingmayer 1987) appear to be somewhat out of touch with experience.

There are three kinds of exemptions from the general rules against contractual restraints.

First, some sectors of the economy are completely or partially exempt, namely, telecommunication which is under the exclusive control of the Federal Post Office (Deutsche Bundespost), traffic, agricultural producer cooperatives and their contractual relationships with individual farmers, banking and insurance, public utilities, and associations engaged in the administration of patent rights of individuals. Traffic, banking and insurance as well as public utilities, in particular, are subject to specific regulations exercised by public authorities. As far as horizontal or vertical contractual restraints of competition in these sectors are concerned, which are exempt from the general ban, an additional supervision by the Federal Cartel Office applies.

The quantitative significance of the general exemptions can be assessed by looking at the gross value added of agriculture, public utilities, traffic, banking and insurance as a percentage of gross value added of all German enterprices. The respective percentage in 1985 amounted to 18.8 (Statistisches Jahrbuch 1988, pp. 542-3). So about a fifth of gross value added of all German enterprises is exempt from the general ban against contractual restraints of competition. Still, it should be recalled that all restraints of competition are subject to the supervision with respect to abuses of market power, besides being regulated by specific public authorities.

It might also be noted that coal mining and the iron and steel industry are exempt from the national law against restraints of competition since they are subject to the regulations of the European law.

Second, particular types of cartels are either exempt per se or can be exempted by decree of the Federal Cartel Office.

Exemption per se obtains for pure export cartels, i.e., those cartels which do not affect the domestic market. If the agreement also affects the domestic market the Federal Cartel Office may permit the cartel, provided the side effect is necessary to ensure its success on foreign markets.

Cartels which exclusively pertain to the terms of contract with customers (Konditionenkartelle) or rebates which do not entail an unjustified discrimination between customers have to be notified to the Federal Cartel Office. The agreement becomes valid unless the Federal Cartel Office raises objections within three months.

Cartels set up for the purpose of facilitating rationalization and specialization between firms may be allowed by the Federal Cartel Office. Cartels which aim at facilitating rationalization may be allowed even if the agreement also pertains to prices and distribution outlets, provided rationalization is deemed to serve the public interest and the agreement does not unreasonably restrain competition. Similarly, in the case of specialization, a substantial degree of competition must be maintained. Cooperations of the aforementioned type may, in particular, be allowed by the Federal Cartel Office if they do not substantially lessen competition and enhance the competitiveness of small and medium sized firms.

Cooperation between small and medium sized firms is exercised by the Co-operatives (Genossenschaften) of retailers and various trades aiming at organizing centralized purchasing and marketing. In fact, the survival of large sections of the economy occupied by small scale business can be attributed to the activities of those Co-operatives which serve as wholesalers and provide managerial advice. The Co-operatives are exempt from the ban on cartels insofar, as they are confined to small scale firms and do not unduly restrain the behaviour of member firms.

Third, in the case of a structural crisis the Federal Cartel Office may allow a cartel to be set up if it is necessary to ensure a systematic reduction of productive capacity and if the arrangement is in the public interest. The permission to form such a cartel shall be given only for a limited time span, subject to prolongation if necessary.

Trade associations are permitted to recommend technical norms, general terms of business transactions and rules of fair conduct. Particularly the latter kind of rules have always been favoured and demanded by spokesmen of industry as a means to achieve what sometimes has been alluded to as "orderly marketing" which, however, actually is nothing else but collusion in disguise. The claim that such rules would be suitable to prevent predatory price-cutting is not well founded since without monopolistic market power of a dominant firm or a cartel predatory pricing is unlikely to occur (see also Mestmäcker 1984, pp. 23 ff.). The original wording of the respective section of the Act Against Restraints of Competition led the Federal Court of Justice (Bundesgerichtshof) in 1966 to confine the permission of rules of fair conduct to those cases only where they were framed in such a way as to solely prevent unfair trading (Mestmäcker 1984, p. 22). Subsequently, however, the wording of Section 28, subparagraph 2 of GWB has been changed to cover also cases where price competition might upset the prevailing structure of industry. This amendment introduced into the law against restraints of competition elements of structural policy.

All cartels with the exception of pure export cartels and all recommendations of trade associations are registered with the Federal Cartel Office. The register is public and thus accessible to anybody.

According to the latest report of the Federal Cartel Office 276 cartels were in existence in 1990, the bulk of which, namely 23, were agreements about rationalization and specialization, 60 pertained to general terms of contract and rebates, 2 were export cartels affecting the domestic market. Among the agreements about rationalization and specialization there were 147 cooperations between small and medium sized firms which have been actively propagated by the Federal Government as part of a policy that aims at compensating disadvantages of smaller firms vis-à-vis large firms. It is remarkable that only one cartel (for synthetic fibres) existed which was formed to cope with a structural crisis.

The bulk of rationalization and specialization agreements are to be found in the quarrying industries and building trades, in metalworking and machine-building industries, independent suppliers for the automotive industry and food processing. Cartels pertaining to terms of contract are mostly found in textile and clothing industries. On the whole it is remarkable that most cartels and recommendations given by trade associations exists in industries where small scale firms abound and where the degree of industry concentration is relatively low.

In fact, there is a statistically significant inverse correlation between the C3-concentration index in 1983 and the total number of registered cartels and all kinds of recommendations given by trade associations in 30 two-digit industries in 1986. The simple correlation coefficient is 0.36 with a *t*-ratio of 1.95. In calculating this correlation coefficient the quarrying industry has been disregarded since a scatter diagram, which is not reproduced here, shows it to be a clear outlier, which would have raised the magnitude of the correlation coefficient substantially. Thus disregarding this industry yields a conservative estimate of the relationship investigated.

Permissible cartels and recommendations by trade associations, although looking innocuous at first sight may serve as a framework to maintain clandestine agreements which go far beyond what has been publicly announced to be agreed upon. The cooperation, as registered with the Federal Cartel Office may just serve as an instrument to create an atmosphere of mutual trust conducive to collusive parallelism with regard to prices and quantities. As already observed by Adam Smith that "people of the same trade seldom meet together, even for merriment and diversion, but the conversation ends in a conspiracy against the public or in some contrivance to raise prices" (Adam Smith, vol. I, p. 144), the likelihood of collusive parallelism increases upon the establishment of a contractual framework even if itself does not explicitly pertain to prices.

This reasoning receives further support by the observation that permissible agreements are inversely associated with industry concentration. In his theory of oligopoly George Stigler (1966) suggested that fewness facilitates the private enforcement of collusion. Hence, given the pervasive inclination to collude, for firms operating in a highly concentrated industry, it will be fairly easy to maintain clandestine agreements. In less concentrated industries it is much more difficult to achieve the same result unless some extra scaffolding is provided such as permissible cartels and recommendations. The inverse relationship alluded to above thus indicates that concentration, which may be achieved by mergers, and cartels, to some extent, are substitutes.

The Federal Cartel Office as well as the respective authorities of the Federal States in Germany face the difficult problems to prevent any violation of the rule against cartels. In fact, in a substantial number of cases violations have been successfully prosecuted. For example, during 1985-1986 the Federal Cartel Office brought to a close by imposing a fine 74 proceedings against violations of the per se prohibition of cartels (Section 1 of GWB), and the respective number of cases handled by the authorities of the Federal States was 78. Although quite a few violations will remain undetected the active prosecution by the authorities entails a substantial risk which can be expected to reduce the number of violations.

Merger control

Mergers and acquisitions, under the law of merger control as embodied in sections 2-224a of GWB, are acceptable if they are justified on economic and technical grounds. The aim of the law is to ensure that markets remain competitive. Thus mergers and acquisitions are unlawful if they are undertaken to establish or increase market power by obtaining or strengthening a dominant market position which entails market control. The law does not oppose the acquisition of a dominant market position through internal growth of an enterprise.

Merger control, according to the regulations of the Act Against Restraints of Competition, is split into two parts, namely formal control and material control, respectively.

The first one requires the firms to notify any acquisition or merger of a specified nature to the Federal Cartel Office. Second, as laid down in Sections 22, 23a and 24 of GWB, the Federal Cartel Office, under specified conditions, may prevent a merger to take place (material control).

The amendment to the Act Against Restraints of Competition which introduced merger control in 1973 also established an independent Monopoly Commission (Monopolkommission) to regularly report about the development of concentration in the German economy and to comment on the enforcement of merger control and the supervision of dominant firms, as exercised by the authorities. The Monopoly Commission may recommend changes in the law which appear desirable in view of the development of concentration.

Notification requirements

To provide a chance to prevent a merger if that is desirable mergers which might significantly affect the degree of competition must be brought to the attention of the Federal Cartel Office. A merger must be notified immediately upon consummation if (Section 23 GWB):

(1) in the Federal Republic of Germany or in a substantial part thereof the merger will increase or attain a domestic market share of at least 20 per cent, or if a participating company, in another market of the same geographical area, already holds control over at least 20 per cent;
(2) in the last accounting year before the merger the participating companies together had at least 10,000 employees or attained a turnover of at least DM 500 million.

Premerger notification is required in the case of major mergers, i.e., if (Section 24a of GWB):

(1) one of the enterprises, which is a part of the intended merger, in the last accounting year had a turnover of at least DM 2,000 million, or
(2) at least two of the parties involved in the intended merger each had turnover of DM 1,000 million or more in the past accounting year, or
(3) the intended merger should be effected through any law or act of souvereignty of the State involved.

Where a premerger notification is not mandatory the participating enterprises can nevertheless voluntarily register their intention with the Federal Cartel Office as a precautionary measure. The advantage of doing so is that the Federal Cartel Office must ordinarily approve of or deny the intended merger within four months after notification.

Legal definition of a merger

Any of the following constitute a merger, as defined by Section 23 of GWB:

(1) The acquisition of assets of another enterprise in whole or a substantial part thereof.
(2) The acquisition of an interest in another business firm where the acquiring company through the acquisition attains
    (a) 25 per cent of the voting share capital or

(b) 50 per cent of the voting share capital or
(c) a majority holding in accordance with Section 16, subparagraph 1 of the German Law of Joint Stock Companies (Aktiengesetz).

(3) Agreements with other enterprises are entered into whereby
(a) a "Konzern" in accordance with Section 18 of Aktiengesetz is formed or expanded or
(b) profit transfers are in whole or in part agreed upon or
(c) the business of an enterprise, either in whole or a substantial part thereof, is leased or assigned.

A merger is not assumed to take place in the case where a bank, upon the foundation of an enterprise or upon an augmentation of capital or otherwise, such as in the case of bankruptcy, acquires shares of capital in order to sell them to the public, provided the sale takes place within one year and the voting rights going with the capital share are not exercised.

When the law was enacted the legal definition of a merger was deemed sufficiently encompassing to catch all kinds or mergers and acquisitions conceivable. Nevertheless it turned out subsequently that loopholes were left. In a few cases the acquiring enterprise bought an interest of only a little less than 25 per cent, the difference to the legally stipulated threshold being held by a friendly bank. In this way the acquisition did not qualify as a merger in the legal sense and thus escaped the governmental merger control. In the latest amendment to the Act Against Restraints of Competition this loophole has been closed by introducing a general clause according to which an acquisition qualifies as a merger by which, irrespective by which means, effective control of the acquired company is obtained.

Control of the market

According to Section 24 of GWB the Federal Cartel Office may prevent a merger where it can be expected that the participating companies, as a result of the merger, will attain control of the market or thereby strengthen an already existing controlling position. Thus the decisive criterion is market control which is legally defined in Section 22 of GWB. It refers to a single enterprise or two or more firms which dominate the market, respectively.

Market control obtains if an enterprise, or a group of two or more enterprises, as either a seller or a buyer, are not exposed to competition or are not subject to substantial competition. Market control also obtains if an enterprise occupies an overriding market position, which is defined by taking account of its market share, financial strength, access to markets as either buyer or seller, and the legal and actual impediments to the entry of other competing firms.

In each particular case the onus of proof is upon the government. Nevertheless some legal guidance is provided in Sections 22 and 23a of GWB as to when market control might be presumed to exist.

According to Section 22 of GWB market control presumably obtains:

(1) if a firm, for a particular kind of commodities, commands a market share of at least a third unless its turnover during the past accounting year falls short of DM 250 million,
(2) if three or less than three firms have a cumulative market share of at least 50 per cent or if five or less than five firms have a market share of two thirds unless the turnover of the respective enterprises during the past accounting year falls short of DM 100 million.

According to Section 23a of GWB a merger is presumed to give rise to an overriding market position or to strengthen such a position if

(1) an enterprise with a turnover of at least DM 2,000 million acquires a firm that
- is operating in a market in which small and medium sized firms have a cumulative market share of at least two thirds and the firms participating in the merger have a market share of at least 5 per cent, or
- is holding control in one or several other markets in which during the past calendar year a total of at least DM 150 million turnover has been attained, or
(2) the participating firms during the past accounting year had a total turnover of at least DM 12,000 million and at least two participating enterprises had a turnover of at least DM 1,000 million.

The legal presumptions can be refuted by the enterprises by showing that even after the merger material competition can be expected to obtain and that overriding market positions do not arise in the cases enumerated in Section 23a of GWB. Thus, in these cases the onus of proof is on the acquiring enterprise.

The provisions of Section 23a of GWB have been incorporated into the law by an amendment enacted in 1980 to cope with the relative increase in vertical and conglomerate mergers and the presumption that small and medium sized enterprises might be extinguished through the financial strength of giant firms.

Enforcement of merger control

The various presumptions constitute a prima facie proof of market control. A major problem of enforcement consists in delineating the relevant market to which the market share presumptions apply. The Federal Cartel Office usually adopts a two stage procedure. First, a relatively narrow definition of the relevant market is adopted. Geographically the relevant market may be even smaller then the area of the Federal Republic of Germany if markets are local because, as in the case of cement for example, transport costs are significant. Second, in a further step, neighbouring markets are taken into account in order to appraise whether they constitute close substitutes. It is investigated, first, whether customers are regarding commodities of neighbouring markets as substitutes for those supplied by the merging firms. It is secondly asked whether firms operating in neighbouring markets might be able to enter the narrowly defined market where the merger is taking place. In doing so the Federal Cartel Office originally disregarded foreign competition in most cases, which was severely criticized by the Monopoly Commission (Monopolkommission 1978/1979, p. 167).

The earlier practice has been changed more recently, however (BKartA 1985/1986, p. 16). Increasingly, both actual and potential international competition has been taken into account. Imports are a part of the domestic market volume and thus directly influence the computation of market shares of individual firms. An example for taking account of potential international competition has been the decision in the case of the acquisition of Werner & Pfleiderer, the largest German producer of equipment for bakeries, by Fried Krupp GmbH. The Federal Cartel Office did not object to the acquisition since the potential competition by Britain's Baker Perkins, with its world wide operations, was considered to prevent market control by the merger. On the other hand there will be doubts regarding the effectiveness of potential competition if an entry has not occurred for a long time, particularly because entry is unlikely due to barriers to international trade. Thus it is not the present market structure that really counts. The dynamism of markets must be taken into account as well. For example, the acquisition of a majority holding of Triumph-Adler by Olivetti met with the approval of the Federal Cartel Office in spite of large market shares involved because the market for typewriters is undergoing dramatic changes under the influence of Personal Computers and related equipment.

Another major problem of enforcement arose in connection with the necessity to take into account financial strength as a criterion for market control. Financial strength may engender a deep pocket strategy of predatory behaviour of dominant firms which might induce smaller firms to sell out to large rivals and discourage entry of smaller firms in the first place. The leading case has been the proposed acquisition of a majority holding of WMF (Württembergische Metallwarenfabriken) by Rheinmetall. WMF holds a dominant market position in the fields of high quality table appointments and large coffee machines. Rheinmetall is a leading supplier in the field of military equipment. So the proposed merger was of a purely conglomerate character intended by Rheinmetall to reduce its dependence on the high risk field of military equipment. The acquisition was disallowed by the Federal Cartel Office on the ground that such a leading firm acquisition by a firm like Rheinmetall with its command of ample financial resources would strengthen market control of WMF. The decision of the Federal Cartel Office has subsequently been upheld by the Federal Court of Justice (Bundesgerichtshof) and thus constitutes a landmark with respect to conglomerate mergers (Monopolkommission 1984/1985, pp. 181-183).

This case contrasts with a series of conglomerate acquisitions by DaimlerBenz, the most conspicuous being the acquisition of AEG, a major electrical and electronics firm. The acquisition was approved of by the Federal Cartel Office since AEG, just as previously acquired aircraft firms MTU and Dornier, was not found to be in control of any of its markets. Although these major acquisitions aroused a lot of public sentiment the Federal Cartel Office had no choice, given the present law.

Joint ventures

Joint ventures may constitute mergers to be handled according to the regulation of merger control. They may alternatively be purely cooperative and thus fall under the verdict of the per se rule against cartels. A joint venture may also occupy a middle ground. For these reasons joint ventures are subject to a twofold examination.

A joint venture qualifies as a pure merger and is thus subject only to merger control if it gives rise to a viable enterprise with all essential enterprise functions and if it renders market-related services rather than acting exclusively or predominantly for the parent companies at a preceding or subsequent stage of the economy and if the parent companies themselves are not or no longer active in the product market of the joint venture.

A joint venture is deemed to be purely cooperative if its organizational structure is shaped in such a way as to primarily coordinate the conduct of the parent companies.

Two cases of purely cooperative joint ventures stand out. In 1975 the Federal Court of Justice upheld a decision of the Federal Cartel Office disallowing four cement producers from jointly selling their production via a jointly owned though legally independent sales organization. In 1980 the Federal Cartel Office prohibited HFGE (Handelsgesellschaft freier Groß-und Einzelhandelsbetriebe GmbH), set up by four trading groups who previously had purchased separately to obtain better terms by concentrated buying, as an illegal buyers' cartel. The decision was upheld in court.

On the other hand, a joint venture set up for exploration and exploitation of manganese nodules from the seabed was regarded as a pure merger by the

Federal Cartel Office in 1976. No restraint of competition was found and the cooperation was deemed necessary since each of the participating enterprises alone was short of the required financial and technological capacity.

In 1984 the Federal Cartel Office turned down a proposal of five leading cable manufacturers in Germany (Siemens, Philips, AEG, SEL (ITT) and Kabelmetall (Cables de Lyon)) to establish a joint venture for the production and distribution of optical fibres. The Federal Cartel Office prohibited this proposal on the ground that it would strengthen the participating firms' dominant oligopoly, continue the former telecommunication cable cartel in a new shape, block the entry to the market, and impair technological competition in the production of optical fibres. The Federal Cartel Office, in this case of a joint venture comprising both cooperative and concentrative elements, found the anticompetitive effects to outweight advantages to the public.

The efficacy of merger control

The review of the practice of merger control by the Federal Cartel Office suggests that, on the whole, it has been cautiously exercised. Although a large number of mergers has been notified only a rather small number of mergers has been disallowed by the authorities, as can be seen from Table 4.1. From a total of 14403 notified mergers only 98, that is less than one per cent, have been prohibited by the Federal Cartel Office. Of these 98, so far only 40 interdictions became valid in law upon litigation. In 14 cases the prohibition has been cancelled, in 19 cases the prohibition was annulled by court decision, an 10 cases are still waiting to be settled by court decision (Monopolkommission 1990/91, p. 36).

Table 4.1. Notified mergers and number of prohibitions, 1973-1991

	Mergers	Prohibitions
1973-1975	773	4
1976-1977	1007	7
1978-1979	1160	14
1980-1981	1253	21
1982-1983	1109	10
1984-1985	1284	13
1986-1987	1689	5
1988-1989	2573	16
1990-1991	3555*	
Total	14403	98

*of which 911 acquisitions in East Germany (privatisation)

Source: Monopolkommission 1990/1991, p. 251

Given the extremely small number of interdictions of mergers one wonders whether merger control had any significant effect on merger activity. Actually, a close look at the evidence will reveal that merger control was far more influential than it might be inferred from the numbers mentioned above.

First, it should be recalled that merger control attempts to curb merger activity only in so far as it is conducive to create or strengthen monopolistic market power. A great many mergers, however, are just reorganizations without significant impact on market structures. Although they have to be notified to the authorities they are completely harmless from the point of view of competition policy.

Second, everybody can read the law and can obtain legal advice from counsel. During the years a substantial number of precedents arose by the decisions of the courts so that the law became to be known by interested parties. If doubts existed firms took the opportunity to address the Federal Cartel Office in an informal way to inquire whether an intended merger would meet with the approval of the authorities. Actually, by the end of 1987, in 162 cases an intended merger was given up after informal talks with the Federal Cartel Office, and in 1986-1987 alone 6 notified mergers were subsequently abandoned. It thus appears that the law of merger control works as a fleet in being which exerts a significant influence on merger activity. It likely has contributed to reducing the number of those mergers which otherwise would have occurred and tended to increase monopolistic market power.

Such an effect might be inferred from the changing composition of the various kinds of mergers. During 1974-1975, i.e., immediately after merger control had been enacted, the share of horizontal mergers in the total number of all notified mergers was 74.5 per cent. The share of this type of merger which is particularly likely to give rise to market control declined to 67.5 per cent in 1985-1986, but rose again to 73.2 per cent in 1989-1990. In contrast, the share of conglomerate mergers increased from 12.0 per cent to 22.5 per cent in 1985-1986 and declined to 16.2 per cent in 1989-1990 (Monopolkommission 1982-1983, p. 213, BKartA 1985-1986, p. 119, BKartA 1989-1990, p. 137).

Industrial policy through merger control

The introduction of merger control in 1973 was based on differing motives. Support for merger control came from adherents of the Ordo-liberal School on the ground that mergers just as cartels might give rise to monopolistic market power and should therefore be inhibited. Believers in a more interventionistic stance of economic policy supported the introduction of merger control on the ground that it would provide for an active structuring and restructuring of the economy.

Merger control, as laid down in the Act Against Restraints of Competition, is clearly dominated by the first approach where knowledge of an optimal market structure to be achieved is not pretended to exist and where the government consequently only attempts to inhibit monopolization. Still, the alternative constructivistic approach has left its traces in the law and its administration.

According to Section 24 subparagraph 1 of GWB the presumption of an attainment or increase of market control put forward by the authorities can be disproved by the enterprise concerned. It has to show that the merger also yields an improvement of the competitive situation and that these improvements outweigh the disadvantages arising from market control. The intention of this clause is to take into account the variety of effects entailed by a merger. From the point of view of the first mentioned approach to merger control which denies the feasibility to identify an optimal market structure ex ante the cited clause is ill-devised. Since the effects of a merger cannot be quantified a weighing of it advantages and disadvantages is not feasible in the first place. Still, the Federal Cartel Office, in its administration of merger control has to apply the clause as part of existing law. Actually, the Federal Cartel Office circumvents the inherent difficulties by adopting an obviously constructivistic stance.

In quite a few cases the Federal Cartel Office has approved of a merger on the condition that the participating firms sell shareholdings in other enterprises, usually of enterprises operating in quite different markets, the guiding idea obviously being that a restraint in competition in the market where the disputed merger occurs can be compensated by an increase in the number of independent competitors operating in another market. This practice has been severely criticized by the Monopoly Commission as being an inadmissible structural policy (Monopolkommission 1986/1987, pp. 174-196, and p. 331).

A further instance of falling victim to the fallacy of constructivism is the practice of the Federal Cartel Office to look more favourably at mergers where a more balanced market structure is achieved, i.e., if smaller firms merge and thereby obtain a market share which approaches the market share of the dominant firm of the industry. I cannot see any theoretical reason why in that way competition might increase. On the contrary, as Stigler (1966) has convincingly demonstrated, increasing concentration facilitates collusion.

Another case of industrial policy within the exercise of competition policy is the possibility of admitting a merger by Ministerial decree. In special cases the Federal Minister of Economics may approve of a merger if it is deemed to be in the public interest (Section 24 subparagraph 2 of GWB). In this case a trade-off evaluation applies where the disadvantages arising from the restraint of competition are to be weighed against the advantages for the entire economy. The approval is subject to the condition that it must not upset the competitive order of the entire economy and that no other less harmful alternative is available.

So far only six mergers out of fourteen which were originally disallowed by the Federal Cartel Office and for which an application for exceptional approval was filed with the Federal Minister of Economics were eventually approved (Monopolkommission 1986/1987, p. 320, BKartA 1989/1990, p. 18). In two cases, i.e., VEBA/Gelsenberg (1974) and BP/Gelsenberg (1979), the merger was permitted on the ground that it would contribute to securing the supply of petroleum products to Germany. In one case, i.e., Daimler-Benz, Messerschmidt-Bölkow-Bohm, the decision was guided by objectives of industrial policy. In the remaining cases the permission was motivated by the desire to save jobs.

A final rather extended intrusion of industrial policy into competition policy is given by the diffused allotment of privileges to small scale firms. As already mentioned above, among small and medium sized firms the formation of cooperations is facilitated which otherwise would qualify as illegal cartels. Another field of exercising industrial policy which is likely to gain still more weight in the future can be found in retailing. During the latest decades a substantial structural change has occurred in retailing, particularly in food retailing. The market share of discounters and chain stores has increased dramatically whereas the share of small independent retailers has declined to half of its past magnitude. During the same time concentration has gone up. In food retailing the market share of the largest five trading firms has increased from 18.5 per cent in 1978 to 33.2 percent in 1984 (Monopolkommission 1986/1987, Anlagenband, p. 29), and the share of the ten largest firms has increased from 46.2 per cent in 1985 to 58.8 percent in 1990 (Monopolkommission 1990/1991, p. 269). Allegedly this increase must be attributed to predatory practices of large firms. Consequently fears were expressed that a continuation of this development would end up in a harmful monopoly, notwithstanding the fact that in the U.S.A. the five largest food retailers in 1987 were holding a cumulative market share of 67 per cent (as calculated from "Business Week" March 14, 1988, p. 73) without competition being extinguished so far. Obviously the drive towards protecting the traditional structure of retailing is coming from pressure groups very similar to those which during the thirties in the U.S.A. brought about the Robinson Patman Act. Actually, the latest amendment to the Act Against Restraints of Competition introduced a provision according to which market control, in the case where dominant buyers are involved, is presumed to exist at a threshold which is lower than the one ordinarily applied in merger control.

In defence of industrial policy favouring small scale firms in various ways it should be mentioned that smaller firms are in fact disadvantaged to some extent not in consequence of inferiority with respect to their economic capabilities but by privileges enjoyed by large firms. These will be discussed in due course.

Abusive practices

Enterprises holding market control and cartels which are permitted due to exemptions or by decree of the Federal Cartel Office must not abuse their market power. Abusive exercise of market control is present

- if an enterprise that is holding market control charges prices or applies other terms of contract in excess of those which can with high probability be expected to obtain in the case of effective competition or if it charges prices or applies terms of contract in excess of those which are charged by the same enterprise on comparable markets, or if a firm as a buyer depresses purchase prices in consequence of monopolistic market power (Section 22, subparagraph 4 No. 2 and 3 of GWB),
- if an enterprise holding market control substantially impedes entry of other firms in an unjustifiable way (Section 22, subparagraph 4 No. 1 of GWB),
- if enterprises with market control or cartels of firms exercising resale price maintenance unduly impede the freedom of action of other firms or discriminate against them in an unreasonable way, or if an enterprise entices another firm to boycott third parties (Section 26 of GWB).

Irrespective of market control, enterprises in command of comparatively high market power must not unduly impede the freedom of action of small or medium sized competitors.

The authorities may prohibit abusive practices, which thereupon become legally invalid, and may impose fines on violators. Table 4.2 summarizes the development of the number of proceedings of the Federal Cartel Office against abuses of market control according to Section 22 of GWB. Somewhat astoundingly the development displays a pronounced downward trend. Whereas in 1973-1975 the number of proceedings amounted to 341 it declined to 14 in 1990-1991.

Proceedings of the Federal Cartel Office against firms for charging excessive prices turned out to be relatively ineffective. The basic requirement for a proof of excessive prices under Section 22 of GWB consists, first, in finding a comparable market, or, second, to construe a fictitious situation of effective competition, and, third, to establish that prices are substantially in excess of competitive prices. All of these proofs are extremely difficult to produce.

Table 4.2. Proceedings of the Federal Cartel Office against abuses of market control pursuant to section 22 of GWB since 1973

1973-1975	314
1976.1977	68
1978-1979	46
1980-1981	48
1982-1983	69
1984-1985	30
1986-1987	14
1988-1989	7
1990-1991	14

Source: Monopolkommission 1988/89, p. 230 and 1990/91, p. 240

For example, in proceedings against Merck for overpricing Vitamin B the Federal Court of Justice (Bundesgerichtshof) found a decrease in market share from 51.9 per cent to 40.6 per cent of revenues and from 32.2 per cent to 22 percent in terms of quantities sold as sufficient to disprove the presumption of the absence of substantial competition. Since according to the view of the Court market control did not obtain any prosecution for abusive exercise of market power was without legal foundation. In the proceeding against Hoffmann-La Roche for overcharging Valium the Federal Court of Justice principally accepted the reference to similar markets but reproached the authorities for not sufficiently having taken account of dissimilarities, such as price ceilings in Britain imposed by the British government, lack of patent protection in Italy, and the requirement of a substantial excess of prices over the competitive level.

Having recourse to price-cost margins does not help much either because of the difficulties to identify actual prices and actual costs. That has been demonstrated in the case of Chiquita Bananas tried before the European Court of Justice in 1978.

This experience led to the conclusion that proceedings against abusive pricing should be handled with utmost caution.

The authorities were more successful in prosecuting abusive practices of dominant firms which consists in impeding entry of competitors. More recently a public enterprise, GFN (Gesellschaft für Nebenbetriebe der Bundesautobahn mbH), refused a well-known fastfood chain to be admitted to take on lease one of the restaurants along the Federal Motorway (Bundesautobahn) owned by the GFN. The Federal Cartel Office considered GFN to be in control of the market and thus being guilty of violating the ban on discrimination (Section 26 of GWB) and erecting undue barriers to entry.

In quite a few other cases rebate schemes of dominant firms were found to entail an exclusion of newcomers by granting a rebate on the basis of total purchases during a full year.

The diminution of the number of proceedings, as shown in Table 4.2, may be attributed to the fact that both sides have learned. The authorities came to realize the difficulties inherent in prosecuting an enterprise for abusive pricing and thus became more cautious. The firms, on the other hand, learned which practices that entailed impediments to other parties could be successfully prosecuted by the authorities, given a series of precedents developed by the adjudication of the courts. Hence they avoided contracts which are amenable to be taken up by the authorities.

IV. Overall Assessment

Development of concentration and competition

An increase in horizontal concentration is likely to reduce competition unless markets are contestable. Since horizontal mergers contribute to rising horizontal concentration an examination of its development may offer some indication regarding the efficacy of merger control. Likewise vertical and conglomerate mergers may give rise to increased market power by utilizing financial strength. Since vertical and conglomerate mergers affect the overall concentration of the economy an examination of its development appears informative.

For seventeen two-digit industries the Monopoly Commission in its report for 1980/1981 (pp. 23-24, 199-204) identified the components which contributed to the change in concentration using the method suggested by Leonhard Weiss. Mergers were shown to have exerted a substantial influence on the development of horizontal concentration. On the average of the sample under investigation concentration, as measured by the cumulative market share of the three largest firms, C3, increased from 1958 to 1975 and decreased until 1980. In that year concentration did not exceed the average attained in 1965.

More recently, from 1978 to 1988 concentration, as measured by the Herfindahl index for 248 commodities in a 4-digit classification, increased for 117 commodities, it decreased for 107 commodities, and remained practically unchanged for 24 commodities (Monopolkommission 1988/1989, p. 85). More detailed information may be gleaned from Table 4.3. A similar picture emerges by looking at the development of the cumulative market share of the ten largest enterprises of 33 two-digit industries. The unweighted average stood at 38.5 per cent in 1958. It increased to 41.8 per cent in 1973, to 43.6 per cent in 1979, and to 44.2 per cent in 1983 and

1985 (Monopolkommission 1986/1987, p. 93).

Table 4.3. Changes of the Herfindahl index in 248 commodity classes, 1978 - 1988

Change of the Herfindahl index (times 10,000)		Number of 4-digit commodity classes
from	to (below)	
1000	2567	2
500	1000	10
300	500	10
100	300	34
50	100	24
10	50	37
- 10	10	24
- 50	- 10	28
- 100	- 50	16
- 500	- 100	45
- 1812.8	- 500	18
Total		248

Source: Monopolkommission 1988/1989, p. 85

Horizontal concentration thus apparently changes only at a glacial pace. Mergers do play a role, but other forces, such as internal growth or decline, entry and exit, also contribute to changes in concentration. The fact that concentration did not increase much after 1973 may be taken to indicate that an average monopoly power has not significantly risen. Whether, and to what extent, that can be attributed to competition policy must remain an open question, however.

A very similar picture emerges if one looks at the share of largest 100 enterprises in manufacturing industry. These firms accounted for 36.6 per cent of total sales of manufacturing industry in 1978. The share increased to 37.0 per cent in 1980, to 39.5 percent in 1982 and 1984, and decreased to 38.2 per cent in 1990 (Monopolkommission 1990/1991, p. 32). It is remarkable that the largest firms were involved in mergers and acquisitions more than proportionally, as shown in Table 4.4. The largest 25 firms were involved in 52.1 percent of all mergers in 1986. In view of disproportionally high merger activity of large firms one would expect them to have increased their share in manufacturing industry more than they did. From this one may infer that there are counterforces tending to reduce the size of the firms.

Table 4.4. Involvement of the 100 largest enterprises in mergers and acquisitions in 1986 and 1990

Firm of rank involved in mergers	Number		Percentage share	
	1986	1990	1986	1990
1-25	302	780	52.1	51.7
26-50	139	294	24.0	19.5
51-75	83	213	14.3	14.1
76-100	56	221	9.7	4.7
Total	580	1508	100.0	100.0

Source: Monopolkommission 1986/1987, p. 165 and 1990/1991, p. 239

As suggested by the theory of contestable markets (Baumol et al. 1982), one would expect plant sizes to be limited by economies to scale which determine the efficient minimum plant size. Given the size of the market concentration would then be determined by the respective minimum efficient plant size. Unless they rise growing markets will thus yield decreasing concentration. This tendency would be enhanced if technologies change in such a way as to provide lower minimum efficient plant sizes.

More recently, it has in fact been shown by Bo Carlson (1988) that the technological development appears to move into that direction. Similarly Scherer, after an extended discussion of economies, comes to the conclusion that "actual concentration in U.S. manufacturing industry appears to be considerably higher than the imperatives of scale economies require" (Scherer 1980, p. 118). It is also noteworthy that structure-performance studies for West German industries and firms invariably came up with a significantly negative impact of absolute firm size on the price-cost margin (Neumann et al. 1984 for 283 manufacturing firms 1965-1977, Neumann et al. 1981 for 316 manufacturing firms 1965-1973, Neumann and Haid 1985 for 96 West German 4-digit industries). That indicates that firms in general are larger than required by economies to scale. It also casts doubts on the suggestion of Demsetz (1973) and other followers of the so-called Chicago School that the favourable influence of concentration on price-cost margins, which was an outstanding finding of the aforementioned studies on German industries, can be attributed to scale economies.

These findings support the view that the increase in concentration, however modest it may have been, must primarily be attributed to mergers and acquisitions. It further suggests that firms which are already large will attempt to gain market control in particular by acquisitions unless they are inhibited by competition policy.

Public policy and concentration

The prevailing degree of competition and the effectiveness of competition policy, as conducted by the Federal Cartel Office, depends to a large extent on the framework established by economic policy in general. In the sequel four aspects will be discussed briefly, namely foreign competition in domestic markets, the role of taxes and subsidies, the regulations of the labour market, and the influence exerted by banks.

From the very beginning economic policy of the Federal Republic of Germany has been guided by the belief in the beneficial role of free trade. Consequently barriers to trade were reduced and the share of imports and exports of merchandise and services in gross value added rose substantially. In 1989 exports went up to 39.6 per cent of gross value added of all enterprises and imports to 32.9 per cent from 21.3 percent and 18.4 per cent, respectively in 1960 (Statistisches Jahrbuch 1991, pp. 630 and 641). On the domestic markets thus entry of new competition occurred to a large extent in the form of increased imports. For domestic enterprises their markets became more and more global, as witnessed by the increasing share of exports.

The competitive impact of imports made itself felt by shrinking price-cost margins of German firms, just as one would expect on the ground of theoretical reasoning. An investigation covering the period 1965-1977 showed that the adverse influence on price-cost margins exerted by the share of imports was particularly pronounced during recessions (Neumann et al. 1985, p. 16).

Thus foreign trade worked as a handmaiden of competition policy. On the other hand several retarding influences can be identified.

First, taxation should be mentioned. In order to avoid multiple taxation of profits within a complex corporate structure the tax code provides for some privileges if shareholdings exceed some thresholds. That creates incentives to acquire shareholdings in excess of those thresholds, i.e., shareholdings that generally entail a decisive influence on the respective corporation. Such holdings, in turn, constitute mergers according to the Act Against Restraints of Competition. Although privileges of this kind have been reduced by the reform of the corporation income tax enacted in 1977, still, some privileges remained (Monopolkommission 1980/1981, pp. 205-210). On balance however, the effects of taxation on concentration must not be overemphasized. Taxation may sometimes tip the balance in favour of a merger. The dominant reasons for mergers must however be sought elsewhere.

Second, some subsidies tend to favour large firms (Monopolkommission 1980/1981, pp. 211-225). Subsidies to enhance R&D activities, in particular, are to a large extent handed out for specific projects. Since large firms are capable of maintaining specialized departments which are liable to exploit all possibilities to obtain government aid large firms will, and actually do, obtain a disproportionally large share in such subsidies. On the other hand, loans at subsidized rates of interest and aids within the framework of regional policy are predominantly going to smaller firms. Whether, on balance, subsidization creates a bias in favour of large firms is a matter of dispute. Looking at the possibility of a bias arising from subsidization which would favour large enterprises in the same industry, the Monopoly Commission came to the conclusion that a bias does not obtain. I would nevertheless submit that some bias is created in so far as the cash flow of large firms is augmented by financial aids from the government which makes it easier for them to acquire other firms. Furthermore in the case of declining industries, large firms which are getting into trouble are more likely to obtain financial support from the government since upon bankruptcy a large number of jobs are at stake and pressures from trade unions and political representatives of the respective region usually induce the government to step in with some help. The taxes that are necessary for covering those expenses fall on large and small firms indiscriminately. The greater likelihood for public support for large firms in trouble reduces their risks and thus makes it more easy for them to obtain credits from banks.

A further comparative advantage enjoyed by large firms arises from regulations of the labour market. Labour in West Germany is heavily protected from dismissal. A long warning is required and with an increasing duration of employment a dismissal becomes more and more difficult and costly for the firm unless the employee to be dismissed can be offered an equivalent employment within the firm. Since large firms ordinarily have more opportunities to do so labour costs may be higher in small firms than in large ones. Consequently larger firms may offer higher wages and thus attract employees with higher qualification which may entail comparative advantages of larger firms to be utilized in the market place.

The influence of banks is ambiguous. Access to capital markets plays a decisive role for the ease of entry of newcomers. Easy access facilitates entry and thus undermines attempts of incumbents to adopt strategies of entry deterrence. Since the stock market is underdeveloped in Germany due to severe government regulations the bulk of financing of business firms occurs by loans from banks. Banking as well as insurance, which offers another source of finance, is closely regulated and, to some extent, exempt from the ban on cartels. Hence competition among suppliers of financial resources is restricted. That, in turn, renders entry of new competitors difficult. Furthermore, since German universal banks are active both in the loan business and in investment banking a conflict of interest may arise. Sometimes, banks have been reproached for neglecting the stock market at the expense of their loan business.

The dependence on bank credit as the main source of outside financing entails some influence of the banks on the conduct of business. As has been demonstrated by Brander and Lewis (1986), a dominant influence of creditors tends to reduce the aggressiveness one might otherwise expect to obtain in the case of an oligopoly which is the prevalent structure of many markets. Certainly, as has been countered by spokesmen of the banking industry, bankers ordinarily command only a limited influence. Still, small as it may be, it moves the conduct of firms affected into the direction of more collusion. On the other hand, the influence of banks exercised as members of the supervisory board of a joint stock company or of equivalent bodies of companies with limited liability may contribute to enhancing the efficiency of the allocation of funds (Cable 1985) because banks usually are far better informed about the business of the company than outside stockholders.

Competition policy and public interest

The review of the development of mergers and acquisitions in the past decades suggests that competition policy, in spite of quite a few impediments arising from the social and political framework, has been fairly successful in the pursuit of maintaining competition. That does not mean, of course, that the German economy is perfectly competitive and that monopolistic market power does not exist. On the contrary, all studies testify to the presence of at least some market power.

As already mentioned above, the finding of a consistently positive association between concentration, irrespective of whether it is measured by a cumulative market share of a group of leading firms of an industry or by the Herfindahl index, and the price-cost margin of individual firms and industries, in conjunction with the finding of an adverse impact of absolute firm size on the price-cost margin, suggests that some monopolistic market power obtains. Further support for this inference can be drawn from the observation that the export share was invariably found to exert a negative influence on price-cost margins of individual firms during the entire period 1965 to 1982. The results for 1965-1977 are published in Neumann et al. 1985. These results were confirmed with an updated set of observations for 1977-1982. The adverse influence of exports on pricecost margins does not mean that exports are unprofitable. It does however mean that exports are less profitable than sales to domestic markets since a domestic firm is exposed to more intensive competition on foreign markets than on domestic markets. To see this let $\bar{m} = m(1-e) + m^* e$ be the average price-cost margin earned on the domestic market, m, and the one obtaining on foreign markets, m^*, weighted with the export share, e, and its complement, 1 - e, respectively. An increase in the export share yields $dm/de = -(m - m^*)$ which is negative if the domestic pricecost margin exceeds the one obtaining on foreign markets. If domestic markets, in consequence of trading costs and barriers to foreign competition, are relatively more protected so that collusion is more feasible at home than abroad sales to foreign markets are exposed to more competition and hence $m^* < m$ (Neumann et al. 1985, p. 9). Conversely, the finding of an adverse influence of an increasing export share on price-cost margins suggests that domestic markets are in fact less competitive than foreign markets. That in turn implies that some monopolistic market power exists.

Given distortionary effects of monopolistic market power on the allocation of resources and a retarding influence on technological change, competition policy that aims at curbing restraints of competition appears to be well founded.

Concentration, international trade and efficiency

More recently markets have become increasingly global. Therefore the market, as visualized by exporting producers, clearly extends the national borderlines. Insofar as barriers to trade have been removed global competition also affects the domestic markets of exporting firms and thus exercises a depressing influence on profit margins, as has been discussed in the preceding section. On the world wide market exporting enterprises ordinarily are subject to competition which is likely to weed out less efficient suppliers or at least repel them to their domestic markets where they may be able to survive insofar as remaining barriers to trade provide protection. In any case global competition tends to bring about a reduction in the number of surviving competitors in the market for a particular commodity. That entails increasing concentration in the domestic markets of countries joining the game of international competition if economies of scale are present. Industries which are successful internationally will therefore be populated by relatively large firms which stood the test of international rivalry and will mostly be more highly concentrated than industries which comprise firms that are less successful internationally and which are repelled to inside the walls of whatever may be left of a protective fortress towards foreign competition. This reasoning suggests a positive association between concentration and the share of sales going abroad.

Such a relationship is evident from the accompanying figure. The coefficient of correlation between domestic concentration in 28 West German manufacturing industries in 1983 and the respective percentage share of exports to total sales in 1987 is 0.78 with a t-ratio of 4.05. Thus about 60 per cent of the variation in the concentration ratio C3 is statistically accounted for by the export share with a probability of error of less than 0.1 per cent. In calculating the correlation coefficient two outliers, which are clearly evident from the Figure 4.1, namely petroleum refining and the tobacco industry, have been disregarded on the ground that both are dominated by foreign multinationals which maintain subsidiaries in Germany.

The positive association between export shares and concentration has sometimes been wrongly construed to imply a causal relationship running from higher concentration to higher exports and evoked demands to allow mergers in order to improve the international competitiveness. There is hardly evidence in favour of such a policy, however.

The outstanding export performance of West German industries has been achieved in spite of the largest German firms being considerably smaller than their U.S. counterparts and the average size of German firms being comparatively low. In 1986, for example, the size of Daimler-Benz, holding the top rank among West German enterprises in terms of sales, was less than a third of the size of General Motors. Likewise, the largest German chemical firms, i.e., Bayer, BASF , and Hoechst, internationally occupied only rank 39, 32, and 34, respectively, and Robert Bosch, an example for one of the world's leading manufacturers of equipment for motorcars, ranked only 54 internationally (Monopolkommission 1990/1991, p. 178). Further examples are given in Table 4.5.

All this lends support to competition policy as exercised by the German authorities. As has been shown in more detail above competition policy in Germany does not aim at preventing mergers as such. It does, however, aim at inhibiting mergers which tend to lessen competition. Insofar as it has been successful in doing so, maintenance of competition at home may very well have contributed to enhancing international competitiveness.

If trade barriers which still remain are removed within Europe by completing the internal market more efficient producers will get a better chance to penetrate once protected markets. That is likely to give rise to increased firm size and increased concentration on national markets as well. It does not necessarily mean increased monopoly power. On the contrary, it may yield increased competition.

Table 4.5. International comparison of firm size in selected industries

Industry	Sales in billion $		
	1962	1986	1990
Automotive Industry			
- General Motors	14.7	102.8	125.1
- Volkswagen	1.4	24.8	43.7
- Daimler Benz	1.2	30.2	54.3
Electrical Industry			
- General Electric (US)	4.8	35.2	58.4
- Siemens	1.4	20.3	39.2
Chemical Industry			
- Du Pont	2.4	27.1	39.8
- Bayer	1.0	18.8	26.1
- Hoechst	0.9	17.5	27.7

Source: Monopolkommission 1990/1991, p. 179

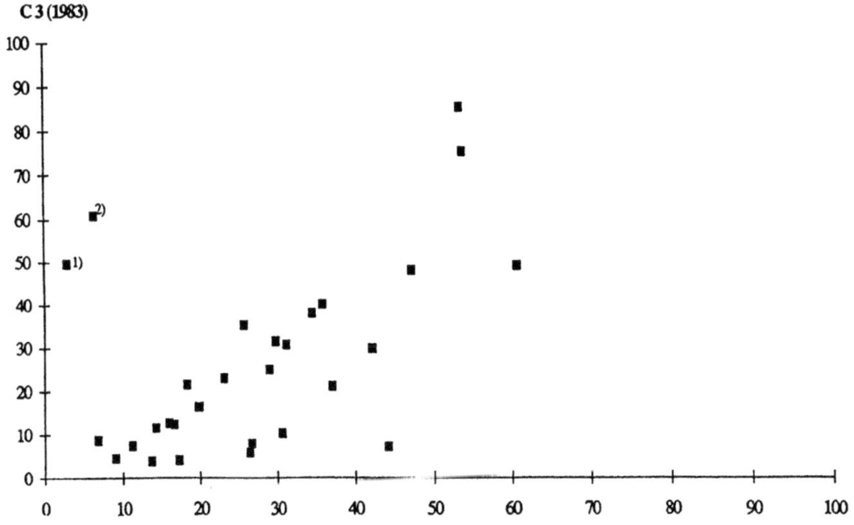

1) Petrolum refining 2) Tobacco industry Export share (1987)

Figure 4.1. Export share and concentration in West German manufacturing industries

V. Conclusions

In concluding it may be reiterated that in view of a pervasive inclination of industry to restrain competition a vigilant competition policy appears to be necessary to secure a competitive order. If cartels were generally allowed they would certainly proliferate as they did in Germany after the turn of the century. On the other hand, if the government attempts to inhibit restraints of competition it is fighting an uphill battle where it has to overcome the resistance of powerful pressure groups which in the past have frequently succeeded in diluting any legislation against restraints of competition. Still, it seems to me that German competition policy, although not always immune from temptations of ill-advised industrial policy, has on the whole been fairly successful in maintaining a competitive order which has been working for the benefit of consumers and significantly contributed to enhance the efficiency of the German economy.

New challenges lie ahead, however. Only two of them shall be touched upon briefly, i.e., the consequences of deregulation and the rise of giant firms.

The completion of the internal market in Europe will remove quite a few regulations which presently restrict intra European trade in commodities and services. In particular, banking, insurance, transportation and public utilities including telecommunication will, and has been, be subject to deregulation. These industries have so far been completely or partially exempt from competition policy as framed by the Act Against Restraints of Competition. Deregulation requires these exemptions to be repealed. A first step have be done by the latest amendment to the Act Against Restraints of Competition.

The completion of the internal market has given rise to a drive towards mergers aiming at firm sizes which allegedly are necessary for global competitiveness. In fact, the removal of internal barriers to trade in Europe will certainly bring about more specialization, longer production runs, and thus, by exploiting economies to scale, lower costs. Although that implies a good deal of restructuring and certainly quite a few mergers and acquisitions to achieve that an increase in absolute firm sizes does not, in all cases, appear to be imperative. The naive comparison of average firm sizes in European countries and those in the U.S.A. and Japan is not compelling given the observation that German firms, in spite of their comparatively modest size, have displayed an outstanding export performance in the past and thus, on average, do not appear to lack international competitiveness. On the other hand it cannot be denied off hand that in some cases giant firms do enjoy comparative advantages. Mergers and acquisitions which give rise to giant enterprises should thus not be prohibited unless those mergers are undertaken to gain market control. In fact, merger control at the European level has recently been introduced. Insofar as mergers fall within the jurisdiction of the EC commission they are exempt from national laws.

Finally, the relationship between the social and political framework on one hand and competition policy on the other hand deserves a concluding comment. As has been shown in Section 4.2. there are quite a few arrangements in the Federal Republic of Germany which tend to favour large firms and thus endow them with a comparative advantage vis-à-vis small and medium sized firms. That has given rise to a policy which attempts to compensate small firms for those artificial disadvantages. In the framework of this socalled "Mittelstandspolitik" small firms are given some privileges to set up cartels which, for large firms, would be prohibited. Furthermore, small firms enjoy some special protection from the inroads of competition of large firms which strain the consistency of competition policy. Thus it appears that in the Federal Republic of Germany, to some extent, arrangements in favour of large firms which are conducive to restraints of competition are attempted to be balanced by favours given to small firms which again engender restraints of competition. That seems to be bad policy which, on the whole, tends to lessen competition and works to the detriment of economic welfare, in particular, because a policy of granting compensating privileges gives rise to rent seeking behaviour which tends to create distortions of its own. It would be preferable to dismantle the advantages of large firms created by public policy and to improve the conditions under which entry of newcomers is possible (Wissenschaftlicher Beirat 1986).

References

Arrow, K., 1962, "Economic Welfare and Allocation of Resources for Inventions", in: *The Rate and Direction of Inventive Activity*, New York: NBER.

Baumol, W.J., Panzar, J.C., and Willig, R.D., 1982, *Contestable Markets and the Theory of Industry Structure*, New York: Harcourt Brace Jovanovich.

Bittlingmayer, G., 1987, "Die wettbewerbspolitischen Vorstellungen der Chicago School", *Wirtschaft und Wettbewerb* (WuW), 709-718.

Böhm, F., 1948, "Das Reichsgericht und die Kartelle", *ORDO-Jahrbuch*, 1, 197-213.

Brander, J.A. and Lewis, T.R., 1986, "Oligopoly and Financial Structure: the Limited Liability Effect", *American Economic Review*, 76, 956-70.

Bundeskartellamt, Bericht über seine Tätigkeit in den Jahren 1985/86 sowie die Lage und Entwicklung auf seinem Aufgabengebiet, Bundestagsdrucksache 11/554 vom 25.6.1987.

Bundeskartellamt, Bericht über seine Tätigkeit in den Jahren 1990/91 sowie die Lage und Entwicklung auf seinem Aufgabengebiet. Bundeskartellamt, Bundestagsdrucksache 12/847 vom 26.6.1991.

Burns, M.R., 1986, "Predatory Pricing and the Acquisition Cost of Competitors", *Journal of Political Economy*, 94, 266-96.

Cable, J.R., 1985, "Capital Market Information and Industrial Performance: The Role of West German Banks", *Economic Journal*, 95, 118-32.

Carlson, B., 1989, "The Evolution of Manufacturing Technology and Its Impact on Industrial Structure: An International Study", *Small Business Economics*, 1, 21-38.

Demsetz, H., 1973, "Industry Structure, Cartel Rivalry, and Public Policy", *Journal of Law and Economics*, 16, 1-9.

Fischer, C.E., 1954, "Die Geschichte der deutschen Versuche zur Lösung des Kartell-und Monopolproblems", *Zeitschrift für die gesamte Staatswissenschaft*, 110, 425-56.

Hayek, F.A. von, 1968, *Der Wettbewerb als Entdeckungsverfahren*, Kiel.

Hayek, F.A. von, 1973, "Rules and order" (1973), reprinted, in: *Law, Legislation and Liberty*, London: Routledge & Kegan Paul.

McGee, J.S., 1958, "Predatory Price Cutting: The Standard Oil (N.J.) Case", *Journal of Law and Economics*, 1, 137-69.

McGee, J.S., 1980, "Predatory Pricing Revisited", *Journal of law and Economics*, 23, 289-230.

Mestmäcker, E.J., 1984, *Der verwaltete Wettbewerb*, Tübingen: J.C.B. Mohr (Paul Siebeck).

Möschel, W., 1972, 70 Jahre Deutsche Kartellpolitik: Von RGZ 38,155 "Sächsisches Holzstoffkartell" zum BGHZ 55,104 "Teerfarben", Tübingen: J.C.B.Mohr (Paul Siebeck), 1972.

Möschel, W., 1983, Recht der Wettbewerbsbeschränkungen, Köln: Carl Heymanns.

Monopolkommission, 1978, Hauptgutachten 1976/1977: Fortschreitende Konzentration bei Großunternehmen, Baden-Baden: Nomos.

Monopolkommission, 1980, Hauptgutachten 1978/1979: Fusionskontrolle bleibt vorrangig, Baden-Baden:Nomos.

Monopolkommission, 1982, Hauptgutachten 1980/1981: Fortschritte bei der Konzentrationserfassung,Baden-Baden: Nomos

Monopolkommission, 1984, Hauptgutachten 1982/1983: Ökonomische Kriterien für dieRechtsanwendung, Baden-Baden: Nomos.

Monopolkommission, 1986, Hauptgutachten 1984/1985: Gesamtwirtschaftliche Chancen und Risiken wachsender Unternehmensgrößen, Baden-Baden: Nomos.

Monopolkommission, 1988, Hauptgutachten 1986/1987: Die Wettbewerbsordnung erweitern, Baden-Baden: Nomos with "Anlagenband".

Monopolkommission, 1990, Hauptgutachten 1988/1989: Wettbewerbspolitik vor neuen Herausforderungen, Baden-Baden: Nomos.

Monopolkommission, 1992, Hauptgutachten 1990/1991: Wettbewerbspolitik oder Industriepolitik, Baden-Baden: Nomos.

Neale, A.D., 1966, *The Antitrust Laws of the United States of America*, Cambridge: University Press.

Neumann, M., Böbel, I. and Haid, A., 1981, "Market Structure and the Labour Market in West German Industries. A Contribution Towards Interpreting the Structure Performance Relationship", *Zeitschrift für Nationalökonomie*, 41, 97-109.

Neumann, M., Böbel, I. and Haid, A., 1985, "Domestic Concentration, Foreign Trade and Economic Performance", *International Journal of Industrial Organization*, 3, 1-19.

Neumann, M. and Haid, A., 1985, "Concentration and Economic Performance: A Cross-Section

Analysis of West German Industries", in: *Industry Structure and Performance*, ed. by Joachim Schwalbach, Berlin: Edition Sigma.

OECD, 1986, Competition Policy and Joint Ventures, Paris.

Scherer, F.M., 1980, *Industrial Market Structure and Economic Performance*, 2nd ed., Chicago: Rand McNally.

Schmidt, I., 1993, *Wettbewerbstheorie und-politik*, 4th ed., Stuttgart: Gustav Fischer.

Smith, A., 1961, *The Wealth of Nations*, ed. by Edwin Cannan, 1, London: Methuen.

Statistisches Bundesamt, *Statistisches Jahrbuch für die Bundesrepublik Deutschland*, 1988 and 1991.

Stigler, G.J., 1964, "A Theory of Oligopoly", *Journal of Political Economy*, 72.

Wettbewerbsrecht und Kartellrecht, 1984, 10. Auflage, Beck-Texte, München: DTV.

Wissenschaftlicher Beirat beim Bundesministerium für Wirtschaft, Wettbewerbspolitik, Gutachten vom 5./6. Dezember 1986, in: Sammelband der Gutachten 1973 bis 1986, Göttingen: Otto Schwartz & Co, 1987, 1359-1391.

5. Merger and Monopoly Policies in the UK

CENTO VELJANOVSKI

I. Introduction

The United Kingdom is experiencing a gradual transition in the regulation of the competitive process. This has not occurred through a major reform of competition laws, or their enforcement, but by the privatisation programme carried out in the 1980s. This chapter examines developments in two key areas of competition policy mergers and the control of the privatised utilities in the telecommunications, energy and water sectors.

The chapter is organised as follows. In Section II a brief overview of the supply-side reforms which occurred in the UK during the 1980s is provided. This is followed by an equally brief description of the structure and administration of competition laws. In Section III the issues raised in the policing of the UK's third "merger boom" this century are discussed. The chapter concludes with a critical analysis of the regulation of privatised monopolies which represents the most significant economic reform of the Thatcher era.

II. Supply-side Reforms in the 80s

The UK entered the 1980s as a corporatist state. It left the decade a more open and competitive economy. Following the election of Mrs Thatcher in 1979 British industry was rapidly baptised into Thatcherism when exchange rate controls were removed. This, coupled with the devaluation of sterling and world recession, was a traumatic experience for British industry. In the face of the ensuing austerity, British management was forced deal with endemic overmanning and inefficiency. There followed a period of major restructuring of the country's manufacturing base.

The 80s were characterised by a strong government committed to the pragmatic application of free market principles. This arose from the conviction politics of Prime Minister Thatcher which permitted the political and intellectual ascendancy of the new right and supply-side policies. Among the more important of these supply-side policies were the:

- reform of trade union and labour laws;
- liberalisation and deregulation of key industries such as the financial, transport and broadcasting sectors; and,

G. Mussati (ed.), Mergers, Markets and Public Policy, 133–162.
© 1995 *Kluwer Academic Publishers.*

- privatisation of state-owned industries in particular the utilities such as telecommunications, gas, water, electricity and airports.

The reform of trade union law was perhaps the most important single legislative initiative of the Thatcher Government. These reforms sought to control the monopoly powers of the trade union movement and to ensure that political strikes were not condoned. They removed a number of trade union immunities, gave employers the right to stop secondary picketing and to obtain an injunction or civil damages, and the Courts were given the power to sequester trade union funds where there were breaches of the law (Hanson & Mather, 1988). The removal of trade union privileges, which should itself have been subject to competition laws, provided a legal environment enabling industry to recapture its right to manage. These reforms cost industry and the economy heavily as trade unions resisted change and confronted management and government, often in hostile defiance of the law. Major civil disturbance was not uncommon, most notably at Warrington with Eddie Shah's use of nonunion labour, the move of Rupert Murdoch's *Times* newspaper group to Wapping, and the long and unsuccessful coal miners' strike.

The deregulation of the financial sector was also critical to developments in competition law particularly toward the end of the 80s. As a result of financial liberalisation and the economic boom of the late 80s the UK, in common with other countries, experienced a merger boom. The number, nature and financing of these mergers raised concerns but resulted in a more open and dynamic economy. This component of the Government's supply-side reforms was marred by new investor protection legislation which imposed heavy costs and was seen as a threat to the City of London's pre-eminence as an international financial market (Seldon, 1988).

The privatisation of state-owned enterprises was the flagship of British industrial policy in 1980s. The major utilities when nationalised raised serious monopoly problems which were never subject to investigation by UK competition authorities. They were organised as monopolies with social objectives, and primitive accounting and management practices. They had failed, after numerous attempts to control their cost and pricing policies, to operate efficiently and provide customers with cheap reasonable quality services. Their performance was described as "third rate", their industrial relations record appalling (one merely has to recall the 1984 Miners' Strike where the country was on the brink of civil war) and their future problematic. These outcomes were inherent in the way the post-war Government of Clement Attlee (1947-51) nationalised gas, electricity, water, rail, road and coal industries. These were brought into the public sector in haste, with no clear objectives other than to act in the public interest and to break-even taking one year with another. As one ex-Chairman of a nationalised industry put it, they were "designed to fail" (Veljanovski, 1988).

Privatisation of the utility sector was slow to develop but accelerated after 1984 to reach a level and extent not even the most ardent supporters of free enterprise predicted. It began slowly with a few undertakings, such as Amersham International, British Petroleum and other small operations which had no special characteristics which would warrant state ownership. The watershed came in 1984 with the privatisation of 50.2% of the equity of British Telecom. This set in train a radical policy of the privatisation of all the utility sectors. To date the telecom, gas, water, airports and electricity industries have all have been transferred to the private sector, as has the Government's ownership of British Airways and road transport enterprises.

III. Structure and Administration

Privatisation brought with it both the prospect of greater competition and a new approach to the control of monopoly abuse-regulation. Thus the UK now relies on two separate, but at times interrelated, bodies of law to control monopoly-competition law and regulation.

The combination of competition law and regulatory approaches has created a complex administrative and legal structure consisting of competition agencies with general responsibility (the Office of Fair Trading and the Monopolies and Merger Commission together with DGI VB and the Merger Task Force) and industry regulators charged with economic regulation, consumer protections and promoting competition by the privatised utilities.

The competition laws (Fair Trading Act 1973 and Competition Act 1980) are administered by the Office of Fair Trading (OFT) and the Monopolies and Mergers Commission (MMC), with the Restrictive Trade Practices Court, the Takeover Panel and the Stock Exchange all playing specific parts in regulating the competitive process. Usually an anti-competitive problem is investigated by the OFT, who advises the Secretary for State for the Department of Trade & Industry whether there should be a referral to the MMC. Hence, the triggering of an investigation is a combination of administrative and political actions. The OFT is headed by a government-appointed Director General who holds a non-political position. The agency is staffed by civil servants and those seconded from other government departments.

The MMC is an investigative body which operates on a referral basis. The MMC operates with a fulltime staff and a number of part-time commissioners who serve on average one and a half days a week. These are drawn from a cross range of businessmen, academics and others with skills regarded as necessary to deal with complex questions. The MMC only has the power to make recommendations. The acceptance of its recommendations and modifications to them is within the power of the Minister.

A merger or competition problem is referred to the MMC by the OFT, the Secretary of State and more recently one of the Director Generals. The referral can be made under a number of different pieces of legislation-The Fair Trading Act, Competition Act or one of the privatisation Acts. The type and number of references made to the MMC over the course of the 80s is shown in Tables 5.1 and 5.2.

As part of the privatisation another layer of economic regulation was added. Each utility was subject to new legislation, awarded a licence or equivalent, and the new regulatory framework was administered by a new agency independent of government butaccountable to it. At the end of 1992 four major economic regulatory agencies with competition briefs had been established - the Office of Telecommunications (Oftel) in 1984, the Office of Gas Supply (Ofgas) in 1986, the Office of Water (Ofwat) and the Office of Electricity Regulation (Offer) (Table 5.3).

These new regulatory "watchdogs" have a range of responsibilities and functions. They typically administer economic regulation under the RPI-X price control where relevant, ensure that the privatised (or liberalised) firms comply with the terms of their licences, have a general brief to "promote" or "enable" competition in the industry, and act as a conduit for consumer complaints.

IV. Mergers Policy

The UK stands out for its permissive attitude on mergers and the large number of mergers, particularly hostile takeovers. The "merger boom" of the 80s, coupled with research suggesting that the gains from mergers have been disappointing and growing concerns about corporate governance, have led to call for a more restrictive merger policy in the UK. These were vigorously resisted by the UK Government.

Empirical setting

During the 1980s the UK experienced its third merger boom this century. The first in the 1920s was driven by technological advances which enable large scale production techniques to be employed in manufacturing industry. The second in the 1960s was seen as a response to the growth of world markets and the need and belief that large size was necessary to obtain economies of scale and that critical mass in the form of large conglomerates were needed to remain competitive (Figure 5.1). The merger boom of the 80s differed from those of the past booms in several important respects:

Table 5.1. MMC References

	Merger	Newspaper Merger	Monopoly	General	Anti-competitive practices	Public sector	Privatisation
Legislation	Fair Trading Act, 1973 ss 67-73	Fair Trading Act, 1973 ss 57-62	Fair Trading Act, 1973 ss 6-7	Fair Trading Act, 1973 ss 6-7	Competition Act,1980 s. 78	Competition Act,1980 s. 11	Telecommunications Act 1980 Ss.13-16 Airports Act 1986 Ss. 36-47 Gas Act 1986 Ss. 24-27 Water Act 1989 Electricity Act 1989
Criteria	25% market share or £30m turnover	Circulation of 500.000 copies per issues	25% market share	Practices regarded as anticompetitive	Specific practices against public interest	Efficiency audit	Specific matters relating to privatised industries
Reference by	OFT via minister	Minister	OFT	Minister	OFT (if failure to. obtain an undertaking)	Minister	Regulatory agencies
Reporting period	6 months	6 months	2-4 months	No limit	6 months	6 months	

Table 5.2. MMC References, 1981-1991

Types of References	1981	1982	1983	1984	1985	1986	1987	1988	1989
Merger	6	5	6	3	5	6	6	4	13
Newspaper Merger	3	1	—	—	2	—	1	1	2
Monopolies	7	2	2	—	3	5	2	3	8
Competition	—	1	1	—	2	—	3	..	2
Public Sector	2	2	5	4	3	3	3	3	3
Privatised Undertaking	—	—	—	—	—	—	1	—	—
Labour Practice	—	—	—	—	—	—	—	—	1

Source: Monopolies & Mergers Commission

Table 5.3. Regulatory Watchdogs, 1993

Agency	Date Formed	Industry	Statute	Regulator
Economic Regulators				
Civil Aviation Authority	1971	Airports	Airports Act 1986	Commission
Office of Telecommunications	1984	Telecommunications	Telecommunications Act 1984	DG
Office of Gas Supply	1986	Gas	Gas Act 1986	DG
Office of Water Service	1989	Water	Water Act 1989	DG
Office of Electricity Regulation	1990	Electricity (England,Wales,Scotland) Electricity(Northern Ireland)	Electricity Act 1990	DG
Office of Electricity Regulation (N.I)	1992		Electricity Northern Ireland Order 1991	DG
Quality Regulators				
National Rivers Authority	1989	Water	Water Act 1989	Commission
HM Inspectorate of Pollution	1987	All	Environmental Protection Act 1990	Chief Inspector
Independent Television Commission	1991	Terrestrial,Cable & Satellite TV	Broadcasting Act 1990	Commission
Radio Authority	1991	Radio	Broadcasting Act 1990	Commission
Broadcasting Standards Council	1990	Broadcasting	Broadcasting Act 1990	Commission
Competition Regulators				
Office of Fair Trading	1951	All*	Fair Trading Act 1973	DG
Monopolies & Mergers Commission	1948	All	Fair Trading Act 1973,Competion 1980	Commission
European Commission (DGIV)	1972	All**	Treaty of Rome 1957 Articles 85,86,90	Commission

*Limited exceptions which includes air navigation services and provision of a licensed cable programme service
**To the extent that affects trade between Member States

- the number and average size of mergers were (Figure 5.1);
- the appearance and extent of hostile takeovers;
- the financing of takeovers by high risk "junk bonds";
- the use of mergers to unbundle companies; and,
- the increase in cross-border mergers and foreign takeovers.

The UK stands out in Western Europe as having the most permissive and conducive environment for merger and acquisition activity. 85% of takeovers in the EC occur in the UK (Table 5.4). The UK also has the largest number of successfully contested or hostile mergers (Table 5.5) and the largest capitalised stock market in Europe (Figure 5.2). With the exception of West Germany and the Netherlands, the low liquidity of equity markets in Europe is perhaps the major block on takeover activity. A large number of mergers involving UK companies are cross-border (Table 5.6).

As can be seen from Table 5.7 and Figure 5.3 the number of mergers actually referred to the MMC for investigation is relatively small, around 3% since 1965 with a slightly higher percentage in the 80s.

Table 5.4. Value and Number of Acquisitions in the EC 1988

Country	Value		Number of Valued Transactions		Average Transaction Value
	£ million	%age	Number	%age	£million
Belgium	160.5	0.3	19	0.9	8.5
Denmark	260.5	0.6	12	0.6	21.7
Eire	379.3	0.8	21	1.0	18.1
France	5,079.9	10.5	90	4.5	56.4
Germany	1,987.9	4.1	49	2.4	40.6
Greece	—	—	—	—	—
Italy	2,337.1	4.8	35	1.7	66.8
Luxembourg	6.6	—	2	0.1	3.3
Netherlands	1,522.4	3.1	46	2.3	33.1
Portugal	6.3	—	1	0.1	6.3
Spain	1,355.3	2.8	29	1.4	46.7
United Kingdom	35,378.8	73.0	1,724	85.0	20.5
Total	48,474.6	100.0	2,028	100.0	23.9

Source: *Acquisitions Monthly* (AMDATA)

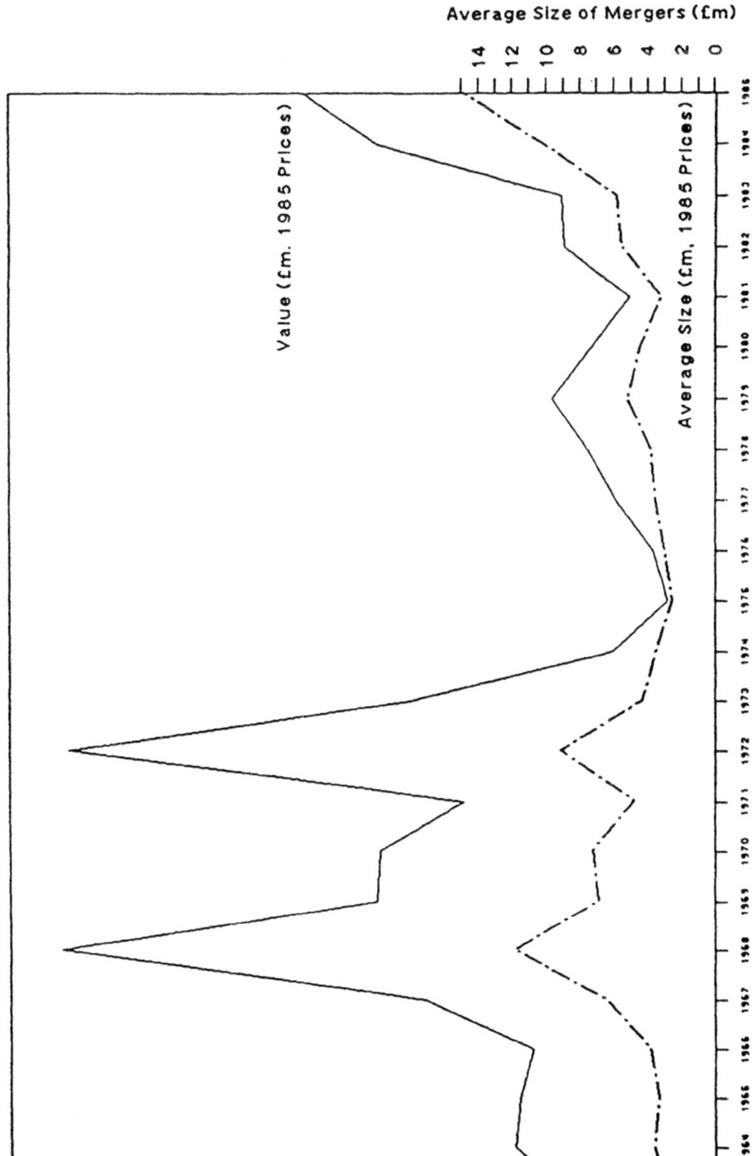

Figure 5.1. UK Acquisition and Mergers 1963-85

Table 5.5. Contested Acquisitions within Each EC Country, 1988

Country	Number	Value £ million
France	1	765.4
Italy	1	**
Netherlands	1	93.0
United Kingdom	23	6,483.7
		7,342.1

Note: ** Not contested
Source: *Acquisitions Monthly* (AMDATA)

Table 5.6. Cross-border Mergers and the EC

Cross Border Acquisitions & Disposals Affecting UK Companies £b.

	1986	1987	1988
Overseas Transactions by UK Co.:			
Acquisitions	8.9	11.5	8.4
Disposals	2.2	3.9	2.1
Transactions in the UK by Overseas Co.:			
Acquisitions	2.9	2.3	5.0
Disposals	0.5	1.2	0.5

Source: *Financial Times*

V. The Merger Debate

A large part of the debate over merger policy has been taken up with differing interpretations of the underlying commercial reasons for mergers, and their benefits and costs. The present merger boom is seen as largely driven not by short term financial considerations industrial concerns.

There are those, including the UK government, who see mergers and takeovers as a necessary and vital part of the competitive process. The ex-

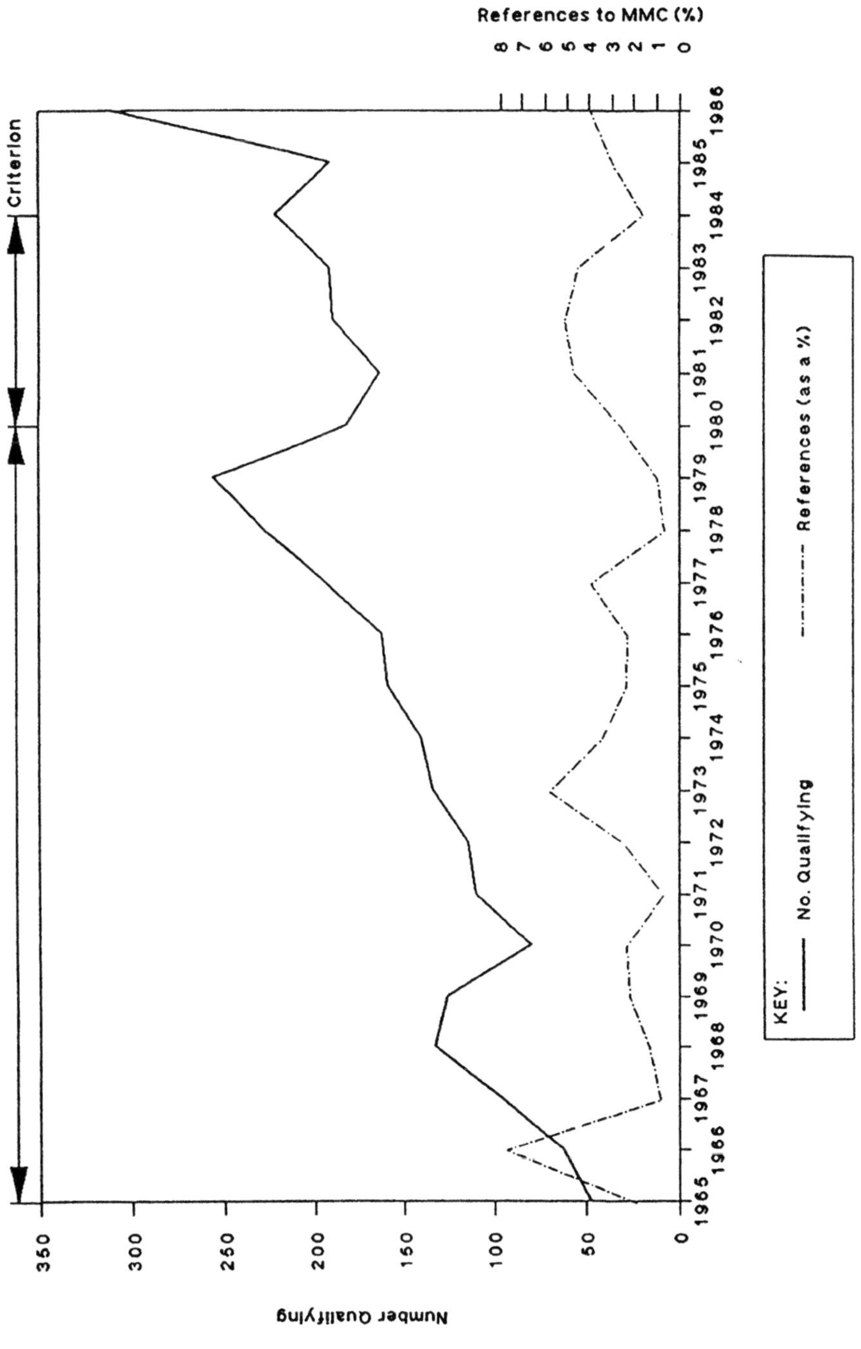

Figure 5.2. Merger Proposal Qualifying for Consideration by Mergers Panel, 1965-86

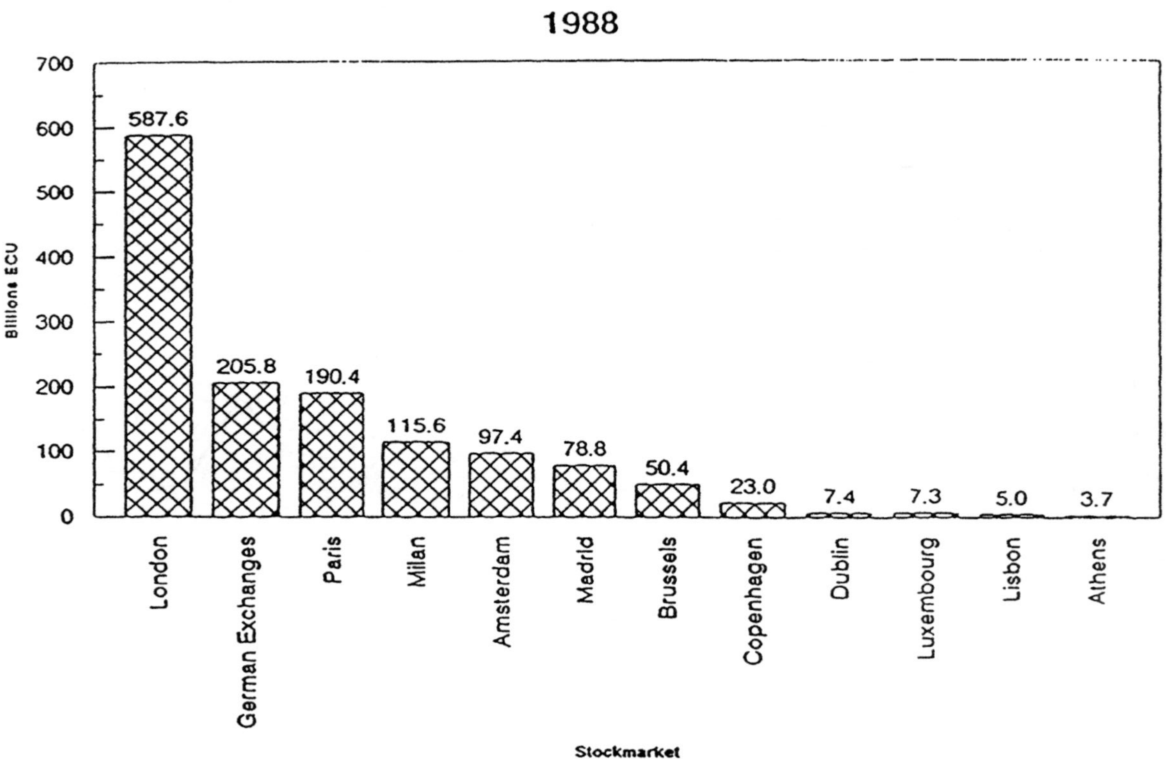

Figure 5.3. Main Market: Listed Securities - Market Capitalisation, 1988

Source: European Stock Exchange, *Annual Statistical Report 1988*, Committee of Stock Exchanges in the EC.

istence of tradeable shares or a stock exchange puts pressure on companies to act efficiently. The logic for this view has been widely debated. First, it leads to specialisation in ownership. Those who own shares in the company do so as an investment and/or because they have knowledge of the industry and particular circumstances in which the firm operates. Second, it efficiently concentrates the risks and benefits of ownership on those who want to bear them. This has an immediate efficiency effect because shares in a company are allocated to those who value them highest. Third, the ability to trade shares creates a competitive market in ownership which disciplines the management of the firm.

This last claim - the market for corporate control - has attracted most controversy. The characteristic of the modern corporation is a divorce between management and ownership. This has led many to argue that the shareholder-owned company is run for the benefit of its managers rather than the profits of its owners. But the capital market acts as a discipline on this potential conflict of interest. If the firm performs poorly and has the potential to increase its productivity and profits, then it will find it difficult to raise equity and debt finance. The share price acts as a constant barometer of the effectiveness with which the management of a public company maximises the wealth of its shareholders. Inefficient or slack management is quickly sent a signal to improve performance by a fall in the company's share price. This, in turn, brings remedial measures either from management itself or via pressure from shareholders. Terminally inefficient management is ultimately displaced by the hostile takeover. Here an acquiring company mounts a bid against the wishes of the existing management of the target company. It must persuade sufficient shareholders that its offer to purchase shares is attractive and that it can manage the company better. The hostile takeover operates to displace and discipline poor management - poor being defined as departing from maximising the long term wealth of all shareholders. This is sometimes referred to as the "market for corporate control".

Most of this analysis is disputed by those who see takeovers as undesirable or else a poor method for disciplining management. It is argued that mergers are largely motivate by short term financial gains. As a result management cannot undertake long term investment, and must constantly exploit immediate business opportunities to keep the share price high. It diverts valuable managerial resources to ward off unwanted takeovers. More sophisticated analysis have been offered. Charkam (1989), for example, argues that there is a two-tier market in shares - a takeover price and the trading price. The fact that the price for a takeover is higher than the trading price indicates that there is a financial gain to be had from control - a bid premium to put the company into play as it were. Charkam argues that this is a positive inducement to takeovers because the fund managers have a legal duty to maximise the wealth of their investors. If a takeover were made more difficult, then investors would exercise more direct intervention. Management, it is argued, should be given greater protection from takeovers.

Others see takeover activity as essential to a well functioning economy, but that they are also an excessively costly way of controlling management. A more direct and effective way is for the large institutional investors which hold the overwhelming bulk of equity in UK public companies to take a more active role in the management of the companies in which they hold shares. However, given the track record of many of the larger financial institutions in managing their own affairs, it is doubtful that this is an effective solution.

A number of commentators and industrialists have called for anti-takeover legislation or devices. They have ranged from reciprocity conditions which would limit foreign companies from countries which did not permit British companies to acquire their companies (such as the Swiss), to devices with exotic labels- poison pills, parachutes, and so on - which entrench management. Notwithstanding this a significant number of companies in the UK remain relatively takeover-proof thorough ownership restrictions. Table 5.7 provides some estimate of "bid proof" companies, although, after the BAT and Consolidated Goldfields bids, one can doubt that size itself is an effective deterrent to a determined bidder.

Table 5.7. Bid Proof Companies as a % of FT-actuaries all Share Index, 1988

Privatised Utilities	9.4
Golden Shares	2.2
Strategic	0.4
Other (Legal Device or Dominant Shareholder)	9.7
Total	21.7

Source: A. Sykes, "The trouble with bid-proof companies", *Financial Times*

Table 5.8. Mergers Considered and Referred to MMC, 1982-1991

Years	1982	1983	1984	1985
Number Considered by OFT	190	192	259	192
Referred to MMC	10	9	4	6
Abandoned before Report	2	2	1	2

Years	1986	1987	1988	1989
Number Considered by OFT	313	321	306	281
Referred to MMC	13	6	11	14
Abandoned before Report	7	0	2	2

Note: On 1 July, 1984 the threshold was raised from £15 to £30m
Source: Monopolies & Mergers Commission

Legal control of mergers

UK merger policy is agnostic as to the relative merits of these two opposing views. The legal framework is permissive with each merger evaluated on its own merits.

Criteria

The key provision governing the control of mergers are contained in the Fair Trading Act 1973. The referral of a merger to the MMC is based on a broad public interest test. The Act requires the MMC to take all matters which they regard as relevant into account, although it specifies some matters which the MMC must consider (see Box 1).

There are two test used for the referral of a merger to the MMC. The first is the "market share test" where the combined share of goods and services of a particular description is at least 25%. Alternatively, there is the "assets test" where the gross value of the world-wide assets taken over by the bidder must exceed £30 million. These criteria merely trigger when a reference can be made, and do not have any relevance beyond this.

When the MMC has found that the merger is not against the public interest the Secretary of State does not have the power to prevent the merger. If it is found against the public interest then the Secretary of State has discretion, but is required to take into account the advice of the MMC. The number of mergers considered, referred and their outcome are listed in Table 5.8.

Box 1: Section 84 of the Fair Trading Act 1973

(1) In determining for any purposes to which this section applies whether any particular matter operates, or may be expected to operate, against the public interest, the Commission shall take into account all matters which appear to them in the particular circumstances to be relevant and, among other things, shall have regard to the desirability-

(a) of maintaining and promoting effective competition between persons supplying goods and services in the United Kingdom;

(b) of promoting the interests of consumers, purchasers and other users of goods and services in the United Kingdom in respect of the prices charged for them and in respect of their quality and the variety of goods 6 and services supplied;

(c) of promoting, through competition, the reduction of costs and the development and use of new techniques and new products, and of facilitating the entry of new competitors into existing markets;

(d) of maintaining and promoting the balanced distribution of industry and employment in the United Kingdom; and

(e) of maintaining and promoting competitive activity in markets outside the United Kingdom on the part of producers of goods, and of suppliers of goods and services, in the United Kingdom.

(2) This section applies to the purposes of any functions of the Commission under this Act other than functions to which Section 59(3) applies.

During the 80s there has been increasing disquiet about the efficacy of British mergers policy. There are those who want merger policy to be clearer, particularly the grounds for referral. The grounds for referral, dependent as they are on the political decision by the Secretary of State for Trade and Industry, and a number of vague and manipulable public interest grounds have come under increasing attack.

The confusion and controversy reached its height in 1984 when the then Secretary of State with responsibility for competition, Norman Tebbit, sought to clarify the referral process by stating that the principal, though not exclusive, grounds for referral was the impact of the proposed merger on competition. Subsequent investigations by the MMC seem to cast doubt on the Government's adherence to the "Tebbit Doctrine", particularly over the referral of Minorco's hostile takeover bid for Consolidated Goldfields in 1987/88. Lord Young (1988, p. 2), a subsequent Secretary of State, was forced to clarify the situation during the Nestlé bid for Rowntrees:

> "... the main consideration in evaluating a merger reference to the Monopolies and Mergers Commission should be the potential effect on competition in the UK."

....

> "A competition-based mergers policy is about the economics of evaluating markets and market shares in terms of the competitive structure."

The White Paper on mergers policy (DTI, 1988, par 2.10) reaffirms this:

> "... the Government believe that those people best placed to make judgement of commercial prospect are those whose money is at stake; it is not the role of Government or statutory agencies to second-guess commercial judgements. Indeed, they are more likely than private sector decision-makers to make mistaken commercial judgements."

Despite the fact that formally there are a number of grounds for the referral of a merger, in practice its effect on competition is the predominant one. Officially, since the Tebbit doctrine was announced, the only referral on non-competition grounds was the increasing equity stake of the Kuwait Investment Office in BP (MMC, 1986) and mergers of newspapers which are governed by different criteria. In BP it was feared that the companies would fall under the control of a foreign government. This decision, while based on political and strategic considerations, proved to be correct with the invasion of Kuwait by Iraq.

There have also been attempts to make the financing of takeover bids a ground for referring a merger to the MMC. In the Goodman Fielder Wattie bid for Ranks Hovis McDougall leveraging combined with other factors was seen to "pose a danger to the public interest". The use of so-called "junk bonds" was brought into sharp relief by the failed Hoylake bid for BAT Industries PLC. This was a £13.5 billion bid - four times larger than the biggest European bid - based on co-called "low quality" debt.

The basis of a "leveraged buyout" (LBO) is the extensive use of debt to acquire a company backed by claims on the income and assets of the acquired company. This is financed by high risk, high yield debt (popularly known as "junk bonds"). In the UK there is *not* a junk bond market and Hoylake was the first hostile LBO with a debt/equity ratio of 340%. It has been argued that this form of bid financing should be prevented or at least become a ground for referral because:

- it damages the health of the corporate bond market;
- it creates financial distress and increases the probability of default. This leads to short-termism;
- that there is not a well-developed market in junk bonds, which can lead to instability and artificial values and trading prices. The recent failure of the US "junk bond" market has given some support to this claim;

and,
- that post-merger divestments are seen as destructive "asset stripping".

Even Sir James Goldsmith (1989), the prime mover behind Hoylake's bid for Minorco, is alive to the dangers of LBOs:

> "In the early acquisition, high leverage was a transitory phenomena. Debt was paid down rapidly from the proceeds of the disposals of diversified assets. The ongoing .... businesses were well capitalised and assumed traditional levels of debt. But in the new transactions which sought maximum leverage, the policy was that even the ongoing ... businesses remained thinly capitalised and heavily leveraged. Debt repayment was to be made out of operating cashflow expected over quite a long number of years."

On the other hand, LBOs subject the management of the largest firms to the threat of takeover. The recent DTI consultative document expresses the UK government's scepticism about the claims that LBOs are bad. It is, it argues, for the market to decide and a LBO will not *per se* be regarded as a ground for referral.

Recent reforms

The major area of reform has not been on the principles and substance of merger policy but its administration. In June 1986 the Government launched a review of aspects of UK competition law and policy, directed mainly at mergers policy and restrictive trade practices (DTI, 1988; DTI, 1989).

The Merger Policy White Paper reiterates that the main consideration in a referral of a merger is its potential effect on competition (para. 2.12) and that "[I]t is the exploitation through market power of UK customers ... that is the appropriate touchstone for UK merger policy". The Government has concluded that the broad thrust of UK merger policy should remain unchanged but that there was room for improvement of the administration and procedures under the Fair Trading Act.

The following recommendations for reform were proposed.

- Voluntary pre-notification of mergers to facilitate more efficient and rapid handling of mergers. There will be automatic clearance if a merger has been pre-notified and the parties do not hear from the OFT within a proposed four week time limit. These companies which do not notify the OFT will be liable to MMC reference for a period up to 5 years.
- Statutory undertaking in place of referral. It is proposed that the DG have the power in appropriate situations to discuss with the parties possible variants on

their proposal with a view to obtaining a suitable legally binding undertaking to remove the competition objections.

- Procedural changes:
  - completion of OFT and MMC investigations within 4/5 months;
  - MMC investigation not to last more than 3 months;
  - exchange of information between OFT and MMC on a more consistent and regular basis;
  - where appropriate, MMC staff and Commissioners to adopt a more proactive investigative approach by gathering facts and developing a working relationship with the parties rather than the current procedure of a formal "Preliminary Hearing" followed by a "Public Interest Hearing" based on written submissions;
  - greater recourse to informal factual presentations;
  - change in style of MMC reports to a terser document concentrating on issues relevant to the MMC's conclusion;
  - decisions based on twothirds majority of a panel of five commissioners;
  - experimentation with smaller panels of a minimum of three commissioners, the appointment of more partcommissioners and more flexible arrangement as regards appointments; and,
  - statutory charge imposed on the parties to a merger under investigation to defray costs of OFT and MMC.

VI. Regulation of Privatised Utilities

Privatisation, the sale of nationalised industries to the private sector has led to a significant increase in competitive forces in key sectors of the UK economy. In the 80s the telecommunications, gas, electricity, airport and water industries have all been privatised. In this sense the UK is unique among countries in the European Community where there have only been tentative plans to privatise the major utility sectors.

The general approach

In nearly all cases nationalisation meant monopolisation. As a consequence privatisation has led to the introduction of competitive forces fostered through a combination of *re-structuring* the previously nationalised industry into a number of separate companies, the fostering of service competition through *interconnection agreements* using the transmission network of the privatised companies, or by assisting new entry to provide direct competition to the privatised entity, so-called *liberalisation*. The general criticism voiced during each privatisation was that there was insufficient restructuring of the sector to foster an adequately competitive environment. As a consequence the majority of consumers continua to face the monopoly provision of essential services.

The acceptance that the privatised utilities are still able to wield significant market power has given rise to a new body of regulatory law designed to foster a number of objectives ranging from universal service, and consumer protection to enhancing competition. Indeed, privatisation has been accompanied by a considerable amount of institutional innovation with the formation of new regulatory watchdogs (see above), and new techniques of economic regulation known as incentive regulation principally in the guise of price caps and an explicit regulatory approach to fostering competition.

There evolved a clear pattern of institutional innovation with each privatisation. In each utility sector at least one new autonomous government agency was established to administered a tailor-made system of economic regulation. In addition, for some industries a second agency was set-up to represent consumers interests (in the gas sector) or to regulate environmental quality (water). The new economic regulators are charged with administering the system of price control, ensuring universal service and quality of service, and encouraging or promoting competition. The general duties of the regulators differ from sector to sector, and the evolution of this new body of regulatory law has been widely criticised as *ad hoc* and lacking consistency in its substance and procedures (Veljanovski, 1993).

The use of a separate body of law to control monopoly and actively foster competition is a subject in itself. While the government wanted the OFT to undertake responsibility for regulating the utilities it was decided, at some stage for reasons not entirely clear, that this was best handled by an industry-specific agency with the referral of contentious matters to the MMC. This contrasts with the approach adopted in New Zealand where privatised utilities are subject only to competition law.

The reason why the UK has adopted a regulatory approach to the utility industry has never been spelt out in any official document. However, it can be assumed that officials believed that the complexity of utility regulation subject to wider public interest considerations (such as universal service) militated against sole reliance on the existing competition laws. But, as we shall see, the regulatory approach is much more interventionist that the application of general UK competition laws. It has given rise to the notion of *entry assistance*; that is, positive and at times discriminatory steps to assist new firms to overcome the obstacles and initial disadvantages when trying to compete with the established dominant privatised utility.

Legal framework

The control of utility monopolies involves both the newly formed regulatory watchdogs and the general competition agencies, and also the provisions of the privatisation acts and the licences issued to the utilities, together with general competition law.

Under the Fair Trading Act 1973 a "statutory monopoly" is held to exist where a company supplies or receives at least one quarter of all goods and services of a particular description. This is known as a scale monopoly. Alternatively, a complex monopoly exists where two or more persons who supply or receive 25% of goods or services of a particular description so conduct their affairs as to prevent, restrict or distort competition. These requirements act as a trigger to enable a monopoly reference. Under UK legislation there is no presumption that monopoly is wrong. The legislation only recognises that when this threshold has been reached there is a possibility that the monopoly may operate against the public interest. The assessment of a monopoly is in rather vague terms but the MMC has in recent years sought to clarify the conditions for a monopoly reference and the public interest test.

The relationship between the regulatory agencies and competition law is diverse and complex. The utilities are subject to general competition law whether it be UK or EC with the exception of designated airports. Prior to privatisation the Secretary of State could, under the Competition Act (s. 11), refer to the MMC any questions relating to the efficiency, costs and services of a nationalised industry and other public sector bodies (so-called public sector references). These references precluded consideration of competition issues focusing on service and internal efficiency of the nationalised industries. After privatisation, the greater emphasis given to new competition matters was reflected in the powers given to regulators and the MMC. In the telecom, gas, water and electricity industries the regulator has the power to enforce the terms of the utilities licence which contain the main aspects of economic and competition regulation. The Director also has the power to seek modifications of licence conditions and to make determinations such as on interconnection terms and access to the network, the level of the price controls and so on. The normal process is for the Director to seek agreement to proposed modifications with the utility. Where he fails to reach agreement the matter is referred to the MMC.

The MMC's new powers to conduct inquiries into these industries are found in the different privatisation acts beginning in 1984 with the privatisation of BT. The MMC has duties to conduct inquiries into the activities of privatised undertakings, under specific conditions contained in five separate statutes the Telecommunications Act 1984, The Airports Act 1986, The Gas Act 1986, the Water Industry Act 1989 and the Electricity Act 1989. The grounds for these references differ for each Act, and are generally much narrower than the usual MMC reference. There are three types of privatisation references:

Licence modifications - All five statutes enable the regulator to refer a modification of a licence term to the MMC where he and the utility fail to reach agreement. The test used by the MMC is not the general public interest test (under s.84 of the Fair Trading Act) but a more narrow one as stated in the relevant Privatisation Act having regard to the duties imposed on the regulator. The MMC's decision is binding although any remedies imposed by the MMC are not. This is a discretionary matter for the relevant regulators.

Modifications of prices - Under the Airports and Water Industry Acts charges can be specifically referred to the MMC. Under the Airports Act the Civil Aviation Authority undertakes a quinquennial review of charges at airports designated by the Secretary of State (currently the three London airports and Manchester airport). It is obligatory for the CAA to refer these charges to the MMC. The CAA has to take into account the MMC's recommendations before making a final decision but the MMC's findings are not determinative. The MMC acts as a "research unit" for the CAA which has the final say. Remarkably, the airport regulator is itself a nationalised industry (because of its provision of air traffic control services) and hence subject to periodic investigations by the MMC to assess its efficiency. Under the Water Industry Act (in fact the "appointments" given to the water companies) the MMC can only be called in when the regulator and industry disagree over price formula modifications. However, when this occurs the MMC's decision is binding.

Water mergers - Under the Water Act mergers are automatically referred to the MMC provided that both companies have assets of over £30 million. The MMC has to apply a wider public interest test than that used in mergers generally. The MMC is required to take into account and give priority of consideration to the proposed mergers impact on "yardstick competition" or "comparative competition". Merger references can also be made under the Fair Trading Act in which case only one party needs to have assets over £ 30m.

To end, before 1944 there have been five airport references, three water merger references and two MMC investigations into British Gas.

Regulatory efforts to promote competition

One criticism of the UK's privatisation programme is that not enough was done to foster greater competition in the utility sector (Barnes & Winward, 1989; Veljanovski, 1989). In the first two utility privatisations the nationalised industry was left intact, and the privatised water companies remain regional monopolies. It was only in the electricity supply industry that radical restructuring occurred, and then it was argued by many experts that the non-nuclear generation sector should have been split into a greater number of generators. However, years after the privatisation of some utilities the restructuring of the industry is still very much on the agenda (Ofgas, 1993).

The debate over competition has focused on three separate avenues of increasing competition *restructuring, interconnection and liberalisation.* These three forms of competition have operated with different intensity in the main utility sectors so far privatised.

British Telecom

British Telecom was the first utility to be privatised in 1984. Of all the utility industries, telecommunications is the one in which the possibility of competition in the provision of services and networks is most real. The speed and extent of technological innovation has been dramatic. This has led to proliferation of new services and technologies, and manyfold reduction in the costs and dramatic increase in the capacity of telecommunications systems.

The privatisation of BT did not involve any restructuring of the company as nationalised (apart from its prior separation from the Post Office). However, the privatisation of British Telecom took place in the context of the prior licensing of a second PTT, Mercury Communications. That is, liberalisation preceded privatisation. However, the announcement of the sale of 50.2% of BT led to the so-called duopoly policy, the latter conferring on BT and Mercury the exclusive right to provide voice telephony in the UK until 1991. The duopoly policy was widely seen as protecting BT's market and establishing a cosy relationship between it and Mercury, while at the same time leaving the real area of BT's monopoly the local loop unchallenged.

Subsequent to privatisation a number of developments took place which diluted the duopoly constraint and *expanded, at least potentially, the competitive pressures on parts of BT's operation.* These included the narrow application of the duopoly to protect only the core voice telephony of BT and the Government's licensing of other operators using new technologies such as mobile and broadband cable networks. As a result BT now faces a large number of competitors in the provision of mobile, satellite and broadband wire network systems and services. Nonetheless, most of these services have a relatively low market share of the total telecommunications traffic.

The most important single pro-competitive action of the regulator (Oftel) to date has been the interconnection agreement between BT and Mercury.

In order for Mercury to provide end-to-end telecommunications services in the UK it must have access to BT's network. It is, therefore, necessary that there be some agreed basis for interconnection and a non-discriminatory charge which permits Mercury to compete on an equal footing to BT while not giving it an unfair subsidy. The regulatory framework leaves it to the parties to come to an agreement on the terms and cost of interconnection and, failing this, for the Director General of the Office of Telecommunications to make a determination which BT can accept or alternatively to seek a separate determination by the MMC. After much discussion the regulator proposed an interconnection agreement which was accepted by BT which many regard as overly favourable to Mercury. This was the first overt application of *entry assistance* which discriminated in favour of competitors to the privatised entity.

The second as yet to be fully realised introduction of competition to the UK Telecom sector, has occurred through the licensing of broadband cable system. This was the responsibility of the now defunct Cable Authority established in 1984 at the time of BT's privatisation. The original intention behind licensing broadband cable systems was that they would provide an alternative means of supply for multi-channel television and eventually provide competition with BT in the local loop at negligible marginal costs. The Government's assumption was that the bulk of the infrastructure costs would be covered by subscription revenue from the provision of television channels. While the growth of cable has been slow, by the time of demise of the Cable Authority over 130 cable systems covering 70% of homes in the UK, most in the major conurbations had been licensed. Nearly all these cable operators have as the main or dominant partner a North American Regional Bell Operating Company (RBOC) or other established media company with a wealth of experience of running telecommunications systems. Thus BT now faces considerable competition at its doorstep as these systems are built, offering business and domestic customers combined video and telephony services.

Notwithstanding these developments BT still has a high overall market share. Even the highly contestable international telephone traffic has been brought into the price control system because of the regulators belief that competitive pressures were too weak. While the stated goal of regulation is to mimic the outcome of a competitive market, the question has been continuously asked whether there has been a tendency to substitute regulation for actual competition, as the regulator, impatient with the pace of entry, takes steps to reduce BT's market share and profitability.

British Gas

British Gas stands out among the utility privatisations for the Government's complete failure to restructure the industry. As a result a large monolithic company was sold to the private sector with weak guarantees that competition, though permitted, would arise. Indeed competition was *not* a major objective of gas privatisation. Yet the subsequent history of gas regulation has been the champing at the bit by the regulator to foster competition against the background of a dominant utility and a very weak regulatory remit to enforce competition in the contract market (for customers consuming 25,000 therms or more).

The regulatory problems and controversy surrounding British Gas concern the use of its transmission network, or more particulary the terms of access to that network. Under the Gas Act 1986 the regulator has a responsibility to enable competition in the contract market. The Act was based on an assumption that this competition would arise naturally without the need for active intervention by the regulator. Thus, in common with other legislation, it gave the regulator the power only to intervene if British Gas and third-party suppliers of gas who wanted to use British Gas's network could not reach agreement on terms and charges.

The gas regulator, Sir James MacKinnon, has sought vigorously to encourage competition, often in terms which made him an unwanted salesman of British Gas' services to its competitors. The regulator formed the view that the dominance of British Gas in the gas industry was unaceptable and the matter was referred by the Office of Fair Trading to the MMC in 1987. The reference applied to sale of gas through pipes to contract customers and was made following complaints about British Gas' pricing policy.

The MMC's (1988a) report concluded that in law British Gas had a monopoly position and that it had engaged in extensive price discrimination which acted against the public interest. The report recommended that British Gas:

- publish a price list and cease price discrimination;
- publish information on common carriage terms;
- contract initially for no more than 90% of any new gas field; and
- not refuse to supply interruptible gas on the basis of the use made of it or alternative fuels available.

The Secretary of State for Trade and Industry asked the Director General of Fair Trading to seek undertakings from British Gas consistent with the remedies proposed by the MMC, and further to initiate a review of their effectiveness after two years.

In 1991 the OFT reviewed the situation concluding that although British Gas had complied with the undertakings obtained in 1990 the "objective of self-sustained competition in the general industrial and commercial contract market has not been achieved". The remedies had been ineffective in creating competition and further action was required. However the OFT asserted that the objective of its report was to establish the effectiveness of competition and not to investigate what additional undertakings would be required. In assessing this point wider issues of public policy would need to be considered and British Gas should be allowed to answer all the issues raised by the OFT inquiry. It therefore concluded that the Director of Fair Trading would be justified in making a further referral to the MMC though it was decided that this should be delayed until the end of the year in order to provide the opportunity for additional discussions and negotiations between the parties. This issue as well as a tightening of the price cap instigated by Ofgas has caused a protracted dispute, often confused by the interplay of several regulators. In order to avoid a reference to the MMC British Gas agreed to undertakings to the OFT to halve its share of the contract gas market by 1995 and to separate its pipeline operation from the rest of the company.

In late 1992 British Gas was again referred to the MMC, which has been asked (through four separate references) to undertake an extensive review of the gas industry. Deep structural changes to the industry have been suggested by Ofgas (*Ofgas*, 1993) to the MMC Inquiry which could lead to the break-up of British Gas.

Water

Water privatisation differs from that of the other utilities in that the service is not priced on the basis of consumption (because of the absence of water meters), and the industry needs major investment to upgrade its network. As a result the price formula includes K factors for each water company designed to make the customer pay for the capital investment.

It is also an industry where the scope for direct head-to-head competition is severely limited. Nonetheless the regulatory system attempts to use competitive concepts as an integral part of regulating the companies. Under the Water Act the regulator must evaluate the performance of the water and sewage companies within a system of *comparative competition*. This uses the performance of the best to evaluate that of other water utilities controlling for differences in the geological and commercial factors affecting each company, a regulatory concept of competition which relies heavily on arbitrary comparators and the ability to adequately control for exogenous factors beyond the control of the companies which would explain different financial and economic performance. It is fair to say that at present the comparators are fairly crude and are still being developed.

Apart from the difficulty of devising acceptable comparators the MMC has the ability to recommend that mergers between water companies should be blocked if they reduce the regulator's ability to compare performance. Therefore, for any merger to gain support this detriment to public interest has to be compensated for by substantial and clear benefits to customers, normally in the form of significant reductions in their bills.

Following the enactment of the Competition and Service (Utilities) Act 1992, the regulator is examining whether direct competition in the supply of water and sewerage service can be fostered through common carriage provisions similar to that in the gas, telecom, and electricity industries. The 1992 Act also extended the powers of the regulator to make inset appointments in the 1989 Water Act to large existing customers. This measure is an attempt to open up competition for large customers; that is, those using more than 250 mega-litres of water a year.

Electricity generation

Largely as a reaction to the privatisation of British Gas, a radical restructuring of the generation sector of the electricity industry took place at privatisation. The nationalised Central Electricity Generation Board was broken up into four entities - a transmission company owned by the Regional Electricity Boards (RECs) which distribute electricity to the customer, two non-nuclear generating companies (National Power and PowerGen), and nuclear power generation which has remained in state ownership. In addition, private generators and the RECs can enter the market for electricity generation.

The Government originally proposed a duopoly structure in order to cross-subsidise nuclear power which was to be included in the larger of the companies (PowerGen). It was vigorously argued at the time of privatisation that the separation of the non-nuclear generating capacity in two posed potential monopoly problems particularly given that the price of wholesale electricity was to remain unregulated. Many argued that at least five profitable generating companies could have coexisted (Henny, 1987 Sykes & Robinson, 1987). The costs of decommissioning power plants and other potential liabilities arising from the nuclear industry led to the nuclear generating capacity remaining in the public sector. Despite this change the Government failed to re-organise the generation sector. As a result, two main generators supply the national grid with a periphery of emerging competition from the regional electricity companies.

The Director General of Offer, Professor Stephen Littlechild, has on two occasions (Offer, 1991, 1992) examined the behaviour of the two generators following price increases. While suggesting that they may have resulted from the exercise of market power, he has refrained from alleging that the price increases are unjustified.

Issues raised by regulatory approach to competition policy

As stated above the growth of economic regulation has altered the control of monopoly in a major sectors of UK economy. Unlike competition law the introduction of a regulatory approach has given rise to new concepts and issues which have yet to be fully analysed.

The myth of temporary regulation

A number of regulators contended that their intention is to work themselves out of a job. They claim that much of the regulatory structure is temporary *stop-gap regulation* which will wither away as the competitive pressures which they have fostered increase. Such views have been expressed both by the telecoms and gas regulators at various times:

> "... if regulation is seen as a process for managing change it should be welcomed as a temporary phenomenon. We at OFGAS see regulation in that way and we aim to get out of the way of business operations as soon as a self-sustaining competitive market gets on its feet. We will measure our success by the speed with which we can withdraw from situations in which competition is developing. These situations include the tariff and industrial gas supply markets as well as the pipeline business" (Ofgas, 1991).

The idea that regulation in the UK begins or is run in the belief that it will disappear within the five year tenure of a regulator is clearly not an adequate working hypothesis. This is particularly the case when the failure of the Government to restructure potentially competitive parts of each sector is taken into account. The existence of large utilities or duopolies (in the case of electricity generation) supplying in excess of 90% of the overall market means that permanent regulation is required to curb monopoly excess. While there have been attempts by some regulators to propose the radical restructuring of the sector, in particular of British Gas, it is unlikely that these will find favour. Thus the withering away of regulation is inconceivable given the presence of persistent pockets of monopoly, particularly the transmission networks. The feasibility of less regulation will be determined in purely economic terms of whether these industries are so characterised by economies of scale, scope and /or density to preclude competition, whether the advantage of the privatised utility is so significant that effective competition is not realisable within any sensible time frame or ever, and the political context of regulation.

Trade-off between regulation and competition

The regulatory approach has as its central feature price regulation. Each utility has retail prices pegged to the rate of inflation minus X percentage points to reflect the ability of the utility to improve efficiency. The exception is the water industry where prices are set at RPI plus K, the K being set to permit greater investment in the industry's infrastructure.

The price cap is designed to deal with the most immediate effects of monopoly and dominance the ability of the utility to charge a monopoly price to captive customers. It has been argued that the operation of the price cap is anti-competitive because it taxes away the profits of entry for competitors. The regulator, by using price controls as a surrogate for competition, prevents competition arising and therefore regulation becomes it own justification. This trade-off poses a serious matter of principle. Clearly in areas where the likelihood of competition is small (transmission networks) this is not a serious concern. But in other areas the extension of price controls to, say, international telecommunications traffic by Oftel on the grounds that competition has been slow to develop is much more dubious.

From entry assistance to managed competition

The regulator's duty to promote competition implies something considerably more than the need to prevent monopoly abuse. If it meant the latter, a competition law approach rather than a regulatory approach would have been adopted. The corollary of promoting competition is overt *entry assistance* by the regulator. In practice this means subsidising entry by extracting favourable interconnection and other terms for the new entrant presumably to overcome the initial hurdles it faces. However, this is a marked departure from the idea that regulation should credit a level playing field.

The duopoly policy was a major test case for the efficacy of entry assistance. The idea was that Mercury would provide effective competition to BT if protected from other competitors for seven years (an infant industry argument) and given favourable interconnection charges (subsidy). The duopoly policy failed and has been replaced by tighter permanent price controls.

In British Gas' case entry assistance has taken a new turn. Instead of promoting competition the regulator is forcing British Gas to reduce its market share to give it away rather than to have it won by competitors. This departure appears to see competition as an end in itself, manufactured by the regulator rather than something which should be initiated by robust entrepreneurs who win market share. The justification for such managed competition appears weak and certainly requires more justification and explanation than hitherto has been the case.

References

Barnes, F. & Winward, J., 1989, *In the Absence of Competition A Consumer View of Public Utilities Regulation*, London: National Consumer Council.

Charkam, J., 1989, "Corporate Governance and the Market for Control of Companies", London: Bank of England, Panel Paper no. 25.

DTI, 1988a, *Mergers Policy. A Department of Trade and Industry Paper on the Policy and Procedures of Merger Control*, London: HMSO.

DTI, 1988b, "Review of Restrictive Trade Practices Policy A Consultative Document", Cm.331, London: HMSO.

DTI, 1989, *Barriers to Takeovers in the European Community. A Study by Coopers & Lybrand for the DTI*, 3 vols., London: HMSO.

Goldsmith, J., 1989, "Paper of Conference on International Mergers and Acquisitions", London.

Hanson, C.G. and Mather, G., 1988, *Striking out Strikes*, London: Institute of Economic Affairs.

Henny, A., 1987, *Privatise Power Restructuring the Electricity Supply Industry*, London: Centre for Policy Studies, 1987.

Lord Young, 1988, "Merger Policy Address to Stock Exchange Conference for Industry" London: Department of Trade & Industry.

MMC, 1988a, *Gas*, London: HMSO.

MMC, 1988b) *The Government of Kuwait and The British Petroleum Company plc*, Cm. 477, London: HMSO.

Offer, 1991, *Review of Pool Prices 1991*, Birmingham: Office of Electricity Regulation.

Offer, 1992, *Review of Pool Prices 1992*, Birmingham: Office of Electricity Regulation.

Ofgas, 1991, *Annual Report 1991*, London: Office of Gas Supply.

Ofgas, 1993, *The Gas Industry in Britain – Future Structure*, London: Office of Gas Supply.

OFT, 1991, *The Gas Review: A Review by OFT Officials in Conjunction with Ofgas of the Industrial and Commercial Market for Gas and Developments Since the MMC Report*, London Office of Fair Trading.

Seldon, A., ed. 1988, *Financial Regulation or Over Regulation?*, London: Institute of Economic Affairs.

Sykes, A., Robinson, C., 1987, *Current Choices: Good Ways and Bad to Privatise Electricity*, London: Centre for Policy Studies.

Veljanovski, C.G., 1988, *Selling the State Privatisation in Britain*, London: Weidenfeld & Nicolson.

Veljanovski, C.G., 1989, *Privatisation and Competition: A Market Prospectus*, London: Institute of Economic Affairs.

Veljanovski, C.G., 1993a, "The Future of Industry Regulation in the UK - A report of an Independent Inquiry", London: European Policy Forum.

Veljanovski, C.G., 1993b, "The Need for a Regulatory Charter", *Journal of Regulatory Law & Practice*, 1.

6. Evolution of Antitrust Policies in France

FRÉDÉRIC JENNY

I. The Emergence of Competition Law in France

Until quite recently, it was widely assumed in international circles that anticompetitive practices were widespread in France and that French authorities were largely unconcerned with promoting competition. This view was fostered by the well-known, long standing French tradition of government intervention in market mechanisms ranging from price controls to subsidisation of key industries and centrally planned restructuring of firms, as well as by an obvious lack of a competitive spirit of French firms dealing in international markets.

Thus the claim of that the enactment of the 1986 ordinance on "price freedom an competition" was a major breakthrough for the promotion of the competitive free market ideal in France, was widely accepted.

To a large extent, the idea that French public policy makers did not care about competition policy was justified until the mid-seventies and although antitrust legislation had been enacted in 1953, its implementation was at first seen by academicians and the business community as little more than window dressing.

However, since the mid-sixties important changes have occured in the attitudes of public policy makers, the business community and consumers with respect to the benefits to be expected from the development of competition. In addition, there have been equally important changes in the nature and the vigour of enforcement of antitrust legislation.

II. The Context of French Economic Policy in the Immediate Post War Period

Four aspects of French economic policy are important to understand what characterised competition policy during the 50s, the 60s and the early 70s

First the need to reconstruct the French economy after world war II and the existence of powerful business organisations led to a particular type of government intervention in the market mechanisms exemplified by the French indicative planning process. Business community leaders and public officials jointly monitored the economy.

Second, concern about black marketeering during the immediate post-war period of reconstruction and about inflation during the subsequent period of

G. Mussati (ed.), Mergers, Markets and Public Policy, 163–200.
© 1995 *Kluwer Academic Publishers.*

rapid economic development led public authorities to rely heavily on price controls.

Third, concern with developing the French industrial potential and an inclination toward engineering achievements reinforced the commonly held idea that distributors did not contribute significantly to the creation of real wealth but were mainly bothersome intermediaries.

Fourth the progressive involvement of France in the European Economic Community at the beginning of the sixties led to the belief that France's main disadvantage in the realm of international competition lay not in an inability to innovate, but was a result of weaknesses in its industrial structure. It was widely held that exports expansion would occur naturally if French firms could benefit from economies of scale in production. Increasing the size of French plants and French firms seemed the obvious way to rapidly achieve the desired result. This view, which was popularised in 1967 by J. J. Servan Schreiber in his book "The American Challenge"[1], led to a merger wave between 1965 an 1975. A policy granting financial aids to firms willing to engage in external growth was supported by public officials in part because they thought that it would be easier to monitor a small number of large firms in each industry than a large number of small firms. It was also supported by the business community which realised that concentration that might possibly lead to a decrease in unit costs of production would also certainly lead to increased market power at the domestic level for the firms involved.

III. The 1953 Antitrust Statutes

The enactment of the first French competition antitrust statute (decrees of August 9 1953 and January 27 1954) was basically at odds with the overall economic approach of public policy makers. At the time, the enactment of a competition law was mainly seen as a complement to the price control ordinance adopted in 1945 (Ordonnance n° 45-1483 du 30 juin 1945 relative aux prix) and the decree of 1953 was an amendment to the 1945 ordinance. Indeed due to a lack of understanding of economic theory, it was generally believed that anticompetitive behaviour should be opposed because it led to higher price levels and therefore contributed to inflation, rather than because competition would lead to a more efficient allocation of resources.

The major characteristics of the 1953 competition statutes can be explained by the afor-mentioned factors.

The newly added Article 59bis of the ordinance of 1945 on prices stated that: "are unlawful, subject to the provisions of Article 59ter, all concerted actions, conventions, express or tacit agreements, or coalitions whatever their form or their cause, if their object or their potential effect is to impair the full exercise of competition by preventing a decrease in costs or in selling prices or by facilitating an artificial increase in prices".

The text of Article 59bis clearly indicated the government preoccupation with price movements.

Article 59ter stated that "are not subject to the provisions of Article 59bis concerted actions, conventions or agreements:

1) if they result from a law or a decree;
2) if their authors can justify that their effect is to ameliorate or increase production or to ensure the development of economic progress through rationalisation and specialisation".

Thus it was assumed that competition was not necessarily the most appropriate way to increase efficiency or production and that concern about competition should not interfere with the industrial policy favoured by business leaders and supported by the French government.

The preliminary investigations of potentially anticompetitive agreements were to be conducted by the Price Division of the Ministry in charge of Economic Affairs. Upon completion of those investigations, the Minister could refer the case to an administrative body (Commission Technique des Ententes) which was to give an opinion as to whether or not the examined practices were prohibited. If the Commission Technique des Ententes considered that there was a violation of the competition statutes, the Minister could either send the firms or organisations involved an official letter asking them to discontinue the practice or he could refer the case to the courts.

The 1953 decree did not establish merger control or a control of abuse of market power by individual firms having a dominant position on a market.

The 1953 provisions were modified on several occasions during subsequent years. A review of those changes reveals a slowly growing sophistication with respect to the analysis of market mechanisms.

In 1963, ten years after the enactment of the original provisions against cartel agreements had been enacted, a provision prohibiting anticompetitive practices by firms having a dominant position on a market or a monopoly was added to Article 59bis of the 1945 ordinance on prices (law n° 63-628 of July 2 1963).

In 1967, Article 2 of the ordinance n 67-835 of September 28 1967 amended Article 59bis of the 1945 price ordinance prohibiting cartel agreements in a way that can be interpreted as a slight move away from the idea that competition was primarily designed to prevent price increases. The revised text of Article 59bis stated that "Are unlawful, subject to the provisions of Article 59ter, all concerted actions, conventions, express or tacit agreements, or coalition whatever their form or their cause, if their object or their potential effect is to prevent, restrain or alter competition; for example by preventing a decrease in costs or in selling prices, by facilitating an artificial increase in prices, by preventing technical progress, or by limiting the ability of other firms to compete freely".

The ordinance n 67-835 of September 28 1967 also amended Article 59ter which now read: "are not subject to the provisions of Article 59bis concerted actions, conventions or agreements:

1) if they result from a law or a decree;
2) if their authors can justify that their effect is to ensure the development of economic progress, in particular by an increase in productivity" (rather than the previous phrasing which stated: "if their effect is to ameliorate or increase production or to ensure the development of economic progress through rationalisation and specialisation").

However these changes were of marginal importance and the promotion of competition on the market place did not figure high on the agenda of government authorities in charge of economic matters until 1977. Besides the obvious unwillingness of public authorities to rely on market forces in a competitive environment to achieve efficiency, the system designed in 1953 was largely ineffective because the legal means of the Minister in charge of Economic Affairs were insufficient to dissuade firms from engaging in anticompetitive practices either because they did not care about the warnings that be could issued or because the courts did not handle speedily and effectively the cases which be decided to refer to them.

IV. The 1977 Reform

The change that occured in 1977 under the premiership of Mr. Raymond Barre was decidedly more significant. Three main factors played a role in the 1977 reform.

First, a personal factor. Prime Minister Barre is an economist by training an therefore familiar with price theory. Prior to becoming Prime Minister of France, be had been chairman of the E.E.C. Commission, which has always actively promoted competition at the European level.

Second, an economic factor. At the beginning of the seventies, research in the field of industrial organisation revealed three major facts that challenged the wisdom of previous policy in the area of industrial structures:

concentration on the market place had increased significantly during the previous decade partly, but not exclusively, due to the merger policy actively pursued by public authorities; the profit rates of firms in concentrated industries were significantly higher than the profit rates of firms in industries that had a more competitive structure; in many industries the largest firms were less efficient than their smaller competitors. These findings, combined with obvious examples of industrial policy failures in industries in which the government had tried to increase concentration (such as in the steel and computer industries) and the slowly emerging feeling that the lack of aggressiveness of French firms on international markets was partly a consequence of weak competition on their domestic market, led a vocal minority of economists and public policy makers to call for a strengthening of French competition law.

Third, an institutional factor. At the 1972 "Paris Conference", the heads of the E.E.C. countries had agreed on the necessity of establishing a merger control law at the European level. This plan was considered a threat by the segment of French bureaucracy in charge of industrial policy, which was still busily involved in promoting mergers among French firms. Indeed, they realised that if it were to come into being, merger control at the E.E.C. level would not necessarily be limited to mergers between firms of different countries. It could well mean that a merger between two large French firms holding a significant share of the European market (such as a merger between two large French automobile manufacturers), even one backed by the French government and considered essential from the point of view of domestic industrial policy, could in the future be challenged by "faceless Eurocrats" on the ground that it might impair competition and trade within the E.E.C. Thus although public policy makers in charge of French industrial policy generally still believed in the positive effect of concentration and mergers, they were led to favour the adoption of some kind of merger control at the French level (as long as that control was exercised by the government rather than by the courts) as a way to defeat the European merger control project. Indeed they reasoned that it would be far easier to argue that the establishment of a merger control at the european level was useless, if they could show that French authorities were trying to curb potentially anticompetitive mergers at the domestic level.

Thus for the all of the above, somewhat contradictory, reasons a major revision of French competition law took place in 1977. Four main provisions of the new law (Loi n° 77-806 du 19 juillet 1977 concerning the control of economic concentration and the repression of illicit agreements and abuse of dominant positions) are worthy of comment.

First, the Minister in charge of Economic Affairs could henceforth impose an administrative fine on firms found, by the Commission de la concurrence (the new advisory body in charge of investigating cartel agreements and the behaviour of firms holding a dominant position on a market), to have engaged in anticompetitive practices. Fines imposed by the Minister could not exceed amounts recommended by the Commission nor could they exceed 5% of the total annual sales of the firms involved.

Second, the Commission de la concurrence was established as an administrative body independent of the Minister of economic affairs. Cases involving potentially anticompetitive practices could henceforth be referred to the Commission by parties other than the Minister in charge of economic Affairs such as trade associations, consumer organisations and local governments.

Third, merger control was established. The control could occur in the case of horizontal mergers, if the market share of the merging firms exceeded 40% on any market "at the national level", and, in the case of non horizontal mergers, if the market shares of two of the merging firms exceeded more than 25% on different markets. The 1977 law stipulated that if Commission de la concurrence found that the disadvantage for competition of the merger outweighed its contribution to economic and social progress, the Minister in charge of Economic Affairs, and the Minister in charge of the economic sector considered could prohibit the merger or order divestiture. However the ministers decisions could not go beyond the Commission de la concurrence recommendations.

Although, the 1977 law did not change the substance of French competition law regarding the definition of anticompetitive agreements and practices of dominant positions, it was an important signal to the business community that public authorities were serious about discovering and curbing anticompetitive behaviour.

Between 1977 and 1986, the Commission de la concurrence investigated 145 cases of potentially anticompetitive agreements (ranging from price fixing to market sharing, illicit exchanges of information among firms, attempts to block entry into an industry, selective or exclusive distribution contracts designed to prevent competition at the retail level, conspiracies in procurement markets etc. ...) or abuses of dominant positions.

Despite this, the 1977 law was, to a certain extent, considered a half measure. Indeed, although it was meant to affirm the commitment of the French public authorities to promoting competitive market mechanisms, the Minister in charge of Economic Affairs retained both preliminary investigative powers and the power to make final decision about the cases. As it was clear that a Minister's decision could be influenced by political considerations, the effort to promote competition was often considered as just another tool added to the already considerable means for government interference in market mechanisms rather than as a way for the government to permit decentralised economic forces to run their course. This impression was reinforced by continued widespread recourse to price controls (until 1983) which enabled the Minister in charge of Economic Affairs to impose ceilings on yearly price increases in some industries.

Nevertheless, French firms slowly but surely recognised that if they engaged in anticompetitive practices, they ran the risk of being caught and penalised. The Commission de la concurrence did not hesitate to recommend significant fines in cases in which firms or their trade associations were found to have flagrantly violated the law (up to 1 million dollars for some firms). The Minister of Economic Affairs concurred with the analysis of the Commission in most cases although in some instances he reduced the fines proposed by the Commission (frequently between 1977 and 1983, more rarely afterwards). It was the imposition of fines in certain cases, more than orders to discontinue prohibited practices, which played a crucial role in popularising the notion that the promotion of competitive market processes was a worthwhile enterprise. This occured because monetary sanctions were considered highly newsworthy by the press and received wide coverage. Thus the idea that firms could individually or collectively abuse their market power and that consumers had a collective interest in the prevention of such practices slowly but surely seeped into the French conventional wisdom.

It is interesting to note that the change that occurred in 1981, when a socialist government replaced the conservative governments which had been in power since 1958, did not slow down the trend towards a more vigorous enforcement of the competition. Indeed, in 1981-1982, although the Socialists did not favour the free market ideal, they were suspicious of economic power and considered competition law a useful tool to curb "abuses" of economically powerful firms. What is more, after 1983, as the 1986 legislative elections were drawing to a close, they chose to undercut the conservative opposition by adopting a more liberal stand on economic issues.

V. Other Restraints on Business Practices

In addition to the prohibition of anticompetitive cartel agreements and of abuse of market power by dominant firms, a number of other business practices were prohibited during the post war period, namely: resale price maintenance, refusal to deal, price discrimination, and reselling at a loss. The prohibition regarding these practices either is, or was until very recently, a per se prohibition. However, these prohibitions were not enforced by the Commission de la concurrence but were handled through the French civil court system or through an administrative procedure.

During the early fifties, the development of large-scale retailers and of discount stores was hampered by the fact that traditional (small-scale) distributors threatened to boycott and in some cases actually boycotted manufacturers who did not maintain resale prices. Such boycotts were not necessarily indicative of the existence of illegal cartels among the retailers involved but reflected the corporatist tendency of a large majority of the distributors.

Partly because it believed that small scale distributors were often inefficient and partly because it was under the mistaken impression that the development of large-scale distributors and discount stores would reduce inflation, the French administration tried to remedy the situation at the end of the fifties by making it illegal for manufacturers to refuse to sell or to impose resale prices.

During the sixties, traditional distributors retaliated by alleging that manufacturers discriminated against them and in favour of large-scale distributors using unfair methods of competition by reselling certain products at a loss (to attract consumers) while making a profit on others. Using the considerable political clout that they derived from their large numbers, traditional distributors were successful in lobbying for legislation making it illegal per se to ask for or to grant a discriminatory advantage or to resell at a loss.

In 1973, traditional distributors scored another victory in their fight against the development of large-scale low margin retailers when the "Loi ROYER" subjected the creation of new retail stores above a certain size to the prior authorisation of local administrative bodies called "Commissions d'Urbanisme Commercial" (CUC) in which local traditional distributors were represented and could make themselves heard.

However, for various reasons, these proved to be illusory victories for the traditional distributors.

The per se ban on price discrimination ceased to be enforced by public authorities around the middle of the seventies not only because in many cases it was often difficult to prove the existence of such discrimination but also because the government slowly but surely realised that in most cases price discrimination enhanced competition rather than hampered it.

The per se prohibition on refusal to deal was easier to enforce and, by and large, manufacturers were forced to sell their products to large-scale distributors even when this displeased traditional retailers. However numerous manufacturers, eager to avoid a strong negative reaction from their traditional small-scale retailers, tended to give a substantial part of the discounts that their large-scale distributors were entitled to in the form of conditional discounts (i.e., discounts paid at the end of each year and based on the total volume purchased during the year by the distributor). As the price below which distributors were prohibited from reselling (by the per se prohibition on reselling at a loss) was the invoice price and not the actual purchase price (invoice price minus year-end conditional discount), in some cases the effect of this practice was to force "discounters" to sell at prices higher than those they would have chosen spontaneously and therefore to somewhat limit price competition among different types of distributors of the same good.

Whenever successful large-scale distributors found it difficult to obtain the necessary authorisation (from the CUC) to open new stores in areas where they wanted to expand, they tended to use their profits to buy existing stores (as no prior authorisation was necessary in much cases). Thus concentration in the retail sector increased significantly, partially as a result of the very laws which had been designed to protect small traditional distributors.

The development of concentration in the retail sector led to an increase in the buying power of some distributors who were in turn able to threaten manufacturers with refusal to buy if they did not offer them additional (discriminatory) rebates. Manufacturers reacted by giving in to the demands of the most powerful or the most determined nation-wide large-scale retailers. As a result, price discrimination by manufacturers became widespread and buying conditions offered to traditional distributors and their large competitors became more and more unequal.

The slowdown of economic growth at the beginning of the eighties intensified competition among nation-wide large-scale retail chains and led each of them to intensify its efforts to lower resale prices and to secretly obtain ever more favourable buying terms from its suppliers. Furthermore competing distributors began to set up common buying agencies ("super-centrales d'achat") in order to increase their leverage over their suppliers. Thus concentration on the buyer side increased even further.

Thus, during the sixties and the seventies significant changes occurred in France regarding the economic relationship between manufacturers and distributors of consumer goods. Large-scale distributors have become a force to reckon with both for traditional distributors and for manufacturers.

At the beginning of the eighties, the complex and burdensome legislation which accrued from successive attempts by the government to monitor the changes in the relationship between manufacturers and distributors was widely denounced as uneconomical, ineffective and unjust. Manufacturers of brand goods, in particular, strongly denounced the per se prohibition of refusal to deal, arguing that this prohibition put them at the mercy of powerful distributors which could force them to grant illegal discriminatory price concessions under the threat of boycott since they were not subject to a parallel prohibition of refusal to buy.

VI. The 1986 Ordinance on Price Freedom and Competition

The afore-mentioned considerations help us to understand the rationale behind most of the important features of the new competition ordinance of 1986 (Ordonnance n° 86-1243 du 1er decembre 1986 relative à la liberté des prix et de la concurrence).

To underline its commitment to the concept of a free market economy, the new administration repealed the unpopular Price control ordinance of 1945. Article 1 of the 1986 ordinance "on the freedom of prices and competition" states that: "prices are freely determined through competitive process". However, the government retained the power to control the prices of a small number of predetermined products or services, mostly in the health or transportation sectors, for which price competition is limited either because of the existence of a natural or legal monopoly or because of an acute shortage.

In addition, the government has relinquished its power of decision regarding anticompetitive cartel agreements and abuses of market power. A quasi-judicial body ("Conseil de la concurrence") charged with prosecuting such practices was created. Composed of 16 members (magistrates, economic and legal experts and members of the business community), this independent body has investigative powers and can impose fines or give injunctions to firms found guilty of having violated the law. The decisions of the Conseil de la concurrence can be appealed to the Paris Appeals Court. Alleged anticompetitive practices can be referred to the Conseil de la concurrence by firms as well as by trade organisations, unions, local governments or the Minister in charge of Economic Affairs.

The Conseil de la concurrence is also charged with advising the government, parliamentary commissions, business and consumer organisations, and unions on general questions related to competition.

As previously mentioned, in spite of the fact that the 1977 competition law established a possibility of controlling mergers and in spite of the poor performances of a number of firms that had merged in the sixties and the seventies, there is still a lingering feeling among French bureaucrats in charge of industrial policy that economic concentration is necessary to ensure the competitiveness of French firms and that the government should play an active role in the area of industrial structures. It is thus not surprising to observe that the government has not relinquished its decision making power in the area of mergers.

The Minister of Economic Affairs retains sole authority for referring mergers to the Conseil de la concurrence; after referral, the Conseil de la concurrence delivers an opinion as to whether the merger should be allowed (and if so under which conditions) or whether it should be prohibited. Whereas in the system established in 1977, the Minister of Economic Affairs and the Minister in charge of the economic sector concerned could not go beyond the recommendation of the Commission de la concurrence, they are now free to follow or ignore the opinion of the Conseil de la concurrence.

As far as the substance of the law is concerned the main provisions prohibiting cartel agreements and abuses of market power by firms holding a dominant position remained largely unchanged. However, the debate concerning the emerging power of distributors and their relationship with manufacturers led to some important changes in the French competition legislation.

Three main questions were raised during the preparatory phase of the new competition ordinance:

- should anti-merger law be revised to enable public authorities to control mergers in the distribution sector?
- should the practices of firms that do not have a dominant position on a market but which wield substantive bargaining power towards their suppliers or buyers be controlled?
- should existing legislation on vertical restraints of trade be revised?

Merger control

Until December 1985, the ability of the Minister in charge of economic affairs to control mergers was limited to two situations:

1) in the case of horizontal mergers, the merging firms had to have a combined market share equal or superior to 40% of the domestic consumption of a product at the national level;
2) when the merger was not horizontal, at least two of the merging firms had to have a market share of at least 25% of the market of a product at the national level.

In spite of the fact that the merger control law was not vigorously enforced, manufacturers consistently denounced it as unfair by arguing that the criteria used to determine which mergers could be controlled should not be the same for the distribution sector and for the manufacturing sector. Indeed, they pointed out that if in most cases manufacturers compete at the national level, competition among distributors is mostly local. Therefore they argued that a merger between two distributors could well limit competition even if it could not be controled because it did not meet the market share criterion written into the law. They further argued that although a large manufacturer might easily have a market share superior to 40% of the national market, not even the largest distributors, who wield considerable buying power (and occasionally have a dominant position at the local or regional level), account for 40% of the retail sales of any given category of goods at the national level.

The clamour of manufacturers convinced that merger legislation was unfair to them, was thus based on their fear of the growing concentration in the distribution system as well as on the fact that if merger legislation could be used to prevent manufacturers from gaining "too much selling power", it could not, in fact, be used to prevent large distributors from gaining "too much buying power".

In December 1985 some changes making it easier to control mergers were introduced in the merger legislation. An amendment to the 1977 competition Law (loi n° 85-1408 du 30 decembre 1985) provided that thereafter any merger, whether horizontal or non horizontal, in which the merging firms bought or sold more than 25% of a product at the national level or on a substantial part of the national market could be controlled if it was likely to decrease competition.

However, for two reasons the amendment to the 1977 law did not quite meet the demands of the manufacturers: first, it was obvious that very few retailers, if any, bought or sold more than 25% of a product at the national or even at the regional level; second, the amendment made it easier for the government to control horizontal mergers among manufacturers since merger control could now be applied whenever the merging firms had market share greater than 25% of a market.

A more significant step towards meeting the demands of the manufacturers was achieved by the 1986 ordinance through the adoption of a provision enabling the government to control mergers that are likely to affect competition whenever the combined total sales of the merging firms is larger than seven billion francs (and provided that the pre-merger total sales of at least two of the parties to the merger was larger than two billion francs) even if the combined market share of the firms involved does not meet the 25% requirement. The significance of this change in merger control law cannot be explained by economic reasoning since, as is well known, there is no direct relationship between the absolute size of a firm and its market power. There is thus no a priori reason to believe that a merger between two firms might impair competition for the sole reason that their absolute size is large. However, as the total sales of a number of distributors in France exceed two billion francs, this provision will make it easier for the government to control at least some mergers in the retail sector.

Abuse of buying power

The debate on the necessity of finding ways to curb "abuses of buying power" was triggered in 1983 and 1984 by the fact that some large distributors (acting either individually or through common buying agencies) refused to buy (or rather refused to continue to carry) some brand food products or beverages unless they were granted special additional (discriminatory) discounts by the manufacturers concerned. In each case, the branded products involved accounted for a minute proportion of the total sales of the distributors. It was also obvious that although these distributors held a significant share of the market of the product at the retail level (say between 10% and 2%), they could not be considered to have a dominant position either as buyer or as seller. Yet, for a manufacturer the sales of the brand product to one of those distributors could represent a major part of its total sales.

The manufacturers claimed they had no choice but to grant the discounts requested by the distributors (or by the common buying agencies) and thus ultimately face bankruptcy.

With this controversy in mind, and because it also wanted to alleviate what it considered a growing imbalance in the economic relationship between manufacturers and large distributors, the Chirac administration introduced a provision in the 1986 ordinance making it illegal for firms (even if they do not have a dominant position on the market) to abuse their economic bargaining power vis à vis other firms (suppliers or customers) when those other firms are dependent on them and when the abuse constitutes a restraint of competition. The ordinance states, among other things, that the discontinuation, by a firm, of an established commercial relationship with a dependant firm because the latter refuses unjustified commercial demands could be considered such an abuse.

The introduction of this provision in the ordinance on competition suggests two comments.

First, one could argue that the fact that a firm (Manufacturer A) is dependant on another firm (one of its suppliers or one of its distributors: firm B) tells us nothing about the general market power of firm B and the ability of firm B to impair competition. Therefore, there is no reason to think a priori that the behaviour of firms holding other firms in their dependency is more likely to be anticompetitive than the behaviour of firms which do not hold other firms in their dependency. Thus the logic of this provision is very remote from the logic of competition and might even be considered in contradiction with it if it were used to freeze commercial relationships between suppliers and customers.

Second, the concept of dependency between a supplier and a buyer is, to say the least, a difficult one to define. If a supplier has chosen to sell all of his output to one particular distributor and has adapted its products to fit the needs of the customers of this particular distributor when he could have chosen a different strategy (such as selling its products to a variety of distributors) should be considered as dependent on his distributor in spite of the fact that his lack of strategic flexibility (at least in the short run) is the result of his own doing?

Individual practices

The question of whether to do away with the four main prohibitions of "individual practices" (price discrimination, refusal to deal, resale price maintenance, reselling at a loss) or to keep them on the books was hotly debated in the government and business communities.

Because the government had at long last realised the difficulties and the inadvisability of enforcing the per se prohibition, it was decided, at the end of 1985, to amend the 1945 ordinance on this point. From December 1985 on (loi n° 85-1408 du 30 decembre 1985), price discrimination was prohibited only if it was likely to impair competition. This change in legislation which gave more freedom to suppliers in their pricing policy was, however, opposed both by small distributors and by some manufacturers of standardised brand products (in particular in the food and beverage industries) because they felt that the relaxing of the rule put them in a weaker position to resist the demands of price discounts by powerful distributors. They argued that, contrary to government belief, what was actually needed was a more rigid enforcement of the per se prohibition on price discrimination and stiffer penalties.

This debate continued with renewed intensity during the preparation of the 1986 ordinance on price freedom and competition. The new (Chirac) administration, which felt that per se prohibition of price discrimination was basically inconsistent with its aim to promote competition and freedom of pricing gave in neither to the demands of manufacturers worried by the buying power of some distributors, nor to the demands of traditional small-scale distributors. It argued that new means to fight illegitimate demands by large-scale distributors had been written into the ordinance (through the prohibition of abuses of situations of dependency and by the possibility of controlling mergers in the retail sector) and that a return to the per se prohibition of price discrimination was therefore unnecessary.

The abandonment of per se prohibition of refusal to sell in the 1986 ordinance on price freedom and competition can be considered as a victory for the manufacturers because such a prohibition was considered to be contradictory with the ordinance's main goal of promoting economic freedom.

One should note, though, that unjustified discriminatory practices on the part of suppliers, unjustified discriminatory demands on the part of buyers and refusal to sell remain civil offences under French competition law.

The per se prohibition of two other "individual" practices (resale price maintenance and reselling at a loss) were also maintained in the 1986 ordinance.

The justification offered for the per se prohibition of resale price maintenance was that it restrains intra-brand competition at the retail level. One may assume that beyond this rather weak justification, public policy makers also continue to favour per se prohibition of resale price maintenance because they still have the misguided impression that allowing this practice would fuel inflation.

Although per se prohibition of reselling at a loss is clearly anticompetitive, this measure was favoured as an attempt to protect traditional small distributors from the rigors of competition with the larger distributors. Heated discussions on this subject centred around two questions: first, whether distributors should be permitted to resell at a loss when they want to meet the price of a competitor; second, what is meant by reselling at a loss or, in other words, wether year-end quantity discounts should be deducted from invoice prices to determine the actual purchase price below which a good cannot be resold.

On the first point, it should be noted that distributors are permitted to resell at a loss only to meet the "legal" resale price of a competitor. In other words they are prohibited from meeting the price of a competitor who, himself, resells at a loss.

On the second point, the ordinance states that the price to be taken into consideration when determining minimum resale price is the invoice price (to which must be added sales tax and transportation cost). This means that the only discounts or rebates which can be taken into consideration are those which the distributors is entitled to at the moment of his purchase. They do not include the year-end quantity discounts.

The provision regarding the per se prohibition of refusal to resell at a loss thus reflects a partial victory for small distributors who actively lobbied to increase the minimum resale price of their larger competitors.

VII. The Enforcement of Competition Law in France

Having reviewed the history of competition law in France, we now turn to the enforcement of competition statutes since 1977.

At the outset it is worth mentioning a few general features of the enforcement process.

First, one should note that the majority of the cases brought to the Commission de la concurrence and the Conseil de la concurrence have been cases involving "concerted actions, conventions, explicit or tacit understandings or coalitions which are designed for or may have the effect of curbing, restraining or distorting competition in a given market". Those practices are now prohibited by Article 7 of the 1986 ordinance and were formerly prohibited by Article 50 of the 1945 ordinance.

Most of those cases have been horizontal (agreements between potential competitors), but a significant number have been vertical cases (and in particular cases relating to selective distribution contracts).

In contrast, it is worth mentioning that cases involving abuses of market power by firms holding a dominant position (now falling under Article 8 of the 1986 ordinance) have rarely been sent to the Council.

Similarly, as was mentioned earlier, only about fifteen merger cases have been brought to the Commission or to the Council over a twelve year period.

Second, one should point out that until 1986 the Commission de la concurrence and since then the Conseil de la concurrence have played a major role in interpreting the ordinances prohibiting anticompetitive agreements and abuse of dominant positions. Up until 1977, firms and trade organisations whose practices were found in violation of the law could file an appeal against the decision taken by the minister in charge of economic affairs (after the Commission de la concurrence had issued its opinion on the case) with the Administrative Supreme Court. Since 1986, the Paris Court of Appeals reviews the decisions of the Conseil de la concurrence.

In the pre 1986 system, the Minister in charge of economic affairs generally accepted the findings and the analysis of the Commission (although be felt free to inflict more lenient penalties than those recommended by the Commission) and the Administrative Supreme Court, restricted itself either to determining whether the facts of the case had been clearly estahlished or to procedural matters, but it never questioned the interpretation of the Commission or the Minisiter as to what constituted an anticompetitive practice

One of the few instances in which the Administrative supreme Court overturned a ministerial decision concerned a case in which a number of perfume manufacturers had simultaneously refused to sell to a discounter. The Commission considered that this parallel behaviour implied a tacit agreement among the manufacturers despite their claim that they had not entered into such an agreement and that each one of them had an independent reason to refuse to sell to the discounter[2]. The Commission based its reasoning for establishing that there had been a tacit agreement among the manufacturers on the fact that the reasons given by each one of them to explain its (independent) refusal to deal with the discounter were either unsatisfactory or contrary to the facts of the case. Thus the Commission considered that the manufacturers had entered a tacit agreement with the purpose and the effect of restraining price competition among their distributors and it suggested that they should be fined. Following the recommendation of the Commission, the Minister imposed a fine on the manufacturers. However the Administrative Supreme Court ruled that the fact that each manufacturer had not been unable to satisfactorily explain why it had refused to sell to the discounter was insufficient to establish a meeting of minds and therefore an agreement (explicit or tacit) among them.

Similarly, since 1986, the Paris Court of Appeal has confirmed most of the decisions of the Conseil de la concurrence and has never reversed a decision of the Conseil because of disagreement with its interpretation of the substance of the ordinance.

Third, to determine whether a particular agreement is or is not prohibited by Article 7 of the 1986 ordinance, the Conseil de la concurrence generally turn its attention to three issues:

1) does the practice violate the condition of independence of decision making by the firms on the market?
2) does the practice diminish the uncertainty which each firm should face regarding the strategy likely to be followed by other firms?
3) does the practice in any way impede the ability of other firms to enter the market or to expand on the market?

It can thus be said that the Conseil looks at the process through which prices and quantities are determined rather than at the result achieved. For example, in a 1987 decision[3] concerning bakers, the Conseil found that in one area the professional organization of bakers had urged its members to increase the price of bread by a certain amount, in January and July 1986. It was also established that most backers had indeed followed the recommendation of their professionnal organization. The Conseil thus considered that the professional organization had initiated an anticompetitive agreement among its memher firms. In so doing it refused to take into consideration a claim by the organisation that in other areas (in which there was no evidence of an agreement among backers) the price of bread was higher (or increased faster) than in the area considered. The reasoning followed by the Conseil was that the actual level or rate of increase of the price of bread elsewhere was irrelevant since it was established that the process through which it was arrived at was not independent decision making.

Similarly, except in cases involving price discrimination, the Commission and the Conseil have refrained from considering the absolute levels of prices or profit rates as evidence establishing the anticompetitive nature of an abusive practice by a firm having a dominant position. The caution exercised by competition authorities in this area can be explained both by their process approach to competition and fear of appearing to reestablish price controls under the guise of competition law.

Fourth, until 1986 Article 50 of the 1945 ordinance and since then Articles 7 and 8 of the ordinance of 1986, state that agreements whether explicit or tacit among firms etc... and abuses of dominant positions are prohibited only if their object was to impair or restrain competition, or if they had or could have such an effect. Thus the onus of proof rests with the competition authority which must establish for each case why the particular practice examined had an anticompetitive effect, could have had such an effect or had such an objective.

Although the wording of the ordinance seems to preclude a per se approach, the question of whether competition authorities in fact apply a per se approach or a rule of reason approach, largely rests on the kind of reasoning they use to determine whether or not a particular practice at hand is illegal. If the reasoning is so general that it could be applied to all cases in which the practice was found, the approach can be described as a per se approach. If the reasoning is based on specific considerations pertaining to the market examined or to the firms under scrutiny, then the reasoning can be considered to be a rule of reason.

Whenever the Conseil finds that firms have engaged in a practice that *had* the effect or the objective of impairing competition, it follows a rule of reason approach in that its opinion is based on the specific aspects of the market examined. However, in a number of cases in which the Conseil (or previously the Commission) has found firms guilty of having engaged in practices *that could have* had the effect of impairing competition (and therefore relieves itself with the burden of proof that the practice in fact had that effect), it follows a per se approach.

The rule of reason approach can typically be found, in the Conseil's decisions on vertical restrictive agreements (such as selective distribution contracts), or on parallel price increases in concentrated industries or on cases involving abuses of dominant positions. In such cases competition authorities try to establish whether the practices examined could have restrained competition on the particular markets examined.

But some other practices, such as exchanges of information among potential competitors prior to submissions for public tender offers, are treated as per se offences.

Over the years more and more cases have ben decided either on the basis of the fact that the objective of the practices examined was (necessarily) to restrain competition or on the ground that such practices could by their very nature impair competition. Thus the per se approach has gained ground in many instances even if the competition authorities have always been reluctant to admit it.

Fifth, firms or professional organisations found to have entered into an anticompetitive agreement or to have abused their dominant position can be exonerated if it is established that their practice was the direct (and inevitable) consequence of a law or, in certain cases, if it contributed to economic progress. However the ordinance places the burden of proof on the firms or organisations themselves.

Competition authorities have generally been reluctant to admit that a competitive practice which restrained competition could contribute to economic progress. Indeed, the Commission de la concurrence chose to take a restrictive interpretation of Article 51 and to require firms to show first that the alleged economic progress was the direct consequence of the practice examined and, second, that it could not have been achieved by any other means than by the adoption of the practice.

The Conseil de la concurrence has followed the path opened by the Commission de la concurrence regarding the interpretation of Article 51 of the 1945 ordinance by imposing the same standards of proof. It should be noted that the efficiency defence is likely to become even more difficult to use in the future because Article 10 of the 1986 ordinance, which has replaced Article 51 of the 1945 ordinance, restricts the possibility of an efficiency defence to cases in which the anticompetitive practice "reserved an equitable share of the resulting profits to the buyers" and did not "enable the businesses concerned to eliminate competition on a substantial portion of the markets involved".

One of the rare cases in which the Commission de la concurrence applied Article 51 of the 1945 ordinance to an anticompetitive price agreement concerned Interflora[4]. In this case the Commission first considered that an agreement between Interflora and its (independent) affiliated florists throughout France to agree on the price that should be charged on orders concerning standardised flower arrangements restricted competition among the affiliates. The Conseil based its reasoning on the fact that a customer from one city who used the Interflora system to order the delivery of flowers in another town was quoted a unique price in spite of the fact that in that town several affiliates could have executed the order and that they could have competed on prices to fulfill the order if they had not been bound by the agreement. However the Conseil also considered that striking down the price agreement among Interflora and its affiliate would lead to a significant increase in information costs for consumers wishing to place a long distance flower delivery order since they would then have to establish contact themselves with the Interflora affiliates of the town in which they wanted to send their flowers. This increased cost would in turn decrease demand for the type of service created and provided by Interflora. In other words the Conseil considered that the restriction to competition was in fact a necessary condition for permitting this particular type of service.

VIII. Horizontal Agreements

A wide array of practices such as price fixing among competitors, price recommendations by trade organisations, market sharing and collusion on tender offers, co-ordinated attempts to exclude competitors or importers, exchange of informations among competitors, etc... fall in this category.

Explicit agreements

Over a ten year period (1977-1988), explicit price and market sharing agreements among competitors represent slightly more than a quarter of all the established violations of French competition law. Collusions in tender offers represent roughly 20% of all cases submitted to competition authorities.

Market sharing agreements, although not uncommon, do not warrant a particular comment other than the fact that they are in fact treated as per se illegalities.

Price agreements are more common and also more varied. The approach of competition authorities in this area deserve further comments.

Under the general heading of explicit price agreements, one should distinguish among explicit agreements among competitors to fix prices actually charged, explicit agreements among competitors to determine tariffs when substantial rebates are common practice, establishment and publication of recommended or suggested tariffs by trade or professional organisations, and the exchange of informations on future prices among competitors.

1) Explicit agreements among competitors to fix prices actually charged, price increases or profit margins are treated as per se offences at least since 1985. Reflecting its view on this matter in its 1987 annual report, the Conseil de la concurrence stated: "its strong attachement to independent decision making in the price area. Indeed, this independance is a necessary condition for the existence of price competition which - although it is but one form of competition - is nevertheless determining factor in forcing firms to be as efficient as possible".

French competition authorities consider that such practices violate the law even if the firms party to the agreement represent only a fraction of the suppliers of the good or the service considered on the market. As a matter of fact, in many cases their decision will not give a precise description of the market identifying all the suppliers (although it will always precisely define the product or the service considered).

This position could be criticised on the grounds that it leads to an inefficient allocation of resources in the enforcement of the competition law, since competition authorities have to busy themselves handling, among others, cases in which the social costs of the practices examined were small at best. However one could equally well argue that in a country in which competition policy is relatively new and in which the " spirit" of competition has not yet fully permeated the minds of business executives, the long run benefits to be gained from adopting a tough and clear stand on price fixing might outweigh the short run cost of going after minor infractions by deterring firms that might engage in potentially more harmful practices from doing so.

If a per se rule has generally been applied to horizontal price fixing agreements since 1985, this was not always previously the case. Between 1981 and 1984, the Commission de la concurrence occasionally exonerated some horizontal price agreements (as well as some other horizontal or vertical practices) from the prohibition of Article 50 of the 1945 ordinance because it considered that the actual or potential anticompetitive effect of those agreements was not sufficiently significant[5].

2) Explicit agreements among competitors to determine tariffs even when substantial discounts are offered by the competitors, or the establishment and publication of recommended or suggested tariffs by trade or professional organisations, have also generally been treated as per se offences. Although competition authorities often explain why they think that such practices are prohibited by Article 50 of the 1945 ordinance or by Article 7 of the 1986 ordinance, the reasoning used is usually general and not specific to the case at hand.

As far as concerted actions among potential competitors to determine tariffs are concerned, competition authorities consider that such actions violate the competition law irrespective of whether or not the prices actually charged to consumers were equal to those mentioned on the tariff. Thus, for example, in a 1985 case concerning cardboard manufacturers[6], the Commission de la concurrence, after having established that the firms involved had held meetings to determine common increases in their tariffs went on to say: although it has not been established that this concertation has had an effect (on prices actually charged), it remains that the objective pursued was to encourage an artificial price increase (and that the firms have violated Article 50 of the 1945 ordinance).

In a recent decision on thread manufacturers[7], the Conseil de la concurrence seemed to indicate that its views on this subject will be the same as the views held by the Commission de la concurrence in previous years. In this case a concerted tariff was applied to small customers (representing only two per cent of total demand) whereas large rebates were granted by the suppliers to other buyers; there was no evidence that the amount of the rebates had been jointly determined. The Conseil found the tariff agreement among the manufacturers to be a violation of the law; it noted that it had an effect on some customers; but it also went on to say that "furthermore, if, as the parties claim, there were differences between the tariffs and the actual prices charged by each firm to other customers, it remains that the concerted tariffs could be used as a common basis for negotiations between suppliers and customers (and therefore could have an anticompetitive effect)".

The reasoning followed by the Conseil de la concurrence regarding the publication of recommended prices by trade organisations appears quite clearly in a 1987 decision concerning architects[8]. In its decision, the Council explained that " besides their purpose, such tariffs may have an anticompetitive effect,......, in that they may decrease the incentive (of architects) to compute their costs individually (and to determine their prices).This potentiality is independent of the number of (firms) that actually apply the tariffs".

Commenting its views on the subject on a more general level, the Conseil de la concurrence wrote in its 1987 report: the publication by trade organisations of price lists, price recommendations or indications on prices to be charged, is prohibited, even in the absence of pressure on the professionals involved to follow the recommendations, because by giving an indication to all firms about the level of what is considered by the profession as a "normal price or price increase, the trade organisations may give an incentive to some or all of those firms to actually adopt those prices or price increases".

Finally one should note that horizontal explicit agreement by retailers to boycott manufacturers so as to protect their profit margins are not infrequent and are considered to be illegal per se. One celebrated case of this type concerned the relationship between pharmacists and pharmaceutical firms[9].

The profession of pharmacist is strictly regulated in France. Pharmacists have a monopoly on the sale of prescription drugs and the maximum price-cost margin on those products is determined by the government. Finally, pharmacists must respect a code of ethics which, among other things, prevents them from substituting other drugs for drugs prescribed by doctors and prohibits them from engaging in "non confraternal" behavior. Pharmacists have always interpreted their code of ethics as meaning that they shoul not engage in price competition. Therefore they stick to the maximum price-cost margin allowed on prescription drugs. At the end of the seventies, when Clin Midi, a large pharmaceutical firm, decided to launch a line of generic prescription drugs, French pharmacists became alarmed because they realised that given the comparatively low price of generic prescription drugs they risked a decrease in their revenues. As pharmacists can neither increase the price-cost margin charged for those drugs nor refuse to sell them if they were prescribed, they decided, with the help of their tade organisations, to refuse to carry all the Clin Midi non prescription drugs products that they previously sold. After six months of this concerted boycott, Clin Midi decided to discontinue the production and sale of generic prescription drugs and pharmacists lifted their boycott. Subsequently, the pharmacists trade organisations were found guilty of having engaged in anticompetitive practices and were fined by the Minister. However Clin Midi never resumed its production of generic prescription drugs.

Tacit agreements and parallel behaviour

Since 1977, French competition authorities have repeatedly stated that evidence of parallel behaviour among competitors (for example simultaneous increases in prices or simultaneous refusal to sell to a discounter or absolute stability of market shares) is not sufficient to demonstrate the existence of a tacit agreement among them and that it must also be established either that "a meeting of minds" lies behind and explains the parallel behaviour observed or that it "cannot be explained by other considerations"[10].

In various cases, competition authorities considered that the observed parallelism of behaviour was insufficient to establish a tacit agreement prohibited by the ordinance because each of the firms involved had an interest in pursuing the practice independently of whether or not its competitors pursued the same practice.

For example, in 1982 the Commission de la concurrence did not consider that the fact that various watch manufacturers had simultaneously refused to sell to a discounter [11] was sufficient to establish a meeting of the minds among them. Indeed it considered that the pressure exercised by traditional distributors on each of their suppliers because they did not want to carry products if they had to compete on those products with the discounter, gave each of the manufacturers a sufficient personal reason to refuse to sell to the discounter, irrespective of the attitudes of the other watch manufactures.

In other cases competition authorities were satisfied that a given example of parallel behaviour was necessarily the result of a tacit agreement, as no other explanation could be found. One such case occurred in 1983 when the Commission de la concurrence examined the pricing behaviour of five brick manufactures in the south of France who had simultaneously increased their prices in the same proportion six or seven times over a two year period[12]. In its opinion, the Commission determined that the structures and the costs of the firms were not identical and that the price of substitutes did not prevent the firms from being profitable. It then stated "when firms belonging to the same industry increase their prices simultaneously and more rapidly than their costs (increase which implies that each one of them could have deferred its price increase or increased its prices less than it did) and when, furthermore, those price increases are on numerous occasions simultaneously and strictly identical (which excludes the possibility that they happened by chance or that they resulted from a competitive process), one must conclude that those price increases results from an anticompetitive agreement prohibited by article 50 of the 1945 ordinance".

However, the number of cases in which competition authorities concluded that a parallel behaviour by several firms implied a tacit agreement is relatively small for two reasons.

First, as was mentioned earlier, the Administrative Supreme Court insisted that proof of a meeting of the minds had to be a direct proof and could not be based only on the fact that the firms' explanation of their parallel behaviour was unsatisfactory.

Second, the competition authorities have had difficulties applying the "meeting of the minds standard" to cases of oligopolistic industries (with homogeneous products and near perfect information) in which parallel behaviour is frequently observed. Indeed, in those industries, the parallel behaviour of firms can be due to the fact that each one decides independently to follow an oligopoly strategy.

Thus, for example, when the Conseil de la concurrence examined the pricing behaviour of the two trench cigarette paper manufacturers (used by consumers who roll their own cigarettes), it observed that they had identical prices and had increased those prices at the same periods nine consecutive times over a two year period[13]. If the firm initiating the increase was not always the same, the other firm always followed within a few days. Each of the firms, however, argued that the reason it had always followed the price increases initiated by its competitor was simply that it could not gain anything from not doing so because the only possible result of a refusal on its part to follow its competitor would have been an immediate cancellation of the price increase by the other firm. Thus, they argued they had not "tacitly agreed" to cancel price competition but had separately recognised their interdependency in this area and had competed through other means, most notably through advertising campaigns aimed at the distributors. Because the evidence showed that distributors and consumers were not very sensitive to the absolute level of price but were very sensitive to price differences between the two manufacturers and because it also showed that market shares were not constant over time in spite of the identity in prices, the competition council considered that it was not established that they had engaged in a prohibited practice.

Exchanges of information

Whereas exchange of information on price to be charged are in fact treated as per se illegalities, the exchanges of information on variables other than prices (such as costs of raw materials, wages etc.) are examined through a rule of reason.

IX. Vertical Restrictive Agreements

For political reasons that have been explained previously, resale price maintenance is prohibited per se independently and is handled by the regular courts rather than by the competition authorities.

Other vertical restrictive agreements such as exclusive dealerships or selective distribution contracts can fall under Article 50 or 7 of the ordinances which prohibit all "conventions" (i.e. contracts) which have the objective or can have the effect of impairing competition.

However, whereas horizontal agreements are mostly treated by competition authorities as per se offences, a rule of reason is used to assess the impact of selective or exclusive distribution contracts on competition.

As the cases of selective distribution systems examined by the competition authorities have been far more numerous than the cases of exclusive distribution, the following discussion will center on the treatment of the first type of cases.

The analysis of French competition authorities on this subject have always been close to that of the European Court of Justice as expressed in its decision Metro II[14].

Selective distribution contracts have contradictory effects on competition.

First, they reduce competition among the distributors of the same product (intra-brand competition) and thus give each of them an incentive to push sales of the product considered (for example through the provision of some specific services that they would not provide if their expected profit margin was lower).

Second, the existence of such restrictive agreements may increase or reflect the intensity of inter-brand competition in various ways.

Third, the efficiency effect of selective distribution contracts (or other vertical restrictions of trade) depends on how much marginal and infra-marginal consumers value the services provided by the distributors.

The consequences of restrictive distribution systems on competition and on consumer welfare are thus complex and raise several questions. Do they provide consumers with a broader range of products available? Does the increase in services at the retail level increase consumer welfare? Does the increase in prices stemming from the lessening of competition at the retail level merely equals the cost of the added services to the consumer or does it enable distributors to enjoy monopoly profits?

Competition authorities have not tackled all the afore mentioned issues when dealing with selective distribution systems. They have mainly directed their efforts at establishing rules that would prevent manufacturers from limiting the ability of distributors to determine their pricing policy independently or from rejecting a priori low-margin distributors in their networks. Thus, contrary to what economic theory suggests, vertical restraints of trade in general, and selective distribution systems in particular, have been analysed primarily through their effects on competition at the distributors level.

In its 1984 report[15] the Commission de la concurrence established some ground rules in its comments on a case involving the selective distribution of perfume in speciality shop by numerous manufacturers.

It first considered that for a particular selective distribution system to be potentially anticompetitive, the manufacturer involved had to have a dominant position on the market of the product or a large number of competing manufacturers had to distribute their products through such a system.

In cases in which the selective distribution agreement could impair competition, both the Commission de la concurrence and the Conseil de la concurrence have imposed similar constraints: the manufacturer must not impose a resale price; the requirements set by the manufacturer for accepting a distributor must be explicit, objective and verifiable; the manufacturer must not exclude a priori any type of retailers which could technically meet the requirements set by the manufacturer; the technical requirements defined by the manufacturers must not be used in a discriminatory way to exclude low margin distributors.

Using this approach, competition authorities ruled that selective distribution systems fell within the prohibition of anticompetitive agreements in the perfume sector and in the cosmetics sector[16] whereas they had not impaired competition in the the tennis raquette[17] or in the wind sail sectors[18] (because in the latter sectors only a small number of manufacturers representing a small share of the market distributed their product through selective distribution systems).

The case relating to the distribution of cosmetics by pharmacists deserves further attention.

A number of pharmaceutical firms distribute their most successful and well-known cosmetic products in pharmacies. Typically their distribution contracts provide that those products were to be distributed only by pharmacists who, as we saw earlier, do not compete among each other on prices. For a member of years large distributors have tried to gain access to these products and have denounced the selective distribution systems used by their manufacturers as being anticompetitive, on the grounds that it unnecessarily suppressed intra-brand competition at the retail level. Although it is likely that the manufacturers refused to sell to large distributors because they knew that as soon as they accepted an order from one of them, pharmacists would refuse to carry their products, there was no evidence of a threat of a concerted boycott analogous to the one that had been found in the generic product case. Thus when the manufacturers' distribution contracts came under the scrutiny of the Conseil de la concurrence, the manufacturers' defence was based on the fact that cosmetic products were dangerous products requiring counselling that only licensed pharmacists were capable of giving. Additionally the manufacturers claimed that inter-brand competition was strong and that their distribution arrangements did not significantly restrain competition. Finally, the manufacturers also pointed out that the cosmetics they sold through pharmacists were competing with cosmetics from other manufacturers who had chosen not to sell through pharmacists but through large retail stores. The distributors on their part claimed that they were willing to abide by any condition imposed by the manufacturer (such as hiring competent salesmen with a degree in pharmacy), that the cosmetics they could sell did not really compete with the cosmetics sold through pharmacies since brand names differentiated them and were a major determinant of demand.

The Conseil de la concurrence came to the conclusion that the cosmetics sold by manufacturers who distributed only through pharmacists were not close substitutes of other cosmetics distributed through large-scale retailers as evidenced by the fact that there was a persistent wide difference in prices between the two categories of cosmetics. Having thus determined the boundaries of the specific market examined (i.e. cosmetics sold in pharmacies), the Conseil de la concurrence then considered that the clauses of the distribution contracts which reserved the distribution of those cosmetics to pharmacists violated Article 7 of the 1986 ordinance on prices for two related reasons. On the one hand, such clauses completely eliminated intra-brand competition since pharmacists did not compete on prices. On the other hand, they prevented distributors who were not pharmacists from carrying such goods even if those distributors were technically able to provide the kind of sale services (such as counselling) that the manufacturers desired. In its decision, the Conseil ordered the manufacturers to spell out the technical objective and verifiable requirements to be accepted in their distribution networks and to sell to any distributor (whether or not be was a pharmacist) who met these requirements.

X. Abuse of Dominant Position

It is first necessary to recall the texts of Article 50 of the ordinance of 1945 and Article 10 of the ordinance of 1986 on this subject.

The last paragraph of Article 50 of the ordinance of 1945 prohibited "the practices of a firm or a group of firms having, on the domestic market, or on a substantial part of the domestic market, a dominant position characterised by a monopoly situation or by an obvious economic power, when those practices are designed for or may have the effect of curbing, restraining or distorting the regular working of a market".

Article 10 of the 1986 ordinance prohibits "the abusive exploitation by a firm or a group of firms of its dominant position on the domestic market or a substantial part of the domestic market when they are designed for or may have the effect of curbing, restraining or distorting competition" [19].

Because these ordinances do not refer explicitly to monopolisation or to attempts to monopolise, French competition authorities have had more leeway to censor anticompetitive practices of powerful firms than competition authorities in some other countries.

Four issues are of importance in relationship with those prohibitions:

1) how do competition authorities define a "domestic market" or "substantial part" of such a market?
2) what criteria are used to define the existence of a dominant position?
3) what kind of practices are found to be in violation of the ordinances?
4) what kind of remedies can be applied in cases of abuses of power by firms holding a dominant position?

Definition of relevant markets

Competition authorities use the traditional criteria of economic analysis to define a market, although hard data on cross price elasticities between various goods or services are rarely available. They thus take into consideration factors such as the technical possibility to satisfy similar demands by various means[20], similarities in prices to consumers, identity in the determinants of demand over time[21], differentiation of products or of distribution channel[22], brand differentiation[22], availability of the products or services offered by different suppliers for a group of consumers, etc...

French competition authorities have generally tended to define markets narrowly. This is particularly obvious for cases in which some brand products of a particular kind are sold through certain distribution channels (such as traditionall distributors) whereas less-notorius products of the same kind are sold through other distributions channels (such as discounters). In these cases, competition authorities have tended to consider that the combination of brand differentiation and differentiation of distribution channels reduces competition between products to such an extent that they can be considered to be on different markets. Thus, for example, the Commission de la concurrence concluded in one case that manufacturers selling pickles and mustard under their brand names through neibourghood grocery stores were not on the same market as manufacturers selling mustards and pickles through discount stores under the distributors brand name[23].

For a number of years the Commission de la concurrence hesitated as to the proper definition of markets in geographical terms when it came to establishing whether or not a firm had a dominant position. The difficulty arose from the fact that in certain cases it was obvious that consumers did not or could not substitute a particular kind of good or service provided by suppliers in a geographical area to goods or services of the same kind provided by suppliers established elsewhere. However, as was mentioned earlier, the 1945 price ordinance referred to anticompetitive practices of firms holding a dominant position on "a domestic market or a substantial part of a domestic market". The legal question was then whether or not a market that happened to be restricted geographically could be considered to be a "domestic" market or whether the law only applied to nation-wide markets.

The hesitation of the Commission is clearly visible in its 1979 report which indicates: "The law states that it is possible to control the practices of a firm holding a dominant position on a substantial part of a domestic market. If the law is interpreted in a narrow sense, it could seriously hamper the control of practices of firms holding a dominant position at the local level, which is a common situation particularly in trade and services. However the Commission has considered in one case that if by nature, or because of legal constraints on the mobility of consumers across suppliers, a market is limited geographically to an area, the law can be applied to a firm holding a dominant position on the local market only if it also holds other local dominant positions on a substantial part of the domestic territory". To arrive at this conclusion, however, the Commission used a rather confusing approach, first establishing the existence of separate "local" markets on which the firm examined had a dominant position and then aggregating those local markets into a "domestic" market on which the firm also had a dominant position because of the large number of local dominant positions it held.

Reasoning of this nature were applied to two cases, one dealing with water distribution systems[24] and the other dealing with undertakers' services[25]. In France, each municipality can choose to grant a concession for the exploitation of one or the other (or both) services to a private firm. In such cases, consumers are faced with a monopoly since either for technical reasons (in the case of water) or for legal reasons (in the case of undertakers' services) they cannot contract with a firm established in a town other than that in which they live. The Commission then held that each local market was separate from the others because consumers could not substitute services offered elsewhere to those offered locally. However, it did not stop there for its assessment of dominant positions. In each of the cases, it considered that since the same firm had been chosen by a number of municipalities that firm held a dominant position on the "domestic market" of those services, thereby contradicting its earlier analysis.

However, over the years French competition authorities came to accept more readily the idea that a market separate from other markets could be considered to be a "domestic" market even if it happened to be a local one. Thus, in 1986, in a case concerning the local and regional press [26], the Commission de la concurrence considered that the different local editions of the same daily newspaper were not substitutes because readers of one town were not interested in the local news of another town (and because each edition was sold only in the relevant town). It thus held that the newspaper involved operated simultaneously on different markets and examined whether or not it had a dominant position on each of those markets.

Criteria used to establish the existence of a dominant position

The criteria used by competition authorities to define the existence of a dominant position on a relevant market by a single firm do not warrant a long commentary. The importance of the market share is examined both in absolute terms and relative to the market share of the competitors of the firm considered. However, a large market share is considered in itself insufficient to establish a dominant position.

In addition to market share, competition authorities also take into consideration factors which may affect the possibility for competitors to develop their market shares or for potential entrants to actually enter the market considered: upward or downward vertical integration of the firm under investigation, superior management, technical superiority or product and image differentiation.

Thus, for example, the Commission de la concurrence considered that Interflora had a dominant position on the long distance flower selling market[27] not only because it had a large market share (eight times larger than the share of its main competitor) but also because it had a strong image and because it had contracted on an exclusive basis with the best-located flower shops in France (before the appearance of its competitor) making it extremely difficult for this competitor to develop its market share even if it managed to increase its own network of affiliated flower shops.

Beyond these criteria, to assess the existence of a dominant position, French competition authorities also take into consideration whether or not the firm examined belongs to a large financial group or holds monopoly power on unrelated markets. Competition authorities assume implicitly that firms with significant market shares and large financial means are perceived by potential entrants or smaller competitors as likely to use predatory pricing to prevent the emergence of competition. Thus barriers to entry in an industry are assumed to be more important (and therefore the position of an already established firm with a large market shares more dominant), ceteris paribus, when the firm under consideration is "financially" powerful. The wisdom of such an approach will be discussed below when we consider how competition authorities define "abuses" of firms holding a dominant position.

Before turning to this question a last comment should be made about the definition of dominant firms. The 1945 and 1977 ordinances prohibit anticompetitive behaviour by firms "or group of firms" holding a dominant position on a market. There has been a fair amount of controversy on the definition of what constitutes a "group" of firms. The main question raised was whether or not a tight oligopoly could be considered to be "group of firms" holding a dominant position. The Commission de la concurrence did not hesitate to give a positive answer to that question in 1979[28]. This rather loose interpretation of the law enabled the Commission to declare illegal what it considered to be parallel anticompetitive behaviour in oligopolies even when there was no evidence of an explicit or tacit agreement between the firms involved. However in recent years competition authorities have considered that different firms held a joint dominant position only in two cases: when the firms involved belonged to the same financial group or when they had entered an anticompetitive agreement[29].

Anticompetitive practices of firms holding a dominant position

A large number of cases in which a firm (or a group of firms) holding a dominant position was found to have engaged in anticompetitive practice involved alleged attempts to drive a competitor off the market or to prevent entry through predatory pricing behaviour.

Empirical evidence seems to suggest that well-entrenched, financially powerful firms are occasionally willing to follow such a strategy when confronted with new competitors.

While some may argue that the adoption of a low price strategy by a dominant firm confronted with a new competitor results in an improvement of the price/quality ratio for consumers, and therefore increases consumer surplus, it would seem that the positive effect of such a strategy can be short lived if the entrant is driven off the market. What is more, if successful vis-à-vis one particular entrant, this strategy can also have the long-run effect of discouraging any other potential entrant from trying to enter the market. Thus the short-run advantages to competition must be compared to the long-run disadvantages.

An example of such a case was examined by the Commission de la concurrence in a general opinion concerning the daily regional and local press[30]. In this sector a small number of powerful regional newspapers publish several local editions, which each have a dominant position or a monopoly in an area or in a given town. Because these large regional newspapers do not usually invade each others territory, the main source of potential competition in a given town comes from small local newspapers with limited ability to incur losses for a long period of time without going bankrupt Thus, when such competitors appear or when small, already established newspapers try to increase their circulation, the dominant firm can be tempted to selectively increase the number of pages of the local edition concerned, to decrease its price for consumers, and to reduce advertising rates, thereby pushing the entrant towards bankruptcy.

The Commission de la concurrence qualified its censorship of such practices by stating that if price discrimination among local editions of the same newspaper was not objectionable in itself, it could become a prohibited practice for a firm holding a dominant position when the objective pursued by the firm was not to meet competition but to prevent entry or to drive a competitor off the market The Commission added that only a case by case examination of the facts could enable it to decide whether a price decrease by a dominant firm faced with competition improved competition or hampered it.

The Commission de la concurrence also examined a case of predatory behaviour in a related sector ("shoppers") [31]. In that case the dominant firm launched new publications with the explicit aim of driving off the market two newly established newspapers in two different areas by using discriminatory low advertising rates (well below average costs). The small entrants did go bankrupt whereupon the dominant firm increased its advertising rates by 400% in one area and by 1500% in the other. This behaviour was found to be in violation of the prohibition of abuses of dominant position.

In another case the Commission de la concurrence found a group of dominant firms guilty of abuse of market power for having used predatory pricing behaviour to force smaller competitors to enter a price agreement with them[32]. In that case, which involved the four largest manufacturers of steel rods used for strengthening concrete, the dominant firms happened to be subsidiaries of the two nationalised steel makers. Having entered a price agreement with Italian importers, they quickly realised that the Italian importers were "cheating" by offering discounts. The dominant firms then drove the price of steel rods down to a level below the price of the steel used to manufacture them for a period of six months. During this entire period the Italian importers stayed out of the French market. Having shown their strength (which was largely based on the fact that they did not care about losses because of their status as public firms) the domestic firms allowed the Italians back on the French market in the context of a new price agreement.

Remedies in cases of abuses of dominant position

In most of the cases involving abuses of dominant position, the competition authorities issued an injunction prohibiting the firm or the group of firms involved from continuing the abusive practice and inflicted a fine.

The ordinance of 1986 (as the ordinance of 1945 did previously) state that structural remedy (such as the dismemberment of the firm involved) can be used only when the dominant position of the firm was acquired through merger and when there is proof that the abuse of dominant position is an inevitable consequence of the merger that gave the firm its dominant position. In such a case competition authorities cannot act directly but can ask the Minister of Finance to undo the merger that led to the acquisition of a dominant position. Because French competition authorities never came across a case where they felt that the abusive practice was an inevitable consequence of the dominant position of the firm involved (and because in many cases the dominant position itself did not result from a merger) they never asked for a structural remedy.

XI. Merger Control

Since 1977 merger control has not been an important tool in the enforcement of competition law in France. An average hardly one merger a year has been sent for review to the Commission or to the Conseil de la concurrence by the Minister in charge of economic affairs, who has sole authority to initiate the control procedure.

If the French government has progressively abandoned the aggressive pro-merger industrial policy it favoured in the sixties, there is still a lingering feeling among public officials that large size firms are better able to withstand international competition than smaller firms and that therefore, in general, one should not interfere with the attempts of French firms to increase their size through mergers.

Most of the mergers which have been sent for review to the Conseil de la concurrence over the last few years involved a foreign firm acquiring either a French firm or the French subsidiary of another foreign firm. This led to claims that merger control was in fact used by the Minister in charge of economic affairs to further protectionist goals rather than to further competition. Thus, for example, the acquisition of Spontex by Minnesota Mining and Manufacturing was opposed by the Minister in 1989 (in spite of the fact that the Conseil had considered that its disadvantages from the point of view of competition were outweighed by its advantages from the point of view of economic progress).

The previous mergers for which the Minister in charge of economics affairs had initiated the control procedure involved the acquisition of the French assets of Rowntree Mackintosh by Nestle in 1989 (the Conseil did not find the merger anticompetitive and the Minister did not oppose it), the acquisition of Saint Louise (a large sugar manufacturer) by Ferruzzi (an Italian agro-food conglomerate) in 1988 and the creation of a joint venture between Colgate Palmolive and Henkel-France (French subsidiary of a German firm), also in 1988. In the latter two cases, the firms decided to abandon their planed mergers (although the Conseil de la concurrence had considered that the Colgate Henkel project to create a joint subsidiary did not qualify as an anticompetitive merger).

No mergers were examined by the Commission de la concurrence in 1985 and in 1986 but it had examined two mergers in 1984, the acquisition of Duolite International by Rhom et Hass France in the chemical sector (the Commission found that the advantages of the acquisition from the point of view of economic progress outweighed its disadvantages from the point of view of competition and recommended that it be allowed; the Minister did not oppose the merger) and the acquisition of Ashland Chemical France by Cabot Corporation in the carbon black industry. In the latter case the Commission de la concurrence considered that the disadvantages of the merger outweighed its advantages and recommended that the merger be prohibited. The Minister opposed the merger but his decision was overturned by the Administrative Supreme Court on procedural grounds.

Whatever one may think of the goals pursued by the Minister of economic affairs in deciding which mergers to control, the competition authorities have tended to stick to strictly technical considerations in their opinions, by seeking answers to four different questions.

The first question is whether or not the merger can be controlled: that is whether the share of the merging firms exceeds 25% (previously 40%) on any market or whether the absolute size of the combined firm exceeds the prescribed level. Thus for example, in 1979, the Commission de la concurrence concluded that a merger between Thorn Electrical Industries (a British manufacturer of TV sets) and Locatel (a TV rental firm) could not be controlled by the Minister because they were operating on the same market (and not on different markets as the government claimed) and did not meet the 40% market share criterion[33].

The second question is whether the merger could have the effect of restraining competition. To answer this question, the competition authorities have taken into consideration concentration on the supply and the demand side, barriers to entry, etc... to assess whether or not it is likely that the merging firms will be able to increase prices as a result of the merger. Thus, for example, in its opinion concerning the proposed merger between 3M and Spontex (two manufacturers of sponges for domestic use having a combined market share of 75%) in 1987, the Conseil de la concurrence based its opinion that the merger was unlikely to reduce competition on three main facts: first there were no significant barriers to entry from the point of view of technology, scale economies or capital costs; second, it appeared that a significant portion of the sponges were distributed through large distributors who wielded significant bargaining power; third, the demand for sponges was bound to decrease with the appearance on the market of new products, paper-derived, manufactured by foreign firms[34].

When it finds that a merger could decrease competition, the Conseil de la concurrence must then ask itself whether or not the merger is likely to contribute to economic progress. Thus it examines whether or not the merger will lead to a decrease in unit costs of production or distribution and to capacity expansion. Looking at the merger from a more dynamic point of view, it also assesses whether or not the merger is likely to result in an increase in the rate of innovation or if will contribute to the diffusion of technological advances. Thus, for example, when the Commission de la concurrence examined the proposed merger between Duolite International S.A. and Rohm et Haas (two manufactures of synthetic resins used in water treatment) in 1984, it considered that the merger contributed to economic progress both because the reorganisation of production would enable the firms to decrease their unit costs by 5% to 7% and because technological innovations developed by one of the firms would be transferred to the other[35].

Finally, the last question competition authorities must answer, and by no means the easiest one, when they have found that an anticompetitive merger contributes to economic progress is whether or not the advantages of the merger outweigh its disadvantages.

XII. Conclusion

Recent change in French competition law must be regarded as a significant step toward promoting competition on French markets to the extent that they abolish price controls, refer the enforcement of competition law to the courts or to an independent quasi-judicial body, and eliminate a number of constraints on the market strategies of firms which previously hampered competition rather than enabling it to run its course.

The importance of these changes is underlined by the fact that they cannot be considered to be the consequence of a haphazard or unexpected evolution (or an "intellectual revolution" as some claimed) resulting from a short-run change in the political persuasion of the administration. Rather these changes are the natural continuation of past change in our legislation and thus reflect a long-run trend towards recognition of the limits of government intervention and of the importance of competition in the market place to insure an efficient allocation of resources.

The importance of the shift towards a stricter enforcement of the ban on anticompetitive practices can be illustrated by the striking increase in the total amount of fines inflicted on firms violating French competition law. These fines went from 4.3 million francs in 1987 to 358 million francs in 1989.

France now considers the fight against anticompetitive agreements and abuses of monopoly power to be a particularly important feature of its economic policy, although it has largely neglected the control of structures. At the same time analysis of the way competition authorities have handled cases examined reveals that an initial tendency to use competition law to regulate markets has given way to an approach which is both more severe (as is clear from the increased frequency with which violators are fined) and less interventionnist. This shift has paralleled an increased sophistication of competition authorities in applying economic theory to antitrust cases.

Because there is now a political consensous as to the usefulness of competition and economic freedom, it is unlikely that this trends will be reversed in the near future. What is more, the acceleration of the construction of Europe in 1993 will mean that the efforts of the Conseil de la concurrence to maintain or restore competition will be supplemented by the spontanenus emergence of new competitive forces, particularly in sectors that have, up to now, remained regulated at the domestic level and been sheltered from the rigors of competition (such as banking, insurance, telecommunication or the airline industries).

Notes

1. *Le défi américain*, Jean Jacques Servan Schreiber, Denoel, Paris, 1967.
2. Décision n. 84-13/DC du Ministre relative à la situation de la concurrence dans le secteur de la distribution sélective des produit de parfumerie, Rapport de la Commission de la concurrence pour l'année 1984, p. 63.
3. Décision n. 87-D-33 relative à des pratiques relevées dans le sectuer de la boulangerie artisanale des Côtes-du-Nord, Rapport du conseil de la concurrence pour l'année 1987, annexe 42, p. 6.
4. Avis de la Commission de la concurrence relatif à la situation de la concurrence dans le secteur de la transmission florale et décision ministerielle, Rapport pour l'année 1985, annexe n. 18, p. 123.
5. Décision n° 81-10/DC du Ministre relative à une entente dans la boulangerie dans le départment de l'Oise et avis, Rapport pour l'année 1981, annexe n° 11, p. 184: Décision n° 81-06/DC du ministre reltive a des pratiques concertées dans le secteur de la réparation automobile et avis, Rapport pour l'année 1981, annexe n° 7, p. 140.
6. Décision n° 85-1/DC relative à des pratiques concertées dans le secteur de la production du carton ondulé et avis, Rapport pour l'année 1985, annexe n° 9, p. 60.
7. Décision n° 88-D-50 relative à des pratiques relevées dans les secteur du fil à coudre, rapport du Conseil de la concurrence pour l'année 1988, annexe n° 54, p. 111.
8. Décision n° 87-D-53 du Conseil de la concurrence relative à la situation de la concurrence dans le domaine des architectes et avis, Rapport pour l'année 1987, annexe n° 62, p. 80.
9. Avis relatif à des pratiques concertées de pharmaciens d'officine pour s'opposer à la commercialisation des médicaments d'orgine et décision n° 81-07/DC du Ministre, Rapport annuel de la Commission de la concurrence pour l'année 1981, p. 194.
10. Rapport annuel de la Commission de la concurrence pour l'année 1981; Rapport annuel du Conseil de la concurrence pour l'année 1987, p. XIV.
11. Décision n° 82-7/DC relative à des pratiques anticoncurrentielles relevées dans la distribution de certains produits horlogers et avis, Rapport pour l'année 1982, annexe n° 11, p. 159.
12. Décision n° 83-6/DC du Ministre relative à la situation de la concurrence dans la production des tuiles et briques dans la région Midi-Pyrénées et avis, Rapport pour l'année 1983, annexe n° 10, p. 191.
13. Décision n° 88-D-02 du Conseil de la concurrence relative à la concurrence dans le secteur de l'approvisionnement des débits de tabac et fourniture accessoires, Rapport du Conseil de la concurrence pour l'année 1988, annexe n° 9, p. 21.
14. See Metro SB-Grossmaerkete II, European Court of Justice, 75/84, October 11, 1986.
15. Avis de la Commission de la concurrence relatif à la situation de la concurrence dans le secteur de la distribution sélective des produits de parfumerie et decision ministérielle, Rapport pour l'année 1984, annexe n° 8, p. 63.
16. Décision du conseil de la concurrence relative à la situation de la concurrence dans la distribution en pharmacie de certains produits cosmétiques et d'hygiène corporelle, Rapport pour l'année 1987, annexe n° 24, p. 43.
17. Avis de la Commission de la concurrence sur la situation de la concurrence dans la distribution des raquettes de tennis et décision ministerielle, Rapport pour l'année 1984, annexe n° 13, p. 112.
18. Avis de la Commission de la concurrence dans la distribution des planches a voile et décision ministerielle, Rapport pour l'année 1984, annexe n° 14, p. 114.
19. As no final decision on cases of "abuses of dependency" have been handed out yet by the Conseil de la concurrence, the following commentaries concern only abuses of market power by firms holding a dominant position.
20. Avis de la Commission de la concurrence a des pratiques anticoncurrentielles dans le secteur de l'assurance construction et décision ministérielle, Rapport pour l'année 1980, an-

nexe n° 6, p. 146.
21. Avis de la Commission de la concurrence relatif à la prise de controle de Locatel par Thorn Electrical Industries, Rapport pour l'année I980, annexe G, p. 89.
22. Décision 87-D-15 relative à la situation de la concurrence dans la distribution en pharmacie de certains produits cosmétiques et d'hygiène corporelle, Rapport pour l'année 1987, annexe n° 24, p. 43.
23. Avis de la Commission de la concurrence relatif à l'absorption de la S.E.G.M.A. par le groupe Générale Occidentale, Rapport pour l'année 1980, annexe H, p. 90.
24. Avis de la Commission de la concurrence relatif à des pratiques constatées dans le secteur de la distribution de l'eau et décision ministérielle, Rapport de la Commission de la concurrence pour l'année 1984, annexe n° 4, p. 108.
25. Avis de la Commission de la concurrence concernant le secteur des pompes funèbres et décision ministérielle, Rapport de la Commission de la concurrence pour l'année 1979, annexe n° 12, p. 60.
26. Avis de la Commission de la concurrence sur les conditions d'application du dernier alinéa de l'article 50 de l'ordonnance n° 45-1483 du 30 juin 1945 à des pratiques d'abaissement sélectif de prix dans le secteur de la presse quotidienne d'information locale, Rapport de la Commission de la concurrence pour l'année 1986, p. 12.
27. Avis de la Commission de la concurrence relatif à la situation de la concurrence dans le secteur de la transmission florale et décision ministéreille, Rapport de la Commission de la concurrence pour l'année 1985, annexe n° 18, p. 123.
28. Avis de la Commission de la Concurrence concernant la diffusion de films cinématographiques et décision ministérielle, Rapport pour l'année 1979, annexe n° 14, p. 176.
29. See, for example, Avis de la Commission de la concurrence relatif à la situation de la concurrence sur le marché des treillis soudés et décision ministérielle, Rapport pour l'année 1985, annexe n° 13, p. 90.
30. Avis de la Commission de la concurrence sur les conditions d'application du dernier alinéa de l'article 50 de l'ordonnance n° 45-1483 du 30 juin 1945 à des pratiques d'abaissement sélectif de prix dans le secteur de la presse quotidienne d'information locale. Rapport de la Commission de la concurrence pour l'année 1986, annexe n° 1, p. 12.
31. Avis de la Commission de la concurrence dans le secteur de la presse gratuite en région Provence Alpes Côte d'Azur et décision ministérielle, Rapport de la Commission de la Concurrence pour l'année 1986, annexe n° 7, p. 51.
32. Avis de la Commission de la concurrence relatif à la situation de la concurrence sur le marché des treillis soudés et décision ministérielle, Rapport de la commission de la concurrence pour l'année 1985, annexe n° 13, p. 90.
33. Avis relatif à la prise de controle de Locatel par Thorn Electrical Industries Ltd, Rapport de la Commission de la concurrence pour l'année 1980, annexe G, p. 89.
34. Avis n° 89-A-05 du Conseil de la concurrence relatif au projet de concentration entre les sociétés Spontex et 3M France dans le secteur des outils d'entretien ménager, rapport du Conseil de la concurrence pour l'année I989, annexe n° 72.
35. Avis relatif au projet de prise de controle de la société Duolite International S.A. par le société Rohm and Haas France S.A., Rapport annuel du Conseil de la concurrence pour l'année 1984, annexe n° 4, p. 42.

7. The Protection of the Market in Italy: The Experience of the Anti-Trust Authority*

FABIO GOBBO and TOMMASO SALONICO

I. Introduction

At the end of 1990 Italy, somewhat belatedly in comparison with the other leading industrial countries, bridged a wide institutional gap in terms of market regulation.

Law No. 287 of 10 October 1990, the 'Anti-Trust Act' established an independent Anti-Trust Authority ("Autorità garante della concorrenza e del mercato"), to guarantee free competition and foster the development of competitive market conditions.

What specifically marks Italy's Antitrust Authority out from other similar bodies in the leading industrial countries is its considerable autonomy and the fact that it is independent of government. This is underscored by the fact that its five-member team is appointed by the Speakers of the two Houses of Parliament (the Chamber of Deputies and the Senate), and that they may not be reappointed for a second term.

The only case where the government may intervene to overrule a decision taken by the Authority is provided by Section 25[1] of the Anti-Trust Act, which empowers the Council of Ministers (in practice the government) to prohibit a "concentration" involving foreign companies if there are essential reasons for doing so in the interests of the domestic economy subject, however, to the principle of reciprocity of treatment between States.

But the power vested in the government by Section 25(1) is quite different. For this is not a decision-making power over-riding the Authority's, but a regulatory power. Under this sub-section, the government may issue further general criteria in addition to those already established by the Act, enabling the Authority exceptionally to authorize "concentrations" that should otherwise be prohibited under the ordinary rules, when substantial general interests of the domestic economy are involved within the context of European integration.

The powers vested in the government do not therefore encroach on the autonomy and independence of the Authority's decision-making powers. In every case, the Authority is required to appraise any "concentrations" which are notified, and must also take account of the criteria laid down by the government, with the obligation of ensuring that competition is not eliminated from the market, or that no restrictions are placed on competi-

G. Mussati (ed.), Mergers, Markets and Public Policy, 201–221.
© 1995 *Kluwer Academic Publishers.*

tion that cannot be justified in terms of the general interests of the domestic economy issued by the government.

It is, however, evident that the degree to which the Authority's autonomous decision-making powers are respected in practice depends on the way in which the government exercises its regulatory powers, since the more specific and detailed its regulations, the less scope for discretion will be left to the Authority.

The Authority's work can generally be divided into two main areas: protecting competition, and merely fostering it.

While the former activities can be carried out using the traditional statutory tools and powers relating to competition which other countries also have, it is its promotional work which constitutes one of the Italian Anti-Trust Authority distinctive features, and where its statute-guaranteed independence and autonomy is of decisive importance. The italian legislators - realistically realizing that competition and the sound working of market forces needed protection not only against the conduct of companies but also against distortions and constraints created by the law, regulations or administrative measures - vested the Authority with the power and duty to seek out such situations and bring them to the notice of parliament, government, and public opinion, by publication in the Anti-Trust Authority's own Bulletin (Bollettino dell'Autorità), suggesting appropriate measures to eliminate or prevent these distortions (Sections 21, 22 and 24 of the Act).

II. Measures Adopted to Protect Competition

Drawing on the principles of European Community competition law, the measures adopted to protect competition have coincided in the main with the cases regulated within the Community. The Authority is therefore required to ensure that no agreements are concluded which restrict free competition, or that companies do not abuse their dominant position on the market to the detriment of other companies or consumers, or create or strengthen a dominant position on the market through "concentrations" which are likely to significantly impede competition on a lasting basis.

The very close similarity between the wording of the Community's and Italy's legislation does not, however, lead to an overlapping of jurisdiction or powers. Applying the theory of mutual exclusion, the Italian legislators defined the scope of the Authority's work by exclusion from the application of Community law (Section 1). In practice, however, this criterion can only be easily implemented to control concentrations falling within Community jurisdiction in terms of the turnovers of the companies involved in the operation[1].

With regard to anti-competitive agreements and abuse of dominant position, since the Community has jurisdiction when trade between Member States is jeopardized and competition is impeded in a substantial part of the common market, the borderline between the jurisdiction of the Authority and the Community is not always easy to define. Moreover the principle of mutual exclusion does not prevent the national authorities from directly applying Community law (Articles 85(1) and 86 of the EEC Treaty) before the Commission institutes formal proceedings[2].

Generally speaking, however, it must be noted that relations between the national Authorities and the EC Commission are only very vaguely defined. Some Member States propose that the national Authorities should have more scope for applying Community law governing agreements and the abuse of dominant position in view of the importance of the principle of subsidiarity in relations between the Community and Member States, following the amendments made to the Treaty at Maastricht.

According to the subsidiarity principle, the Community, in areas outside its exclusive jurisdiction, should only takes action when the Member States themselves cannot do so with the required degree of success, so that, for the magnitude and the effects of the measures, that action on the part of the Community itself is likely to be more successful.

Moreover, with regard to controlling concentrations, following the first three years' experience with applying Regulation No. 4064/89, the Commission is inclined to lower the threshold turnover for its jurisdiction, thereby broadening the scope of Community intervention at the expense of the Anti-Trust Authorities of the Member States.

Concentrations

Controlling concentrations is the Authority's main activity in terms of numbers (1,014 concentrations have been examined in three years). This is due to the fact that section 16 of the Act requires any planned concentration to be notified in advance, where the companies concerned have an aggregate domestic turnover of more than 500 billion lire, or when the company which is to be acquired has a domestic turnover in excess of 50 billion lire[3].

Since the turnover of the acquired company is a sufficient basis for requiring notification, operations which are often quite insignificant have to be reported, and companies with a turnover in excess of 500 billion lire are required to report any concentration, however small, which it is planning to effect.

Section 5 of the Act, which is based on Article 3 of the Community Regulation on concentrations, considers the following to be concentrations: a) when two or more undertakings merge; b) when direct or indirect control of the whole or parts of one or more undertakings is acquired by other companies or by other persons controlling an undertaking; c) when a joint venture is created. Since there is no express mention of independent undertakings, it is not been possible to exclude concentrations between non-independent undertakings from the operations to notify , even though it is difficult to envisage any structural changes that they might create that might impede competition.

Like the provisions of Section 16 mentioned earlier, these have greatly added to the Authority's workload[4] and imposed an additional burden on companies. It is to be hoped that they will be amended as soon as possible to make them fully consistent with the Authority's institutional functions[5].

The obligation to submit prior notification is deemed met when it reaches the Authority before the formalities establishing the concentration have been completed. If a concentration is completed before notification has been submitted, any undertaking which fails to notify the Authority (or submits the notification late) may be liable to an administrative fine (Section 19), but once the notification has been made it can then immediately proceed with the concentration. The Authority has the statutory powers not only to prohibit a concentration which would create or strengthen a dominant position on the national market with the effect of eliminating or restricting competition appreciably and on a lasting basis, but also to require steps to be taken to restore conditions of effective competition, and remove any effects that distort it when a concentration has been proceeded.

However, it is now a widespread practice to include a contractual clause suspending the effects of a concentration until the Authority authorizes it.

A concentration may also be suspended by the Authority (Section 19), but only after an investigation has been formally opened: in other words, only when the Authority has ruled that it may be subject to prohibition.

In order to provide legal guarantees, the Act provided very tight deadlines within which the Authority is required to issue a decision: 30 days for a preliminary assessment, where well-founded reasons exist for suspecting that the operation might distort competition, and 45 days (which may be extended once by a further 30-day period) for the final ruling on a particular case following a formal investigation during which both parties have been able to make their respective representations.

The guarantee provided by such tight and absolute deadlines for initiating and completing the investigations is based on the assumption that the information supplied by undertakings in their prior notification is complete, true and accurate. In order to help undertakings comply fully with this obligation, the Authority has produced a special form for notifying concentrations, which contains all the information normally required for an initial assessment of the effects of the operation.

The broad notion of control which the law defines in order to establish which concentrations are subject to assessment by the Authority has proven extremely useful. It coincides substantially with the definition given in Article 3 of the Community Regulation.

This has made it possible to examine operations in which the acquisition of a controlling interest in a company was not guaranteed by the possession of a majority shareholding, but arose in essentially equivalent terms as a result of having taken out leases over the assets of the undertaking[6], or by entering into voting agreements with other shareholders[7], or agreements regarding the appointment of members of the Board of Directors or the Executive Committee.

The Italian legislators also felt the need to exclude from the application of the provisions governing concentrations the purchase of securities by banks or financial institutions being of a temporary nature, and used in connection with the provision of securities brokerage services. However, the conditions laid down for this exclusion are much more stringent than those provided by the Community Regulation, requiring, so long as the securities are in the possession of these institutions, which may never exceed two years (Section 5(2)), they may not exercise voting rights.

When examining concentrations it is essential to identify the relevant market which, in geographic and product terms, provides the context for evaluating the market share which the company will hold following the concentration.

The conceptual benchmark used so far has been to consider the relevant market the one in which, if the company were to become a monopoly, a price could be set by the monopoly-holder which would be substantially higher than a competitive price, enabling him to keep it at that level for a substantial period of time. This approach is useful in order to accurately identify the sphere within which a dominant position can be created, making it necessary to take account of all the information available on the possibilities of substitution open to the purchasers of the product, and on any restrictions on the capacity of competing companies to meet the demand.

In some cases, account has also been taken of the company's supply capacity in order to define the relevant market. Where the production facilities are designed for other products, but could be converted rapidly and without incurring significant costs to produce goods that are satisfactory substitutes for those directly involved in the concentration, account has been taken of the relevant production capacity when establishing the relevant market[8]. Similarly, where there is a wide range of different products in a particular sector, the Authority has identified what prospective purchasers might view as alternatives, carefully examining also the market entry capacity of each of the companies already operating in that sector[9].

In many cases, after identifying the relevant market, with all the appropriate qualifications, a comparison between the market share acquired as a result of the concentration and the market share held by competing companies has made it possible, to conclude that the operation did not create or strengthen a dominant position.

When an examination of the market share does not provide sufficient information to be able to evaluate the concentration within the meaning of Section 6 of the Act, it is examined further in terms of all the other variables that influence the company's market strength.

On the basis of experience gained so far, the following variables may be recalled:

- the capacity of the purchasers of the product to produce it for themselves[10];
- the prospects for a change in the present state of competition among the companies, connected with the developments of the regulations[11];
- the insignificance of barriers to market entry[12].

In only four cases has the Authority held that the notified concentration that substantially raised market entry barriers created or strengthened a dominant position sufficiently to justify prohibiting it. In only two of these cases[13] has the Authority actually prohibited the operation, judging it to be incompatible with the normal development of competition as a result of the increased market strength acquired by the purchaser company. In one of these two cases, the operation related to the acquisition of public telephony equipment manufacturers by companies belonging to a group in which one company was the exclusive provider of the basic telephone service in the field of public telecommunications equipment and systems. The fact that the exclusive carrier of the basic telephone service was not strictly bound to take acquisition decisions on the basis of cost considerations or production efficiency was used by the Authority to conclude that even if it was only potentially possible that, following the take-over, the company's supply policy might be tilted in favour of companies belonging to the group, this in itself represented a substantial and lasting raising of existing market entry barriers such that the development of competition on the equipment market would be substantially reduced.

Two other take-overs[14] were authorized, but with the proviso that specific measures were taken, mainly proposed by the companies themselves, which the Authority held to be appropriate to prevent any substantial and lasting distortion of competition to which the operation would otherwise have given rise.

In one case the companies concerned undertook specific commitments, and since during the course of the investigations the competent Office changed the regulations governing the relevant market, the Authority was able to issue a clearance for that particular take-over, even though it strengthened the dominant position of the purchasing company, on the grounds that the changes that had been made and the commitments that had been entered into were likely to prevent any possibility of substantially eliminating or distorting competition on a lasting basis[15].

Agreements

The number of agreements examined (42 in the first three years) was far smaller than the number of concentrations. The main reason for this was that agreements do not have to be notified, with the result that the investigations only take place when the Authority discovers agreements in the course of its own investigations or when they are reported to it by interested third parties or by government departments. Even though there is no obligation to do so, sometimes the companies actually involved in the agreements bring them to the notify of the Authority. This is a possibility open to them under the Act, which companies can use if they wish to be certain that the agreement is lawful, and knowing that if the Authority does not carry out an investigation to ascertain whether the agreement violates competition law within 120 days of the communication, it cannot subsequently rule against them (Section 13).

In order to acquire the information needed to discover agreements which distort competition, the Authority has conducted many fact-finding investigations into such matters as trading patterns, price trends, or other circumstances suggesting that competition was being impeded or distorted.

These investigations have related to concrete and dairy industries, harbour services, cellular telephones, rolling stock, the high-speed railway and the motion picture industry.

The rules governing agreements differ greatly from those governing mergers. Section 2 of the Act provides that agreements are forbidden whenever their object or effect is to prevent, restrict or substantially distort competition on the national market or in a substantial part of it. This requires the Authority to ascertain any infringements of this prohibition, as the judicial authorities are enjoined to do: indeed, anyone wishing to ascertain whether the law has been broken may apply directly to the courts as an alternative to the Authority (Section 33).

However, the Authority's work is underpinned by wide-ranging investigative powers to enable it to discover all the relevant facts, and by its authority to impose fines of up to 10% of the company's turnover in the case of serious violations, and suspend company operations for up to 30 days in the event of repeated failures to comply with the Authority's rulings.

It also has the power to revoke the statutory prohibition, and authorise otherwise prohibited agreements for a limited period, where it is shown that despite the restrictions on competition there is an improvement in the market supply conditions having the effect of producing substantial benefits for consumers (Section 4). However, any restrictions on competition must be kept down to what is strictly necessary to bring about these benefits.

On the basis of the broad definition of "agreement" provided by Section 2(1) of the Act, the Authority has extended its work to include analyzing any case in which it has been possible to identify the express or tacit intention of two or more companies to regulate market behaviour, with or without creating associations or consortia.

In this way it has taken agreements to comprise the following: accords concluded between individual companies or associations of companies[16], regulations or provisions in the Articles of consortia or consortia companies[17], agreements accessory to mergers[18], exchanges of shareholdings[19], and agreements to establish associations of companies[20], new companies[21] or joint ventures[22].

The Authority has also ruled decisions by consortia companies[23] or associations of companies[24], whether or not taken in implementation of the provisions of their Articles or regulations, to be agreements, expressly emphasizing the relevance of the existence an organization that is able to take decisions binding on all the member companies, independently of the specific legal status of the organization, its objects or purposes, or whether or not the decisions adopted are likely to produce legally binding obligations.

Although most of the agreements examined by the Authority have been designed to distort competition between the participating companies ("horizontal agreements") there have also been examples in which free competition has been distorted as a result of agreements in which restrictions have been imposed on third parties ("vertical agreements")[25].

When appraising agreements, particular attention has been paid to the intensity of the distortion to competition which the Act requires before it can be prohibited, by providing that the object or the effect of the agreement must be such that it substantially distorts competition on the national market or in a substantial part of it. This wording introduces an innovation compared with Article 85 of the EEC Treaty, by not applying the prohibition on agreements that do not impede "workable competition" on the market.

The more stringent provisions governing agreements also apply to concentrations that are shown to be exclusively or mainly designed to make it possible to coordinate the work of the companies involved in them (Section 5 (2)). These are normally cases in which any formal changes that are made as a result of the creation of a joint venture do not really create an economic entity that is able to operate independently on the market, with the result that it is not so much a case of a concentration of the relevant market, as the establishment of a stable organization to coordinate the operating strategies of the parent companies. In the cases examined by the Authority, the main benchmarks referred to have been the criteria laid down by the Community and set out in Notice 90/c 203/06.

The only provision which makes express reference to independent companies is the one excluding from the sphere of concentrations any operations whose main object or effect is the coordination of the actions of the companies concerned. At least here, even the Italian legislator has ruled that cooperation initiatives within the same economic group are irrelevant for the purposes of protecting the market.

Abuse of dominant position

Acquiring a dominant position on the market is still lawful, even with the enactment of the Anti-Trust law. In some areas of the economy special laws have provided restrictions which - at least in theory - are designed to preempt certain positions of strength from emerging on the market (in publishing, broadcasting, relations between corporations and banks, or corporations and insurance companies), but to attain purposes other than to protect market competition.

If a dominant position is created or strengthened as a result of a concentration, the operation is monitored by the Authority but cannot be forbidden unless it can be shown that the dominant position is likely to eliminate or substantially distort competition on a lasting basis.

However, any company that lawfully occupies a dominant market position is under a statutory obligation to act fairly on the market, and is forbidden to abuse that position by exploiting it to acquire advantages which it would not otherwise be able to obtain in a regime of real competition.

Nowhere does the law define "dominant position". The Authority has therefore followed the well-established Community case-law principle that a company occupies a dominant position when it is a position of such economic strength that it is able to prevent effective competition on the market and is able to act quite independently of competitors, customers and consumers.

Abusive practices are therefore prohibited, whether they are to the detriment of present or potential competitors, or suppliers and users.

The Authority is empowered to order a company to refrain from abusive behaviour, and has the same investigative powers to ascertain its existence that it has to appraise agreements and mergers, and when it detects serious violations it may impose penalties.

The cases of abuse dealt with by the Authority clearly reveal the particular nature of Italy's economic structure, especially the State's wide-ranging intervention in the economy in terms both of the activities over which the public sector has a monopoly and of the State's direct market presence. Virtually all the measures taken for abusive conduct was against franchise-holders or corporations controlled by the State.

Three measures were issued[26] against the national telephone carrier, designed to prevent it from exploiting its dominant position as the franchise-holder to broaden its presence on adjacent markets outside the scope of its exclusive franchise (public telephone payment systems, the sale of cellular telephones), and to derive undue advantages from the cellular telephone market using the GSM system to the detriment of other potential competitors.

With regard to an airport handling services franchise-holder[27], the Authority found that it was discriminating between the users of its services in order to favour an Italian airline belonging to the same (State-controlled) group of companies as the handling services franchise-holder, in essence by refusing to allow the other airlines the right to take charge of their own handling services at Rome's international airport.

The Authority took account of the government grants given to a State-controlled shipping company to enable it to assess the company's degree of independence on the market, and find that it had abusively practised anti-competitive behaviour likely to damage a competitor company[28].

Abusive behaviour was also attributed to Cerved[29], a company whose shareholders include a large number of Chambers of Commerce, which operates on the commercial intelligence market over which Cerved enjoys an exclusive position by virtue of the fact that it manages the information system of Italy's Chambers of Commerce.

The conclusions that may be drawn from the results of these investigations are a great stimulus in the present phase in which the whole issue of State intervention in the economy is being re-thought out, and provide further proof of failures in the system of State-owned corporations, at least with regard to the need to reorganize the market to make it more consistent with the general public interest.

When identifying cases of abuse of dominant position the Authority considered the list of the cases set out in Section 3 to be merely examples of the prohibition on abuse of dominant position expressed in general terms. Some measure of the objective importance attributed to the notion of abuse of dominant position, irrespective of any assessment of the intent of the company holding a dominant position to derive any specific economic advantage from it, can be seen from the reasoning behind the Apca/Compag[30] decision. In this case, the order to refrain from abusive activities was considered to be a general prohibition of any behaviour by a dominant company that was not objectively justified and was likely to influence the structure of a market on which competition was already weakened by the very presence of that particular company.

With regard to the subjective area to which the prohibition on abuse is applied, the Authority uses a very broad notion of "undertaking", to comprise any entity that performs an economic activity, whatever its legal status, and however it is financed. This was demonstrated by its ruling that a non-profit association[31] had violated the prohibition on abuse of dominant position, according with the principles of EEC law.

Powers to investigate and impose penalties

In order to ascertain infringements of the prohibition on anti-competitive agreements and abuse of dominant position, and to appraise the conditions for authorizing otherwise prohibited agreements and the effects of concentrations notified to it, the Authority is empowered to undertake investigations to gather all the facts and information it requires. It may ask anyone it believes to be in possession of information or relevant documents to disclose them, or it may directly check company records, conducting inspections (Section 14). Where the specific features of the case make it advisable, it can also acquire expert evidence, and order economic and statistical analyses to be conducted.

To implement these powers a formal administrative procedure must be opened in order to guarantee the undertakings and the individuals concerned full disclosure of the investigative materials, the opportunity to defend themselves against any accusations, and to have meetings with them placed officially on record[32]. Anyone likely to suffer direct, immediate and actual loss or damage by the violations forming the subject matter of the investigations, or by any measures which the Authority might adopt, is also entitled to make representations.

Transparency during the investigations is only limited by the need for corporate or industrial confidentiality which, at the request of party concerned, the Authority may grant if it deems the request to be well founded on the basis of the documents or information supplied. Naturally, all the officials of the Authority are bound to secrecy. In view of the investigatory powers of the Authority, anyone requested to supply data or information is under a statutory duty to be truthful and accurate, with administrative fines for failure to comply.

Once the investigation phase is completed and infringements of the prohibitions provided by the Act are ascertained, the Authority not only orders the removal of these violations but may also impose administrative fines where they are serious violations (Section 15). The amount of the fine is not proportionate to the economic advantage obtained or the damage caused; it is calculated in terms of the turnover of by each company for the products forming the subject-matter of the agreement or the abuse of dominant position, in an amount of between 1% and 10%, depending upon the gravity of the violation and any action that may have been taken to mitigate its repercussions.

The Authority is also empowered to issue penalties against companies that go ahead with a concentration operation after being order to desist by the Authority, or fail to comply with the instructions issued to restore the competitive conditions following a prohibition order against a concentration that has been properly notified but carried through before the Authority's decision is issued.

In the case of repeated failures to comply with the order to remove the violations in the matter of agreements and abuse of dominant position, the Authority may order the undertaking concerned to cease operations for up to 30 days.

III. Measures to Promote Competition

One of the decidedly innovative aspects that constitutes a distinctive feature of the italian competition Act is, as already mentioned, the fact that the Authority has the right and duty to report distortions on the market brought about by laws or regulations (Sections 21 and 22). In the performance of this function, it is extremely important for the Authority to identify the general economic interests justifying statutory provisions that distort competition and the market.

Its powers to report such distortions is of particular topical relevance today, at a time of far-reaching technological and legislative changes, particularly in relation to market deregulation that has been introduced by the European Community.

One telling example of the complementary nature of the need to protect competition and the need to remove statutory restraints on free trade can be seen from the action taken by the Authority in the telecommunications industry.

When restricting the ability of exclusive telephone franchise-holder (or rather the group to which it belongs) to extend its market strength over markets open to competition, by the acquisition of companies or by abusing its dominant position, the Authority noted that the development of technology is making it possible today to introduce competition even into markets which have traditionally been considered natural monopolies, in line with the deregulation policy that has already begun at the Community level to promote the national services and infrastructure markets[33].

The corret incorporation of Community directives and their underlying principles into the Italian legal system is a fact of extremely importance in introducing greater competition into the telecommunications industry. In this regard the Authority submitted a report to the government on its draft legislation to enact Directive No. 388/90, pointing out that it restricted the scope of deregulating the sale of production capacity more narrowly than Community legislation, and it was inadequate to remove all forms of discrimination between telecommunications services providers, with reference to network use conditions[34].

Last year, in order to encourage the opening to competition in markets where this is technically possible, the Authority carried out a fact-finding investigation into cellular telephony, on which it submitted a report to the government. In particular, the Authority noted that since the exclusive telephone service franchise-holder had begun to market the new GSM mobile telephony service on a number of traffic routes, further delay in awarding franchise agreements to other companies to enter the market might permanently jeopardize the future structure of competition in the new digital telephony market. To prevent prior entrenched advantages from being established on the GSM mobile telephony market, the Authority prohibited the franchise-holder from marketing the service so long as it was the sole service provider[35].

Another example of the strict complementarity that exists between the measures to promote competition is the denunciation made by the Authority in a special report[36] regarding the serious distortions to the market caused by the government's regulations on fuel distribution, designed to regulate market entry conditions, the possibility of enlarging and transferring fuel sales outlets, the contractual relationship between production and distribution companies, the range of products that can be sold, and the statutory business hours.

The reason why the Authority was led to submit this report to the government was that it considered that an agreement being envisaged between fuel distributors[37] would be anti-competitive. This agreement, according to the intentions expressed by the parties, was designed to restructure the national distribution network in order to bring it up to the higher efficiency levels of the markets of other Community countries. Even after the concerted action had been banned, the Authority nevertheless used all the instruments at its disposal to foster greater efficiency, promoting a broader competition policy.

After analysing current legislation and regulations, the Authority came to the decision that many of the existing provisions were not only useless but were counter-productive as far as making the distribution network more efficient and holding down costs, and hence prices, were concerned. In its proposals to make the regulations consistent with greater competition, the Authority placed particular emphasis on the need to overcome the rationale of government programming of the distribution network, and hence repeal all the statutory instruments designed to control the structure of supply.

Many of the critical assessments of the government regulation of the fuel distribution market were also set out in another report to the government[38], identifying and suggesting actions to be taken in order to make Italy's commercial retail distribution regulations more competitive.

After comparing Italy with the other leading European countries, the Authority found that there was a certain backwardness in the structure of the Italian markets, both in terms of the uneven development of more modern and efficient distribution systems across the country and because of the general lack of willingness to innovate. The Authority identified the existing system of regulations as being responsible for this state of affairs. Since it limited market entry (permits) and the freedom of choice of the production scale (planning) and the range of products sold (commodity tables) it prevented full competition acting as a stimulus to more efficient forms of production and the choice of retailing sites which would be more beneficial to the consumer.

A further constraint on the development of free competition was envisaged in the regulations governing business hours and closing days. The regulations have been used to establish the maximum uniformity of opening days and business hours by commercial operators in the same commodity sector. Considering opening hours, on a par with price and the features of the service, to be an important element of competition and of benefit to the consumer, the report urged existing constraints to be eased, because they also discouraged any move in the direction of more modern distribution systems.

The need to keep a careful eye on the development of national legislation to guarantee that the principles of competition being adopted by the Community are fully incorporated into Italian law also emerged with regard to public contracts, in which the specific problems of controlling and preventing anti-competitive behaviour are compounded by more general problems relating to the need to ensure fairness and transparency in the area of public tenders[39].

A comprehensive and more detailed analysis of Italian legislation governing public contracts was also the subject matter of a specific report submitted to the prime minister under Section 24 of the Act[40]. This report emphasized the limitations and shortcomings in the present system, and offered a number of criteria and guidelines for reform, mainly designed to reduce the lack of standards in the statutory framework, the ineffectiveness of controls and the often cavalier use of contractual devices and procedures - such as awarding public works under franchise or without competitive bidding - which make it possible to skirt the principles of competition and the guarantees of sound and transparent management of government funds.

The Authority also used its reporting powers in relation to the shipping industry, in addition to taking action to remove the abuse of dominant position on the part of State-controlled corporations. It reported to the government and parliament on distortions to competition resulting from grants given to State-owned shipping lines leading to discrimination against private companies operating on the same markets[41]. The Authority ruled that government aid was not vital to support routes which were being serviced by several Italian and foreign, public and private shipping lines, competing with one another. It therefore expressed the hope that the whole question of public aid for State-owned shipping lines would be reviewed.

It also raised the need to give careful consideration to promoting and protecting competition when defining the criteria and the procedures for implementing the programme adopted by the government reorganizing State-owned enterprises, which is expected to lead shortly to the implementation of specific privatization policies also in Italy[42].

In its report, the Authority felt it necessary to point out that opting for a privatization policy does not, in itself, cover with all the problems connected with the process of re-organizing State-owned enterprises. These problems not only relate to the question of private versus public ownership of companies but also indeed, first and foremost require a definition of rules and general conditions to ensure the sound operation of the market. It will therefore be necessary to ensure that none of the take-overs and mergers that occur after the privatization of State-owned enterprises create or strengthen dominant positions. This must be guaranteed not only by the Anti-Trust Authority, but also by the government, which must adopt policies in line with the aim of guaranteeing and promoting competition in the Italian economic system.

This is a sphere which includes not only manufacturing and banking, but also public utilities and services where a legal monopoly or a franchise system operate, and in which technological progress and market developments today call for deregulation and liberalization.

The Authority felt it appropriate to point out that when establishing the procedures for privatization, due consideration should be given to the possibility of encouraging the development of a production system with a larger variety of independent companies, both by selling equity to foreign investors and, where appropriate, by envisaging the possibility of carrying out de-mergers before floating the companies on the market. For this would make it possible to restore greater competition on markets which are presently dominated by State-owned enterprises.

Lastly, the Authority emphasized the close linkage that exists between protecting competition and ensuring impartiality with public asset disposal operations, in order to guarantee total equality of treatment to all potential investors and prevent any discrimination which, if it were tilted in favour of Italian companies, would violate the general principles of Community law, above all other considerations.

What must be borne clearly in mind here is that in the process of transforming the public utilities, the Authority is in favour of the proposal to set up statutory agencies to regulate the conditions of access to their operations, the procedures under which they are provided, and to draw up pricing criteria and quality control and efficiency standards. With such agencies, it will be possible to draw a clearcut distinction between the responsibility for regulation public utilities and services, and the responsibility for providing them.

However, protecting competition must remain the responsibility vested in the Anti-Trust Authority. Guaranteeing competition and regulating specific industries do not always share the same objectives, with the result that if all the various interests at stake are to be guaranteed, these objectives must be pursued by different institutions. Assessing the impact on competition of actions and conduct by companies requires a specific type of know-how and expertise which is very largely independent of the features of the industries concerned.

IV. Limitations on the Action of the Antitrust Authority

There are both objective and subjective constraints on the Authority's powers.

Objective constraints

These stem from the fact that the powers to protect competition in the publishing, broadcasting and banking industries (section 20) have been taken away from the Authority and vested in the Publishing and Broadcasting Authority (Garante dell'editoria) and in the Bank of Italy, respectively.

However, while the Authority's powers have been weakened - even though it is still required to express a non-binding opinion to the other two "watchdog" bodies - no specific legislation has yet been enacted for the protection of competition in those two industries. The rules to be observed to protect the market are therefore the general rules governing competition, which means that any specific actions taken with regard to banking, publishing and broadcasting are the exclusive responsibility of the agencies that are responsible for enforcing discipline, whose powers of supervising these industries are now extended to protecting competition.

Having opted to share responsibilities in terms of the activities of the undertakings, instead of the public interests at stake, any operations carried out by companies under the supervision of the Bank of Italy or the Publishing and Broadcasting Authority are likely to be appraised according to different yardsticks depending on the different specific aims, namely, the protection of free competition, on the one hand, and protection savings, ensuring stability in the banking system, and guaranteeing freedom of information, on the other.

However, the law makes no provision for solving cases, which are by no means impossible, in which permission is given for an operation to proceed as a means of protecting the stability of the banking system or guaranteeing freedom of information, but is not for the protection of competition[43]. The only exception is with the banking system, where the possibility exists for authorizing otherwise prohibited agreements for a limited period of time, where it is necessary to guarantee the stability of the monetary system.

Practical experience has shown that responsibilities can only be allocated in terms of the individual entities concerned when all the parties to an operation being assessed belong to the industry which has been taken away from the jurisdiction of the Anti-Trust Authority, and is subject to the control of its own sectoral "watchdog" Authority. However, in many instances only a few of them belong to only one sector, in practice. When this occurs, the same operation is appraised both by the Anti-Trust Authority and by the watchdog Authority for their industries concerned, each appraising the aspects relating to their specific terms of reference.

Inevitably, however, any measures adopted as a result of having ascertained a violation of the prohibition on anti-competitive agreements or concentration operations, even when issued by only one of the Authorities responsible for the aspects within their particular jurisdiction, are bound to have repercussions on the agreement or on the concentration as an indivisible whole.

Subjective constraints

These are the constraints set out in Section 8, according to which the provisions governing agreements, abuse of dominant position and concentrations do not apply to undertakings with the statutory responsibility of providing services of general economic interest, or to which a specific activity is reserved by law.

Unlike the cases examined in Section 3.1 above, this is an absolute exclusion through which the legislator intended to protect such undertakings from the principles of free competition, because their activities are for the general good of the community, excluding them from the rules of the free market because their operations are wholly governed by the political Authorities. It was an attempt to strike a balance between the protection of private enterprise, for which the Act was introduced, and the protection of the public interest by making statutory reservations for the activities of specific companies or enterprises.

The practical effects of these "safe conduct passes" have nevertheless been significantly mitigated by the statutory requirement to ascertain the existence of a "close linkage" between the behaviour of the undertaking enjoying a statutory monopoly or providing services of general economic interest, and its attainment of its statutory objects of general interest.

This exclusion therefore only applies where there is a very cogent need for the enterprise to attain these objects and there are no viable alternatives compatible with the market protection principles.

Support for this interpretation comes from the fact that the exclusion provision is seen as an exception to the general principle of equality of treatment of private and State-owned enterprises provided by Section 8(1).

Restrictive criteria for interpreting Section 8(2) have been applied by the Authority from the very beginning, in order to emphasize the close relationship that exists between this provision and Article 90(2) of the EEC Treaty. As we have seen above, these criteria have enabled the Authority to consider that it is also empowered to take action against exclusive franchise-holders providing public services for conduct which cannot be justified by an objective need to attain objectives of public interest justifying the statutory exception in their case[44].

Notes

* The opinions and views of the authors are personal and do not imply the expression of any opinion on the part of the Italian Anti-trust Authority.

1. Council Regulation 4064/89 on the control of concentrations between undertakings empowers the Community to control "concentrations with a Community dimension", meaning operations that meet all the following three conditions: 1) combined aggregate worldwide turnover of all the undertakings concerned is more than ECU 5,000 millions; 2) the aggregate community-wide turnover of each of at least two of the undertakings concerned is more than ECU 250 million; 3) at least one of the undertakings concerned achieves one-third of its aggregate community-wide turnover in one Member State other than any State in which it achieves the other two-thirds.
2. Article 9 of Council Regulation 17/62.
3. These amounts are increased each year by the equivalent of the price deflator index of the

gross domestic product. As a result of this indexing system, the invoicing thresholds were 536 and 53.6 billion for 1992, and 562 and 56.2 billion lire for 1993.

4. During 1992, 179 of the 380 mergers examined involved non-independent companies. 137 of the remaining 201 cases referred to operations in which the acquired company had a turnover of less than 53.6 billion lire, and was therefore only notified because the acquiring company had a turnover in excess of 536 billion (*source*: Anti-Trust Authority Report, 1992).
5. A Bill (Senate Bill No. 36, promoted by the Hon. Franza) has been tabled before parliament to amend section 5(1) and section 16(1) of Law 287/90).
6. Lucana Latte/ESAB, in Bollettino no. 9/1992; Generale Impianti/Falsura Costruzioni, in Bollettino no. 21/1992 and Bayer/Bayer Diagnostici, in Bollettino no. 23/1992.
7. Cariplo/Cassa Risparmio Calabra, in Bollettino no. 16/1992.
8. Cereol/Continentale, in Bollettino no. 6/1992.
9. Fininvest/Amef, in Bollettino no. 3/1992.
10. Finsiel/Eurosystem, in Bollettino no 5/1992.
11. Stet/Finsiel, in Bollettino no. 5/1992.
12. Gilfin/OMSA, in Bollettino no. 8/1992.
13. Italtel/Mistel and Italtel/General 4 Elettronica Sud, in Bollettino no. 23/1992; Emilcarta/Agrifood Machinery, in Bollettino no. 7/1993.
14. Cemensud/Calcementi, in Bollettino no. 8/1992; Unichips Finanziaria/Alidolce, in Bollettino no. 4/1993.
15. Alitalia/Malev, in Bollettino no. 4/1993.
16. Cardile/Bros, in Bollettino no. 19/1992.
17. Procal, in Bollettino no. 5/1992.
18. Cirio/Torre in Pietra, in Bollettino no. 11/1991.
19. CementirlMerone, in Bollettino no. 12/1992.
20. Agip Covengas, in Bollettino no. 4/1992.
21. Sip-Apple-IBM-Olivetti, in Bollettino no. 10/1992.
22. Cementir/Sacci, in Bollettino no. 9/1992.
23. Cedic, in Bollettino no. 22/1992.
24. Federazione Nazionale Spedizionieri, in Bollettino no. 21/1992; Ania, in Bollettino no.19/1992.
25. Vevy Europe/Res Pharma in Bollettino no. 4/1992; INA/Banca di Roma, in Bollettino no. 5/1993.
26. 3C Comunications, in Bollettino no. 5/1992; Ducati/SIP, in Bollettino no. 21/1992; SIP/GSM, in Bollettino no. 32/1993.
27. IBAR, in Bollettino no. 6/1993.
28. Marinzulich/Tirrenia, in Bollettino no. 7/1992
29. Ancic/Cerved, in Bollettino no. 7/1992.
30. ApcalCompag, in Bollettino no. 13/1992.
31. Aici/Fiv, in Bollettino no. 22/1992.
32. This procedure is governed by DPR 10.9.91 no. 461.
33. Fact-finding investigation into the mobile cellular telephone industry, in the ordinary supplement to Bollettino No. 15/16 of 1993, and the report to the government in Bollettino No. 4/1993.
34. Report to the government on the legislation to incorporate EEC Directive 96/388 in Bollettino No. 4/93.
35. SIP-GSM in Bollettino No. 32/93.
36. Report to the government and parliament on "The system governing vehicle fuel distribution and competition", in the ordinary supplement to Bollettino No. 14/93.
37. The restructuring of the fuel distributors' network, in Bollettino No. 14/83.
38. Report to the government on "The regulation of commercial distribution and competition", in the supplement to Bollettino No. 1/93.

39. Report to parliament on the automation of the Lotto gambling system in Bollettino No. 24/1992.
40. Report to the government on "Public tenders and competition" in the special edition of the Bollettino, July 1992.
41. Report to the government and parliament on the financing of the Finmare group, in Bollettino No. 2/1993.
42. Report to parliament on the programme for the reorganization of the State-owned industries, in Bollettino No. 6/1993.
43. In this connection there are two important cases relating to an agreement between advertising agencies (Manzoni/Spi/Spe/Publikompas, in Bollettino No. 12/1993) and a merger between banks (B.Sardegna/B.Popolare Sassari, in Bollettino No. 6/1993) which the publishing Authority (in Bollettino No. 17/1993) and the Bank of Italy (in Bollettino No. 7/1993) deemed to be compatible with the principles of competition, while the Anti-Trust Authority had expressed qualified reservations about the lawfulness of the agreement and the anticompetitive effects of the merger on the relevant banking market.
44. These are measures taken against SIP (3C Comunication, in Bollettino no. 5/1992; Ducati/Sip, in Bollettino no. 6/1992; Sip/Gsm, in Bollettino no. 32/1993); Aeroporti di Roma (IBAR, in Bollettino no. 6/1993; Aeroporti di Roma/Gruppo Sicurezza, in Bollettino no. 35/1993) e Ferrovie dello Stato (Fremura/Ferrovie dello Stato, in Bollettino no. 1/1993).

References

Alessi R., Olivieri G., 1991, *La disciplina della concorrenza e del mercato*, Giappichelli.

Amorelli G., 1991, "L'amministrazione con funzioni regolatrice: le autorità di disciplina della concorrenza sul piano interno e comunitario", in *Rivista Italiana Diritto Pubblico Comunitario*, 943.

Assonime, Associazione fra le società italiane per azioni, circolare n. 9 del 17.1.1991.

Autorità Garante della concorrenza e del mercato - Relazione annuale al Presidente del Consiglio dei Ministri per il 1990, 1991 e 1992.

Banca d'Italia, 1992, *La tutela della concorrenza nel settore del credito*, Banca d'Italia.

Bianchi P., Gualtieri G., 1993, *Concorrenza e controllo delle concentrazioni in Europa*, Il Mulino.

Bortolotti F., 1991, "La legge antitrust: ambito di applicazione e status delle intese compatibili con la libertà di concorrenza", in *Contratto e Impresa*, 597.

Cerrai A., 1992, "Le imprese editoriali", in Colombo-Portale, *Trattato delle società per azioni*, UTET, vol. 8, 343.

Charrier G., 1992, "Parallèle entre la loi italienne pour la protection de la concurrence et le système français", in *Journal of Public Finance and Public Choice*.

Clarich M., 1993, "Per uno studio sui poteri dell'Autorità garante della concorrenza e del mercato", in *Diritto amministrativo*, 77.

Costi R., 1991, "Le concentrazioni bancarie e la legge antitrust", in *Banca Imprese Società*, 399.

Da Empoli D., 1990, "The Italian Law for the Protection of Competition and the Market", in *Journal of Public Finance and Public Choice*.

De Nicola A., 1991, "Disciplina della concorrenza e del mercato: il controllo delle concentrazioni in Italia", in *Giurisprudenza Commerciale*, I, 527.

Donativi V., 1989, *La disciplina della concorrenza nei disegni di legge antitrust*, Luiss.

Donativi V., 1989, *Introduzione alla disciplina antitrust nel sistema legislativo italiano*, Giuffrè.

Franceschelli V., 1991, "La legge antitrust e la nuova disciplina delle concentrazioni", in *Rivista Diritto Industriale*, I, 286.

Franceschelli V., "Concorrenza antitrust", in *Trattato di diritto privato* (a cura di Rescigno), UTET, vol. XII, 765.

Frignani, Pardolesi, Patroni Griffi, Ubertazzi, 1993, *Diritto antitrust italiano*, vol. 2, Zanichelli.

Ghezzi F., Notari M., 1990, *Diritto antitrust nei mercati finanziari*, Università Bocconi.

Hommelhoff P., 1993, "La disciplina antimonopolistica italiana. Osservazioni dal punto di vista tedesco", in *Giurisprudenza Commerciale*, I, 507.

Lacey Eric F., 1990, "The Italian Competition Law Compared with Other OECD Countries' Competition Laws", in *Journal of Public Finance and Public Choice.*

Menis C., 1990, "Les rapports entre le droit communautaire et la nouvelle loi italienne relative à la protection de la concurrence", in *Journal of Public Finance and Public Choice*

Munari F., 1992, "La legge 10 ottobre 1990, n. 287 e il diritto comunitario della concorrenza", in *Rivista Diritto Internazionale privato e processuale*, 233.

Oppo G., 1993, "Costituzione e diritto privato nella 'tutela della concorrenza'", in *Rivista Diritto Civile*, 543.

Papetti G., 1990, "Legge antitrust: un commento economico all'art. 3", in *Rivista Internazionale di Scienze Sociali.*

Pardolesi R., 1993, "Analisi economica della legislazione antitrust italiana", in *Foro Italiano*, V, 1.

Patroni Griffi A. Sabato F., 1992, "La legge antitrust", ESI.

Pieri S., 1991, "La legge antitrust ed il diritto comunitario della concorrenza", in *Diritto del Commercio e degli Scambi internazionali*, 45.

Pinnarò M., 1993, "Diritto di iniziativa economica e libertà di concorrenza. Di talune ellissi e pleonasmi nella Legge antitrust n. 287 del 10 ottobre 1990", in *Giurisprudenza Commerciale*, I, 530.

Pulitini F., 1993, *Le vestali del mercato. Qualche appunto sull'antitrust italiano, Università di Siena.*

Saja F., 1991, "L'Autorità garante della concorrenza e del mercato: prima esperienza e prospettive di applicazione della legge", in *Giurisprudenza Commerciale*, I, 455.

Siragusa M., Scassellati Sforzolini G., 1992, "Il diritto della concorrenza italiana e comunitario: un nuovo rapporto", in *Foro Italiano*, IV, 243.

Spolidoro M.S., 1990, "La disciplina antitrust in Italia", in *Rivista delle Società*, 1292.

Toffoletto A., 1991, "La disciplina della concorrenza e del mercato", in *Giurisprudenza Commerciale*, I, 1002.

Zito A., 1989, "Mercato, regolazione del mercato e legislazione antitrust: profili costituzionali", in *Jus*, 219.

GPSR Compliance

The European Union's (EU) General Product Safety Regulation (GPSR) is a set of rules that requires consumer products to be safe and our obligations to ensure this.

If you have any concerns about our products, you can contact us on ProductSafety@springernature.com

In case Publisher is established outside the EU, the EU authorized representative is:

Springer Nature Customer Service Center GmbH
Europaplatz 3
69115 Heidelberg, Germany

Batch number: 10830943

Printed by Printforce, the Netherlands